The Complete Idiot's Reference Card

Using Political Skills to Get Ahead

I use my political skills to advantage on the job by always trying to:

- ❏ 1. Play fair by treating others as I would like them to treat me.
- ❏ 2. Protect myself against backstabbers, office bootlickers, and other odious colleagues who obviously didn't read the previous item on this list.
- ❏ 3. Support my co-workers and my supervisors.
- ❏ 4. Take an active role in my own success.
- ❏ 5. Look for projects that can increase my visibility, teach me new skills, and make a meaningful contribution to the company's success.
- ❏ 6. Take educated risks.
- ❏ 7. Control my own destiny.
- ❏ 8. Learn new skills and keep current on knowledge, especially technology.
- ❏ 9. Embrace challenges rather than reject them.
- ❏ 10. Know how to enlist the aid of others.
- ❏ 11. Use the rules to my advantage—and change the rules, if necessary and prudent.
- ❏ 12. Bounce back from mistakes, rather than being defeated by set-backs.
- ❏ 13. Have a clear, strong personal agenda.
- ❏ 14. Dress and act in a professional manner.
- ❏ 15. Come to work on time.
- ❏ 16. Think before I act, especially when it comes to making crucial decisions.
- ❏ 17. Deal with the realities of today's multicultural workplace.
- ❏ 18. Use flattery and other ingratiation techniques upward, downward, and across the board.
- ❏ 19. Turn problems into opportunities.
- ❏ 20. Figure out who holds the real power within the organization.
- ❏ 21. Share news of my victories and triumphs.
- ❏ 22. Reap benefits from the office grapevine.
- ❏ 23. Deal effectively with the demands of business travel.
- ❏ 24. Fit in with the corporate culture.
- ❏ 25. Realize when it may be time to move on to a new job.

alpha
books

tear here

Getting the Power You Need and Deserve

Power is like money. Not everyone is obsessed with power or money, but few people would refuse either if it were offered to them. Like money, power is an almost universal currency. Possessing power helps you get what you want on the job. Power can help you avoid unfavorable or unpleasant situations, too. You especially need power at lower levels of an organization to qualify for more responsibility or your slice of the corporate pie.

Here are some techniques for getting the power you need and deserve.

1. Develop expertise. Almost every powerful and successful person began by being especially good at some tangible, marketable skill. Nobody will give you a chance to display your executive skills until you have shown a reasonable degree of technical competence. Here are some areas to consider:
   - Printing
   - Accounting
   - Purchasing
   - Editorial
   - Negotiation skills
   - Computers
   - Manufacturing
   - Fund-raising
   - Production
   - Sales and marketing

2. Maintain expertise. Even after a promotion or two, it's crucial that you maintain your skills in an area other than management.

3. Form alliances with powerful people. In part, power comes from forming alliances with one or more of the powerful people you have identified in the company.

4. Think, act, and look powerful. On the way up, there's something to be said for acting the role of a powerful person:
   - Consider the big picture as well as the little details.
   - Appear in control. Try never to lose your cool.
   - Dress the part.

5. Acquire responsibility. The nature of the work you are performing is not the key factor in determining whether you are line or staff. What is significant is how vital your function is to your employer. Make yourself useful.

6. Take care of minor problems to gain the confidence of your colleagues and bosses. Then build to bigger and bigger issues.

7. Develop a network of useful contacts. The people in your network can be an important source of information about potential customers, reliable suppliers, new developments in your field, important trends, and job openings. Develop contacts by:
   - Exchanging information with others
   - Doing favors for others
   - Sharing credit for successful projects
   - Staying honest and trustworthy

8. Display a commitment to your job. All you need to get ahead is in-depth planning, years of hard work, and a willingness to sacrifice your family for your job. It's really not that bad, but to reach the top in corporate America, sometimes you will have to sacrifice your personal life for the company.

9. Do your homework. Be prepared; never try to "wing it." Never.
10. Cover yourself.
    Set up backup personnel you can rely on when people are out sick, systems crash, and other emergencies arise.

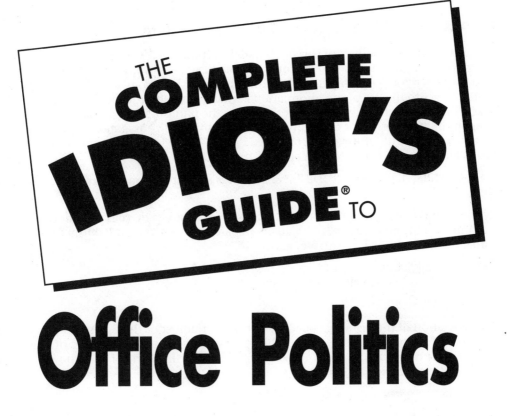

THE COMPLETE IDIOT'S GUIDE® TO

Office Politics

*by Laurie E. Rozakis, Ph.D.,
and Bob Rozakis*

alpha
books

A Division of Macmillan General Reference
A Simon & Schuster Macmillan Company
1633 Broadway, New York, NY 10019-6785

Macmillan Publishing books may be purchased for business or sales promotional use. For information please write: Special Markets Department, Macmillan Publishing USA, 1633 Broadway, New York, NY 10019-6785.

International Standard Book Number: 0-02-862397-5
Library of Congress Catalog Card Number: 98-85128

00 99 98   8 7 6 5 4 3 2 1

Interpretation of the printing code: the rightmost number of the first series of numbers is the year of the book's printing; the rightmost number of the second series of numbers is the number of the book's printing. For example, a printing code of 98-1 shows that the first printing occurred in 1998.

Printed in the United States of America

Contents at a Glance

Contents

Foreword

Are you perplexed at being left behind at work while others who are less skilled move ahead? If so, your dilemma is solvable. Every day, the workplace rewards the less skilled and minimally talented only because they've learned to play the "Idiot's" game of office politics. Yes, idiots do move ahead faster and stay there. They often leave their competent and diligent counterparts behind biting the dust. The saddest part is that they haven't got the slightest clue as to why their careers never took off.

Politics is simply the discipline of getting and retaining power. The first thing you need to know is that whenever there is more than one person, there is going to be politics. You can be certain that in your career you will always be around at least one person who interferes with your quest to get ahead.

This book is a unique opportunity for you to learn how to get your fair share of the pie and catapult you to success. The authors are two "done that–been there" workplace experts, Laurie and Bob Rozakis, who have made this guide humorous and fun, and, more importantly, have packed it with strategies that are easy to implement. Laurie and Bob have treaded the corridors of business and will share with you ways to avoid the hidden and dangerous corporate minefields. They uncomplicate the hypocrisies of corporate America so that you can navigate this minefield and get what you want and go where you want. Armed with this knowledge, you will be able to confront and seduce the backstabbers, upstagers, gossipers, and outright liars. You'll be able to disarm and charm the worst of corporate enemies. You'll develop a power image and get to know the right people, thereby building loyalty, alliances, and teams.

Today, people are spending more hours at work than ever before. The average work week for a woman has risen to 44 hours from 39 hours in 1977. Men report spending 49.9 hours on the job, up from 47.1. So, with so much of our day being spent at work, there's no running or hiding from office politics. It's woven into the fabric of every corporate culture. People are behaving in the workplace today the way we drive our cars…it's anything goes. You need to learn to fend off the corporate sharks and appear confident—and do it all with charm and charisma.

I know you'll gain the knowledge and insight from this guide. No need for paranoia, but if you don't believe everything that you're told (or that you "accidentally" overhear around the water cooler), you'll be off to a good start. Whether you're entering or re-entering the job market, or navigating your way up the ladder, you can make it with this guide at your side. Good luck, and let's get started. I'll meet you on the way up.

—Rosemary Maniscalco

Introduction

Post-O.J., all famous people must be considered powder kegs until they have managed to get through their entire lives without killing someone. And more than ever, we realize that Sartre was close, but not quite, on the mark: Hell *is* other people, most especially the ones in the next cubicle. Why? It's office politics, baby, the jockeying for power and position that consumes most workers' days. Everyone wants to be the head weenie at the roast, but some people just don't play nice.

Not only are office politics more complex today than they were in the past, but now the stakes are at their highest. In an era of corporate downsizing, rightsizing, shakeouts, restructuring, and takeovers, mastery of political tactics is essential for job survival—no matter what your job.

To add to the pressure, too many baby boomers are vying for too few jobs in private and public organizations. At the same time, the number of middle management jobs has been chopped to the bone. Even Kate Moss has more fat than most successful businesses. Today's companies are lean and mean, with the emphasis on the *mean*. Corporate America is a cold, cruel world, as frosty as a snowman.

Before you take a life at work—or lose your own in the Office Wars—read this book. It could save your soul.

What You'll Learn in This Book

In *The Complete Idiot's Guide to Office Politics*, we'll tell you how to cope with some of the most common—and distressing—problems you're likely to encounter at work. This book will give you effective strategies for dealing with your bosses, co-workers, and subordinates. It will teach you powerful tactics for coping with the various personalities and power plays you're likely to encounter when you play in the Big Leagues.

We can't promise you that if you find a dream job, you'll experience heaven on earth (that's a pint of rocky road, a fluffy comforter, and a Ginger Rogers–Fred Astaire movie), but we *can* guarantee that by the time you finish this book, you'll have the tools you need to deal with even the most difficult work situations.

This book is divided into six parts that take you through the process of developing effective strategies for playing the game of office politics without losing your soul. Here's what you'll find in each part of this book.

Part 1: A Cubicle's-Eye View surveys typical office situations, explores your work style, and explodes some common myths about office life that can block your advancement. Then we define "office politics" and probe the interaction of ethics and office politics. Along the way, you'll learn about unavoidable political situations in the workplace and how they can affect your career. You'll also discover the importance of first impressions, alliances, and collegiality.

Part 2: Empowerment Plays explores "power" as it relates to business and office politics, including the different kinds of power. In addition, you'll see why speeches, public presentations, and power go hand-in-hand. Then we give you the inside scoop on meetings, from two power-players (us!) who have attended more than their share. See how to use office politics to get your share of the booty. You'll also learn how to use office gossip, whether transmitted in person or electronically, to advance your career.

Part 3: Dealing with the Suits and Ties shows you how to deal with all different kinds of bosses. We cover the toxic boss, the wishy-washy "puzzler," and the grumbler. There are also clear instructions on dealing with bosses who play favorites. Next we take you on a stroll through the gender minefield, so you can avoid *that* explosion!

Part 4: Games People Play opens with a discussion of dirty tricks used by colleagues, including failure to communicate key information, throwing up roadblocks, and taking credit for your work. You'll also learn how sycophants and toadies manipulate colleagues and bosses—and how you can adapt their techniques to get ahead and win friends. You'll also discover how to cope with people who try to avoid work so they can get all of the credit but none of the blame. The section concludes with advice for out-maneuvering the office star, the player skilled at self-aggrandizing and showing off.

Part 5: Socializing shows you how to recognize the open culture and hidden subcultures within a company. You'll learn the importance of socializing in the office, too. There are also practical tips for overcoming the minefield of office romance. Next, we'll show you how to use your political skills to deal with sexism, sexual harassment, and other forms of discrimination. Last, you'll discover how to sidestep the pitfalls of company travel.

Part 6: Upward Bound opens with a discussion of performance reviews to teach you how to negotiate for what you want—and what you deserve. Then you'll explore how to survive downsizing, rightsizing, and plain old firings. Finally, you'll delve into the myth of burnout, so you know when it's time to move on. We even give you great tips for searching for a new job.

More for Your Money!

In addition to all the explanation and teaching, this book contains other types of information to make it even easier for you to learn to use office politics to your advantage. Here's how you can recognize these features:

Fly on the Wall

These are interesting, useful bits of background information that give you even more of an "inside edge" when it comes to dealing with office politics. You could skip these tidbits, but you won't want to because they're much too tasty!

Protect Your Assets
Use these hints to make it easier and more enjoyable to get along with your supervisors, colleagues, and employees.

Corporate Mumbo-Jumbo
Like every other skill worth knowing, office politics has its own terminology. Here's where we explain these terms.

Watch Your Back!
These warnings help you stay on track. They can make it easier for you to avoid the little goofs—and the major pitfalls—that can sink a career.

Special Thanks to the Technical Reviewer...

The Complete Idiot's Guide to Office Politics was reviewed by Hilary Bland, a human resources representative, who double-checked the technical accuracy of what you'll learn here, to help us ensure that this book gives you everything you need to know to begin building your political office arsenal.

Part 1
A Cubicle's-Eye View

What, in your opinion, is the most reasonable explanation for the fact that Moses led the Israelites all over the place for 40 years before they finally got to the Promised Land?

    a. *He was being tested.*

    b. *He wanted them to really appreciate the Promised Land when they finally got there.*

    c. *He refused to ask for directions.*

Some workers—call them losers*—slouch around looking aggrieved. They're volatile and bellicose, slow to form alliances and loath to reconcile after a spat. But while the losers scrap over the crumbs, other workers—call them* winners*—stay busy maintaining a wide network of allies. They master challenges without resorting to whining, complaining, or procrastination. Why do they fare so well? They know how to win at office politics.*

It's time to ask directions, snookums. And in this section, you'll learn the basics of surviving and prospering in business by mastering office politics.

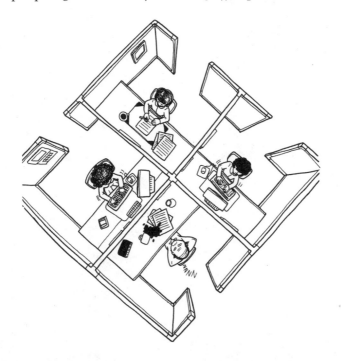

So You Want to Play in the Big Leagues

In This Chapter

- ➤ Some typical office situations
- ➤ Your work style
- ➤ Shared concerns
- ➤ Common myths about office life that can block your advancement
- ➤ The truth behind the myths

An engineer had an exceptional gift for fixing all things mechanical. After serving his company loyally for 20 years, he was fired because he ticked off the wrong person.

Several years later, his company contacted him regarding a seemingly impossible problem they were having with one of their zillion-dollar machines. They had tried everything to get the machine fixed, but to no avail. In desperation, they called on the discharged engineer.

The engineer gleefully took the challenge. He spent a day studying the huge machine. At the end of the day, he marked a small × in chalk on a particular component of the machine and calmly stated, "This is where your problem is." The part was replaced, and the machine worked perfectly again.

The company received a bill for $50,000 from the engineer for his service. They demanded an itemized accounting of his charges. The engineer responded briefly:

| One chalk mark | $1 |
| Knowing where to put it | $49,999 |

It should only happen to you, chum. *You* know you're bright, talented, dedicated, and hard-working. After all, who designed the widget that saved the day—and a bundle of bucks? Who missed the kid's Little League game to finish that Big Report, so it would be ready first thing in the morning for the boss to review? And who worked through lunch for a month to bail out the firm? It wasn't the big shot in the next office, the suck-up, or the boss's nephew, either. It was *you*, my friend.

So why no raise? How come your bonus this year is thinner than Kate Moss? How come the bozo in the next cubicle got the promotion that had your name written all over it? Why is your office the size of a shoe box? How come you get no respect?

Could it be office politics at work? Barring bad breath or the fact that you've been wearing the same clothes all week, you can bet your bippy that office politics are what's holding you back from your rightful place on the corporate ladder.

In this chapter, you'll discover that you're not alone in the cubicle trenches. We'll survey some typical adventures among those paper-thin walls where people battle for respect, raises, and office supplies. We'll see how you react to the realities of the modern, reengineered office (five-foot-high partitions and no windows)—and what your reaction reveals about your ability to use office politics to your advantage.

Protect Your Assets
Often, *what* happens at work is not as important as *how* you react to it. Your reactions are often the key to turning a win-lose situation into a win-win situation.

Then you'll take a look at some typical office experiences. You can compare and contrast these to your own close encounters of the corporate kind. They'll help you discover that we're all in the same boat—only some people are sailing at the helm rather than bailing in the stern. Finally, we'll explore some of the common myths about office life that stand in the way of workers reaching their full potential—or at least getting a 100-square-foot cubicle rather than a 64-foot one.

Total Quality Management

Whether you're building floats for the "Quality Pageant," being the poster child for "Diversity Day," or helping co-workers "empower" themselves, there's no doubt that the workplace is getting weirder and weirder. Lately, no one seems to understand you, no matter how loudly and slowly you talk. The daily grind is draining the life force from your body. You've had it up to *here* with Employee Recognition Days designed to expand your "Productive Zone." You've been reengineered, redesigned, revamped, and reeducated. You feel like you're a part of the Donner party because you're being eaten up alive. (Whose foot *is* that you're gnawing?)

Unfortunately, you're not alone. As a matter of fact, you're just one more wage slave in the third (or is it the fourth?) ring of Cubicle Hell. Forget Dante's Inferno; his imaginary description of the afterlife for the naughty has nothing on the current life of the average worker.

How bad is it? Check out these real-life tales from the front lines:

➤ In response to a recent suggestion by an eager employee, a boss said, "At your salary level, it should be clear we pay you to *do*, not to think."

➤ A supervisor running a "Computer Information Services Department" often asks his employees to add "techno-babble" to technical documents.

➤ On one worker's first day, a boss said, "I really didn't want to hire you, but it's clear no one listens to me."

➤ A boss wandered into an employee's office to ask, "Have you got the 12th of October on your calendar?"

➤ A worker needed two days off, but did not have any vacation time left. When the worker offered to work extra hours to offset this time, the boss said, "Absolutely not. You are salaried and expected to work extra hours. How would I distinguish between the extra hours you are expected to work and the extra hours you want to work?"

No matter what absurd business story we hear, someone says, "That's *nothing*. Let me tell you what's going on in *my* office." Here's the topper of the week, courtesy of a friend:

I provided my department with the best productivity improvements. For years, though, I received no recognition. My boss, however, got constant praises and large raises. After some investigation, I learned my boss wanted to hide my contributions to keep me in his department. To do that, he put the following comment in my personnel file:

"My ranking for him was an adequate, but after further discussions I decided to give him the benefit of the doubt and raised his ranking to a - satisfactory."

See, it's not you—no matter what they tell you at the office. You have vision. You have priorities. You have next-generation systems and acronyms. You even have that rarest of rare commodities in business: a real brain. It's just that no one knows it—or cares much. Read on to get some more news from the front lines.

Truth or Consequences

Let's try a little quiz to see what experiences you've had in the office and how you react to them. Following are 10 paired statements. For each pair, check the one that best describes your behavior.

Office Experiences Quiz

❑ 1. You try to cover the fact that your boss had three martinis at lunch "to calm the nerves."

❑ 2. You hand *your* pocket flask to the boss as he begins stammering through his presentation.

❑ 3. You eat lunch with your colleagues often even if they don't pick up the bill.

❑ 4. You only spend time with the people you're sure can help your career, so everyone knows you're movin' on up.

❑ 5. Every once in a while, you bring some donuts or coffee cake to the office for everyone to share.

❑ 6. You ask a colleague to bring you coffee because you want to make it plain who's the Alpha dog in *this* pack.

❑ 7. You lend someone five bucks until payday.

❑ 8. You borrow five bucks to tide you over until payday. So what if you forget to pay it back? It's only money.

❑ 9. You have a talent for looking and acting calm, even if you're about to go postal.

❑ 10. You believe that venting is good. What's so terrible about a little bellowing, name calling, and swearing?

❑ 11. You keep personal business to yourself.

❑ 12. You believe in letting it all hang out. For instance, you couldn't wait to tell (and show) the whole office your new naval ring.

❑ 13. You find the person sitting two cubicles down from you attractive—and have noticed some glances in your direction too—but don't want to get involved in an office romance.

❑ 14. All work and no play makes Jack (or Jane) a dullard. There has to be something to look forward to at work—why not a little romance?

❑ 15. You briefly commiserate with the boss's secretary about her recent separation, after she brings it up first.

❑ 16. You hear that there might be some juicy gossip about the boss's secretary and, under the guise of confidant, pull the info out of her. Then you run to the nearest water cooler to dish the dirt to one and all. Hey, inquiring minds want to know.

❏ **17.** You join the office softball team.

❏ **18.** You bring your bat to the office on a day when the league *doesn't* meet…and carry it with you all day.

❏ **19.** You ask to see a picture of the boss's new child and manage to say something nice about the kid's appearance (even though it looks just like Winston Churchill).

❏ **20.** You fail to acknowledge that the boss just had her first child, even though she's been as big as a FedEx truck for the past six months.

Score Yourself

Give yourself 2 points for every odd-numbered statement, and take away 2 points for every even-numbered statement.

15–20 points	We like your style—and so does everyone else.
10–14 points	Now you know why you weren't picked to be the office Santa Claus.
5–9 points	Can we talk?
0–4 points	You need us; you really need us.

> **Protect Your Assets**
> Ability to do the job is taken for granted. Otherwise, you wouldn't have been hired in the first place. Attrition will remove some of the contenders for advancement. Promotion to the next rung on the corporate ladder is usually predicated as much on personality as it is on how well you do your job.

Whack 'Em and Stack 'Em

Side-swiping, undercutting, and kneecapping. No, we're not talking about a kindergarten sandbox at lunchtime or a New York City subway at rush hour. We're talking about the average office. "*My* company is great," you protest. "It's like heaven on earth." Maybe so, kiddo, but just wait. Into each life a little office terror will come. Your number hasn't come up yet, but that office roulette wheel is still turning.

Here are three typical tales from the ledge. See how they compare to *your* experiences in a cubicle that even has a real window. So what if it's blocked by a wall?

Exhibit A: Sorry You Asked

Our friend—let's call him "Job"—works as an art director for a small magazine. Over lunch the other day, he recounted this tale of woe:

> One day, a group of us were invited by our publisher to a meeting to "brainstorm" possible improvements. As the meeting began and the words, "Anybody got any ideas?" left my boss's lips, there fell an awkward silence. My colleagues sat there as dumb as toast. I saw my opportunity to chime in with all the great ideas I had since my employment began two months prior, so I went for it.

> My boss and I got into a tremendous dialogue while my work mates remained silent. I felt I was really making a difference. After the meeting was over, every one of my fellow workers commended me on my obvious passionate desire for the success of our magazine and the great ideas I had shared.

> The following morning, my boss asked me to step into her office. I felt certain I was to be praised for my sure-fire plan for success. Instead, I was reamed for suggesting that our magazine was less than perfect. It seems that all my colleagues complained that I was making them look bad. At the end of the meeting, my boss ordered me to apologize to everyone in the office for implying that they were less than competent professionals.

Watch Your Back!
Never assume that your office doesn't have office politics because it is too small, too large, too public, too private, too well-decorated, and so on. Office politics, like TV reruns and traffic jams, are unavoidable.

Exhibit B: Rubbed Out

A colleague we'll call "Drone" shared the following intriguing tale of office sleight-of-hand; she works as a Web page designer for a major southern university:

> I was called by a prominent organization that we belong to and told that I had won first place for a design. The prize was going to be given to me at a banquet in California.

> Immediately, I told my boss that I wanted to go and accept the award. Without offering congratulations, he said that the budget was tight and that the university couldn't afford to send me.

> The following week, my boss went to accept the award for me. After seeing the award, he discovered that my name was engraved on it. He made the Committee reissue the plaque, blank.

> Now, my award hangs in his office.

Exhibit C: A Friend in Need...

A buddy of ours, we'll call her "Gullible," was once the manager of a secretarial pool. One night, a sales rep came to her office in a panic. Here's Gullible's travail:

> The sales rep said he had a very important proposal that *had* to go out that night. It was 5:00 p.m., and I had to get home to feed the cat, so I refused. Before I could dash out the door, the sales rep convinced me to get it done.
>
> Before I started the proposal, I told the sales rep that I would miss my ride and as a result, I would be without a way to get home. With clear salesman charm, the rep offered to take me home. He said he would be waiting in his office upstairs.
>
> Without that worry, I started to work. I worked nonstop until 8:00 p.m. Proud of my accomplishment, I carried the proposal up to the salesman's office.
>
> The floor was empty, and his office was dark. The cleaning crew said he left at 5:30.

Watch Your Back!
When it comes to supervisors, one size doesn't fit all. Supervisors vary in personality, reactions to minor and major situations, concepts of delegating authority, and their feel for the sensibilities of others. *Never* make the mistake of assuming that all bosses are the same.

And these are the *mild* examples. We're saving the goodies for later on, when we've eased you into the office wars. Hey, we wouldn't want to terrorize you before you've gotten used to swimming with the sharks.

Liar, Liar, Pants on Fire

You may have thrown away the last shred of your tattered baby blanket, stuffed teddy bear, or beloved doll, but that doesn't mean you still don't have something you cling to for security. We all have security blankets, only they take the form of myths that help us deal with a seemingly arbitrary business world.

How many of the following statements do you think are true? (And no cheating; we're looking over your shoulder. We want the truth, the whole truth, and nothing but the truth.) For each statement, check true or false.

Myths of the Business World

True	False	
❏	❏	1. Executives make decisions about the people in their corporations based solely on merit.
❏	❏	2. Bosses use objective facts—rather than attempts to please people or pay back favors—when they allocate money and material.

continues

continued

True	False	
❏	❏	3. There's very little favoritism where you work.
❏	❏	4. You don't have to toot your own horn; people will notice you because you do good work.
❏	❏	5. Management knows who's *really* doing the work.
❏	❏	6. Eventually, all the lousy workers will be revealed for the goldbrickers they are.
❏	❏	7. Every dog has his day, and in due time, my co-workers will realize how much I contribute to the smooth running of this office.
❏	❏	8. The company would fall apart without me; I really am indispensable at work.
❏	❏	9. I'm safe in my job because I have tenure, a contract, or top-notch skills.
❏	❏	10. Socializing with my co-workers isn't important.
❏	❏ **Bonus.**	Someday your ship will come in, and no one will find out that you stole a really nice chair from the VP.

Score Yourself

Every statement is false.

Here's why:

1. *Executives make decisions about the people in their corporations based solely on merit.* No, they don't. They also factor in many other criteria. And I know about this from a bizarre first-hand experience...

   About 20 years ago, I was going to get laid off from my job as a high school English teacher. The principal, a kindly fellow, called me into his office to break the bad news in person. He said, "I'm sorry that I have to lay you off, but you'll be okay. You're young and married. Your husband has a job, and you can stay home and have babies. Your job will go to Mr. S—, a social studies teacher who is the sole support of his family."

   I replied, "But I make more money than my husband, and we don't want to have any babies right now."

   And he said, "Oh, dear. I didn't know that. Then you're going to have to keep your job, aren't you?"

   And I did, for more than a decade.

2. *Bosses use objective facts—rather than attempts to please people or pay back favors—when they allocate money and material.* Quote from a telephone inquiry: "We're only hiring one summer intern this year, and we won't start interviewing candidates for that position until the boss's daughter finishes her summer classes."

3. *There's very little favoritism where you work.* Hmmm…and we saw Elvis talking to Judge Crater and Amelia Earhart at a 7-11 last night.

4. *You don't have to toot your own horn; people will notice you because you do good work.* More likely, someone will be looking for a way to take credit for what *you* did.

5. *Management knows who's really doing the work.* See #4. Remember our friend "Gullible?" That sales rep took all the credit for getting the job done on time.

6. *Eventually, all the lousy workers will be revealed for the goldbrickers they are.* Need we say it? Don't we all know at least one person at work who seems to lead a charmed life?

7. *Every dog has his day, and in due time, my co-workers will realize how much I contribute to the smooth running of this office.* Dogs rarely get their days. That's why so many of them bite.

8. *The company would fall apart without me; I really am indispensable at work.* Yes, and the *Titanic* really was unsinkable. All ego aside, here's the sorry truth: no one is indispensable.

9. *I'm safe in my job because I have tenure, a contract, or top-notch skills.* I was laid off from my job teaching high school English not once, not twice, but three times when the school was closed. I had tenure and had even been 11th grade lead teacher.

   And how many executives with contracts have been fired? I'm not sure I can count that high without getting a nose bleed.

10. *Socializing with my co-workers isn't important.* It is. People skilled at office politics form crucial bonds at work that enable them to get what they want and need.

Protect Your Assets

Few of us accept employment for the sole purpose of keeping body and soul together. Those who languish in their jobs do so until their effectiveness is drained or economic conditions catch up with them—then they find themselves searching for a new source of sustenance. To achieve even a drop of effectiveness in any job, you must be motivated to accomplish and be rewarded.

Fly on the Wall

South Carolina: A man walked into a police station, dropped a bag of cocaine on the counter, informed the sergeant that it was substandard, and asked that the person who sold it to him be arrested immediately.

Indiana: A man walked up to a store cashier and demanded all the money in the register. When the cashier handed him the loot, he fled...leaving his wallet on the counter.

North Carolina: A man shot himself when, awakening to the sound of a ringing telephone beside his bed, he reached for the phone but grabbed instead a Smith & Wesson 38 Special, which discharged when he drew it to his ear.

And you think *you're* working with idiots?

The Least You Need to Know

➤ *All* offices are political.

➤ An inability to use office politics to your advantage can hold you back at work.

➤ Executives don't make decisions about the people in their corporations based solely on merit.

➤ There's favoritism in every office.

➤ If you want to get ahead, you have to make your accomplishments known because management rarely knows who's really doing the work.

➤ No one is indispensable or safe in their job—not even you.

➤ Socializing with your co-workers is very important to your success on the job.

Chapter 2

Strange Bedfellows

In This Chapter

➤ Office politics explained

➤ Ethics and office politics

➤ Your approach to getting ahead through office politics

➤ The importance of office politics to your career

1st Person: "Do you know anything about this fax machine?"

2nd Person: "A little. What's wrong?"

1st Person: "Well, I sent a fax, and the recipient called back to say all she received was a cover sheet and a blank page. I tried it again, and the same thing happened."

2nd Person: "How did you load the sheet?"

1st Person: "It's a pretty sensitive memo, and I didn't want anyone else to read it by accident, so I folded it so only the recipient could open it and read it."

It's a truth universally acknowledged that the world is full of cement heads. It's also no secret that you're going to end up having to work with a good portion of them because great-aunt Hortensia forgot to mention you in her will. That's why you need the tools to work with many different kinds of people. This chapter introduces you to those tools.

First, we'll define *office politics*. The definition includes lots of detail, so you'll know exactly what skills you're going to master—and why. Then you'll learn our three rules for getting ahead in the corporate jungle, an alternate universe filled with vision, task forces, and zones of comfort. It's a place where your computer can be programmed to alter your DNA, so you better be good and read *very* carefully. Finally, you'll assess your own approach to office politics.

What Are Office Politics?

Rita very much enjoyed her job as an assistant vice-president at a bank. She had been in the position for six years and was highly respected for her intelligence and ability to get things done. She did her job very well and efficiently, so that she had her evenings and weekends for friends, family, and hobbies.

So when Rita's boss retired and Rita was not offered the position of vice-president, she was ready to erupt like Mount Saint Helens.

"Why didn't I get the job?" Rita asked her boss. "You know that no one works harder than I do."

"Well, there really was no one reason," the boss stated. "Some people felt that Nicole was the better choice because they knew her better. You know, she socializes with everyone at office functions." The boss's final advice to Rita was to be more social and to get more exposure in the company.

Watch Your Back!
Never assume that just because people have a *need* to know that they *will* know. If you want someone to know something, you have to open your mouth.

Rita didn't get the job because she had never campaigned for it. There's no doubt that Rita had the experience to move up to vice-president, but she had not positioned herself for the job. Sitting in the front row doesn't guarantee you'll be the first one picked—unless you have your hand raised. Rita had ignored the reality of *office politics*.

In the Know

Some people say love makes the world go 'round. Others swear that it's money. Trust me on this: They're all wrong. Office politics make the world spin on its axis. Today, you need one vital ingredient to get your share of the organizational loot: political savvy. You must be able to practice sensible and ethical office politics.

Corporate Mumbo-Jumbo
Office politics are the strategies that intelligent people use in both public and private organizations to gain or maintain a competitive advantage in their careers.

How many of these things have happened to *you* on the job?

➤ The promotion you expected was given to someone with less experience or expertise—someone the boss liked better.

➤ You were the scapegoat for someone else's blunder.

➤ You were openly criticized at a meeting.

➤ You weren't invited to the boss's birthday party, and everyone but Iggy-who-never-takes-a-bath was.

➤ You were the subject of unpleasant gossip.

➤ You feel the life force is being sucked right out of you.

If so, you've been the victim of office politics. No longer just a power game, utilizing office politics for your benefit is now an important skill for developing a competitive edge and surviving in the global marketplace. Having political smarts is vital to the success of talented individuals in a fiercely competitive business world.

Protect Your Assets
Remember to be nice to the people you meet on the way up, because you're certainly going to meet them on the way down.

It's also nifty when you're trapped in a focus group where you're forced to "embrace change"—that is, accept yet another bonehead management fad that will result in slow-thinking employees being duped into leaping in the path of an oncoming train. (We're speaking metaphorically, of course. There is no train. It's really a wireless modem hooked to a turbo-charged neuro-spectrum field quantum calculator.)

Attila the Hun Is Alive and Well in Your Office

Clans of long ago that wanted to get rid of their unwanted people without killing them used to burn their houses down—hence the expression "to get fired." Extreme, but effective.

To some people, office politics is a justifiable form of deceit, cunning, and fraud. These workers define office politics as an accepted deception, perpetrated in the name of self-interest and self-preservation. To this crowd, office politics is on the order of cheating on your taxes, rolling back your odometer, and shaving a few years off your admitted age. We all know it's dishonest, but hey, everyone does it.

No, they don't. And the pond scum who think that everyone cheats to get ahead are deluded as well as dishonest.

Corporate Mumbo-Jumbo
A *consultant* is someone who is called in at the last moment and paid enormous amounts of money to assign the blame.

Play Fair

Office politics aren't smarmy and deceitful, like the dirty old man in the park or the scandalized politician du jour. Instead, office politics are the subtle and informational methods successful people use to gain power and advantage. Office politics explain the difference between the corporate fate of equally talented people. Skill at office politics helps you find more effective methods for surviving in the corporate jungle. It also enables you to deal with content-free communication, consultants, and life in the trailer park you call a company. This can help you take the elevator to the top and avoid getting the shaft.

The Force Be with You

Office politics are also:

➤ The ability to control people or resources

➤ The skill to get others to do things you want done

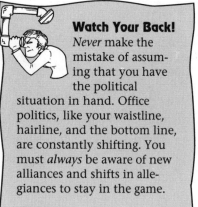

Watch Your Back!
Never make the mistake of assuming that you have the political situation in hand. Office politics, like your waistline, hairline, and the bottom line, are constantly shifting. You must *always* be aware of new alliances and shifts in allegiances to stay in the game.

➤ The desire to build mutual understanding and respect in the workplace

➤ Ways to remain flexible and make concessions without losing face

➤ Social skills

➤ Techniques for dealing with unfair situations with confidence and diplomacy

➤ The ability to master negotiations

➤ Often, the most important aspect of getting ahead at the workplace

➤ Underrated by those not in the know

➤ The most mystifying, confounding, and irritating aspect of being successful in a job

The Rules

Here are Rozakis' Big Three rules for savvy employees (that's *you*, kid):

Rule 1: All business is competitive.

Pretend all you want; we're telling it straight.

Rule 2: All groups have leaders.

And that's where you want to position yourself if it suits your personality, skills, and goals.

Rule 3: Winners get the prizes.

There are many prizes that winners accrue. Among the best are pride in a job well done, respect of your peers and superiors, lots of money, and sometimes even fame.

That's why you have to understand how office politics work and how you can make them work for you. By the time you finish this book, you will:

➤ Have a competitive edge over those who deny that the workplace is a political arena

➤ Be more likely to succeed than your politically naive counterparts

➤ Climb the corporate ladder faster

➤ Become the one with the power

➤ Bounce bullets and proprietary backward compatible RAM off your chest

> **Watch Your Back!**
> It's important to generate trust as well as respect in a business relationship. Inspire trust in others, and they will support you more often than not.

Know Thyself

Office politics aren't simple. If they were, we'd all be where we wanted to be on the corporate ladder—and you'd have saved the price of this book. Before you can get where you deserve to be, you have to know exactly where you are. That's what the following self-assessment can help you discover.

For each question, check "Agree" or "Disagree"; be honest.

> **Corporate Mumbo-Jumbo**
> People in business often band together to confront a common enemy—the so-called "us vs. them" strategy.

Self-Assessment Worksheet

Agree	Disagree	
❏	❏	1. Honesty, like beauty, is relative.
❏	❏	2. Never tell anyone anything that can be used against you.
❏	❏	3. Hire only people who will help you look good and get ahead.
❏	❏	4. It's a waste of time to help someone who won't help you in return.
❏	❏	5. When the issue is crucial, it's important to act as fast as you can.
❏	❏	6. Never share good ideas if they won't personally benefit your career.
❏	❏	7. If you get wind of a juicy tidbit of information, don't hesitate to use it to your own advantage.
❏	❏	8. Diplomacy is far more important than performing well on the job.
❏	❏	9. Always tell your boss the office scuttlebutt, even if you're not sure it's true.

continues

continued

Agree	Disagree	
❏	❏	10. It's a dog-eat-dog world, so it's okay to steal someone else's ideas if they will help your career.
❏	❏	11. When you get angry at a colleague, be sure to share your feelings with everyone in earshot.
❏	❏	12. It's unwise to discuss current issues without first knowing other people's opinions.
❏	❏	13. It's political suicide to hire someone who's smarter than you are.
❏	❏	14. Tell the big bosses what they want to hear rather than the brutal truth.
❏	❏	15. Getting even can't help you in business.
❏	❏	16. You should tell a colleague you like their work even if it stinks.
❏	❏	17. When all else fails, intimidation is a valid option.
❏	❏	18. There are times when it's good policy to make others feel bad about their work.
❏	❏	19. It's a good idea to tell colleagues when you're working on a successful project.
❏	❏	20. You should keep a secret if it will help a friend to get ahead without any benefit to you.

Score Yourself

Give yourself 3 points for every "Agree" and 1 point for every "Disagree."

51–60 points	A master of the universe. So what if ethics get kicked out of the way as you climb to the top?
36–48 points	You wannabe, you. But since you've kicked aside anyone who can help you, don't expect an easy time of it.
24–33 points	We like you. You've got average political skills and diplomacy reinforced by a strong helping of self-control and decency.
20–23 points	What color is the sky on *your* planet? Not only don't you play the game, you're not even aware that there *is* a game.

As this assessment shows, there are two ways to get to the top: nasty and nice. Because you'll get there just as fast—if not faster—by playing fair, why not be a mensch and use the Golden Rule to govern how you use office politics?

Don't Sit Out This Dance

Riddle me this:

Question   What did the 45-year old executive say when he was forced out of his corporate position?

Answer   "I can proudly say I never played office politics one day in my career."

Like death and taxes, you can't escape office politics. They're like air: all around us and necessary for survival.

Unless you're willing to play the game of office politics, you'll find yourself benched and baffled—not to mention broke.

By now, you know that we're advocating an ethical approach to playing and staying in the game. You're not going to learn any corporate kneecapping from us. We're not going to ask you to cook 30-minute brownies in 20 minutes, speak with Elvis, or tread water for three days in a row. We won't even ask you to become a low-level, cubicle-dwelling field sales organizer.

Instead, you'll learn how to play to win, but also how to keep your heart, soul, and integrity in the process.

Once upon a time, when the world was young (say, the 1950s), it was thought that office politics were restricted to the men in the gray flannel suits who were trying to make it to the corner offices. We now know that people in all jobs at all levels use politics to keep their positions and move on up.

Here's what our friend Harry told us:

Protect Your Assets
The Golden Rule, for those of you who slept through catechism (or had no religious reasons to attend it in the first place), is, "Do unto others as you would have others do unto you." It's not: "He who has the gold, rules."

Watch Your Back!
Information is power. Remember that not everyone can access information simply because they have a "need to know." Gather what you can...and use it.

> My parents are very real people, the salt of the earth. They had both worked their way up from entry-level jobs to supervisory positions. They believed in the traditional work ethic that hard work is its own reward, that diligence would eventually be rewarded. When I first started out, I followed their lead. In my part-time jobs in high school and college, I plugged away and bided my time. Their philosophy worked, too. The system failed when I took my first "real" job in a brokerage house, however.

> It became obvious within a few weeks after I was hired that I was with the "take-no-prisoners" crowd. Everyone was looking to make it big and retire at 45, with a

mansion, vacation home, fancy cars, and pots of money. In order to get ahead, it was kill or be killed. My colleagues never missed a chance to trash each other to get in good with the bosses. At meetings, they sat on the edge of their chairs and nodded in approval at anything the boss said.

Protect Your Assets
New business relationships, triggered by role changes (such as promotions), enjoy a honeymoon period. You can sometimes get things done during that time that you otherwise could not accomplish as easily.

They competed with each other to see who could stay the latest at work every night. Of course, they ran out the door right after the partners left. On their off hours, they played golf and tennis with big clients. If someone heard that a client bungee jumped, did barefoot aluminum foil dancing, or practiced underwater fire prevention, they rushed out to take lessons. Soon, I was playing the same games as everyone else. I felt I had to in order to survive.

Maybe you don't have to follow Harry's example to the extreme, but his final point rings true. To compete, you have to do what you can to make sure the playing field is as even as you can get it.

The Least You Need to Know

➤ *Office politics* are the strategies that intelligent people use in both public and private organizations to gain or maintain a competitive advantage in their business.

➤ To survive in today's cut-throat economy, you *must* be politically savvy.

➤ Every business is competitive. The leaders of the pack get the goodies.

➤ Like death and taxes, office politics are inescapable. Like it or not, you have to join in.

➤ Play fair; it pays off big.

Chapter 3

Shoot the Moon

In This Chapter

➤ Inevitable political situations in the workplace

➤ Close encounters of the political kind

➤ Important political and career goals

➤ Personal political strategies

We know you play to win (don't we all?), but sometimes competition gets just *a little* out of hand. Conventional wisdom dictates that the person who dies with the most toys wins, but we all want to be around as long as possible to play with those toys.

No matter what toys you want—a shower in your Rolls, a house the size of Graceland, or a coveted spot on the Oversight Committee—you're going to work hard to get them. But you've learned so far that working hard at your actual *work* counts for little without working equally hard at office politics. Now, don't get us wrong; this isn't a bad thing. After all, toys *are* fun, and competition can be healthy as well as invigorating. Competition for the corner office is inescapable, like infomercials on late-night TV and that guy who calls during dinner to sell you vinyl siding.

In this chapter, you'll first discover why political situations go with the workplace like Michael Jackson goes with cosmetic surgery. Then we'll show you how to rank your levels of involvement in office politics. Along the way, we'll help you decide how deeply you want to get involved in the politics in your office, focus on your personal goals, develop individual strategies, and formulate a mission statement.

Live and Learn

"At last!" Matt thought. "A project that will blow them out of the water. It will make my career. It's going to establish my reputation throughout the publishing world." Jim, Matt's closest friend in the company, agreed. "Your ship has come in, good buddy," Jim said. "This is the one-in-a-million project you've been waiting for your whole career. How come you get all the luck? Well, you might as well tell me about it."

Watch Your Back!
Some workers are more interested in "psychic income," such as a good working relationship and friends, than in money, power, and career prospects. That so many workers choose friend-ships over business is not sur-prising when we consider that some people establish a sense of identity through the con-nections they forge between themselves and others.

Jim had shown such enthusiasm for the project that Matt had shared all the details. Jim had even taken notes. At the time, Matt hadn't thought anything about Jim's interest. After all, it was clearly Matt's project, and they were good friends and colleagues.

Imagine Matt's shock, then, when he walked into the meeting ready to blow his colleagues away with his terrific proposal, only to find that Jim had already asked if he could open the meeting with his "great idea."

Jim stole the idea and ran with it all the way to the top. Jim's career took off for the stars...and Matt was left in the dust.

Matt got duped by his colleague and so-called "friend." We wish we could tell you that this is an uncommon situation, but it's very common. Hey, if life was fair, Elvis would be alive, and all the impersonators would be dead.

Here's Laurie's experience:

"I learned about Machiavellian methods first-hand when a louse snookered me out of credit for a project early on in my career. Me? Me! What can I plead but youth and ignorance. I was such a trusting soul in those days. Even now, more than a decade later, I still can't look at the snake without wanting to throttle him."

What political situations have you been involved in during your career? Take a few minutes to think back. Use the following worksheet to help you organize your thoughts.

Political Situations Worksheet

1. When was the last time you got snookered at work? What was the situation and the outcome?

   _____

   _____

   _____

2. How long did it take you to realize that you were being hung out to dry?

   _____

   _____

   _____

3. When you do realize that you've been sucked into a morass, what usually happens?

   _____

   _____

   _____

4. What do you see as your *strengths* in dealing with office politics?

   _____

   _____

   _____

5. What do you see as your *weaknesses* in dealing with office politics?

   _____

   _____

   _____

6. What is your overall attitude about using tactics and strategies to improve your position in the company and business world?

   _____

   _____

   _____

7. What political skills do you admire in others and would like to acquire for yourself?

_____

_____

_____

8. What do you see as your greatest political challenge in your present company?

_____

_____

_____

9. What *short-term* political strategies have you developed for yourself?

_____

_____

_____

10. What *long-term* political strategies have you developed for yourself?

_____

_____

_____

Goal Tender

Snap Quiz: Answer true or false:

> You either understand innately how office politics work or you don't. Some people are naturally savvy. The rest just can't learn.

The answer is *False*.

Now, it *is* true that all kids come into this world knowing how to raise a ruckus in a restaurant or movie theatre. Some lucky people are born with the ability to find the last parking space in the city or the last chocolate chip cookie in the bag. Heck, some of us even come with silver spoons in our mouths, but none of us comes equipped with a political sense. And every single one of us can learn to master office politics.

How?

Start by exploring your political goals.

When I Grow Up, I Want to...

Lily Tomlin once said, "I always wanted to be somebody, but I should have been more specific." In the past few years, it has become very chic to talk about career planning and career goals. All hype aside, few of us have the slightest clue where we want to be in 10 minutes, much less in 10 years.

There are five reasons why you *must* have political and career goals.

1. Your career goals affect your participation in office politics.
2. It is most efficient to use your energies to work toward something you want.
3. Goals give your work motivation as well as meaning.
4. Having goals gives you objective standards by which to measure your success.
5. Finally, setting goals helps you assess the risks of any career strategy you decide to use.

Here's an easy way to order your priorities. Following are 15 common goals. Arrange them on the line from most to least important. There's no right answer here; it all depends on what you want out of life. Once you know what you want, you can go after it—in the office and outside it.

Watch Your Back!
There's no magic in risk analysis. Basically, there are three factors to consider: probability, cost, and motive.

Prioritizing Your Goals

Goal	Most Important	Important	Least Important
admiration	❏	❏	❏
big money	❏	❏	❏
comfort	❏	❏	❏
fame	❏	❏	❏
family	❏	❏	❏
fancy office	❏	❏	❏
impressive title	❏	❏	❏
knowledge	❏	❏	❏
leisure time to do well	❏	❏	❏
material possessions	❏	❏	❏
power	❏	❏	❏
praise	❏	❏	❏
respect	❏	❏	❏
security	❏	❏	❏

Object Lesson

Now, let's kick it up a notch to focus your goals more closely. Just answer each question. Use the goals and your results from the previous worksheet.

Focusing Your Goals

1. What three career goals are most important to me? Why?

    _____

    _____

    _____

2. What do I like most about my present career?

    _____

    _____

    _____

3. What do I like the least about it?

    _____

    _____

    _____

4. Where do I want to be in a year?

    _____

    _____

    _____

5. Where do I want to be in five years?

    _____

    _____

    _____

6. Where do I want to be in 10 years?

    _____

    _____

    _____

7. What do I have to do to achieve my goals?

_____

_____

_____

8. What stands in my way?

_____

_____

_____

When You Wish Upon a Star

A friend recounted this amazing tale from the ledge:

> When I was hired, my boss promised that I would be making a very handsome salary by the new year. Although the starting salary was less than I wanted, I took the job based on his promise.

> Over the next few months, it became apparent that his promise might not be kept. When I confronted him, he said, "I tried to get that raise for you, but the front office won't allow it."

> "Why, then, did you quote me a figure that you weren't authorized to give?" I asked.

> He said, "When I made you the offer, I quoted you the salary that I *wished* you could get."

Watch Your Back!
The adage "It's not what you know but who you know" often applies to companies that lack clear-cut standards of performance and evaluation. This is very disheartening to employees.

Getting ahead in the office requires more than wishing; instead, it demands active political strategies. But before we can nudge you to get rolling, we must explain what you have to do to avoid getting caught up in special projects, status reports, and executive hair (that's the kind of power hair that deflects radioactivity).

So here are the top 10 political strategies. This is not a Chinese menu; you don't get one from column A and one from Column B. That's because there's only one column—and you get them all.

Top 10 Political Strategies

1. Socializing in the company
2. Networking in the company
3. Networking in the industry

Watch Your Back!
Office politics require some leadership. You have to be able to lead people to do or not do whatever you want done or left undone. People call this "manipulation" if they dislike it and "leadership" if they admire it. We call it the name of the game.

4. Focusing yourself on political realities
5. Maintaining control
6. Setting goals
7. Showing positive attitude
8. Learning to negotiate
9. Communicating persuasively
10. Being patient

Movers and Shakers

By now, you know that people who go out of their way to avoid using political strategies find themselves as cranky as a sleep-deprived two-year-old or a formerly fast-track manager who has just been "rightsized." Therefore, smart people (that's you) know that they have to play the game on some level. Hey, you can't win it if you're not in it.

Here are the three levels of involvement, from heavily involved to lightly involved.

Born to Be Wild

Here's how involved you should be if you're as smooth as silk, like to dominate a conversation, and drive a Mercedes 560SEL:

➤ Cultivate relationships outside the company
➤ Socialize with only the most influential people
➤ Become an expert in your field
➤ Make things happen
➤ Impress high-ranking people
➤ Develop followers
➤ Exaggerate your talents
➤ Recognize that leadership pays much more than a con job and doesn't require fast thinking

Born to Be Filed

If you're born to be filed, you see yourself as a faceless member of the crowd, a worker bee in the hive. You realize that the world is populated by shallow and ignorant people; that's why form will always be more important than substance. That's okay; each to his own taste. Here are the choices for someone like you, a person who never overdresses, never dominates a conversation, and goes to bed early.

➤ Negotiate for raises and other signs of advancement.

➤ Promote yourself.

➤ Seek additional responsibility.

➤ Obtain access to top executives.

➤ Work on key projects.

➤ Compliment and support decision-makers.

➤ Volunteer to be the office Fire Warden (and so risk death in a high-rise inferno while the Born to Be Wild Boss scrambles over your back).

Born to Be Mild

The following list shows your political strategies if you don't care whether your socks match your pants *or* your shoes (or each other, for that matter), are known around work as "the quiet one," and wish you could have voted for Eisenhower.

➤ Build relationships.

➤ Network.

➤ Project a successful image.

➤ Work in teams.

➤ Gather information.

➤ Make yourself known and visible.

➤ Ditch the plastic pocket protector and take the electrical tape off your glasses.

Change Is in the Air

Snap Quiz: As you grow older, what lost quality of your youthful life do you miss the most?

a. Innocence

b. Idealism

c. Cherry bombs

Age has an impact on us all, especially when it comes to career advancement. The first day of your first job, you probably had that bright-eyed, idealistic enthusiasm of an innocent babe. Of course, things change as some of that innocence and idealism erode away. But that doesn't mean you can't effect change or have to thanklessly plod away in a cubicle for 40-some-odd years.

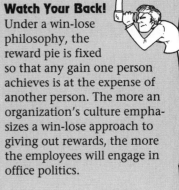

Watch Your Back!
Under a win-lose philosophy, the reward pie is fixed so that any gain one person achieves is at the expense of another person. The more an organization's culture emphasizes a win-lose approach to giving out rewards, the more the employees will engage in office politics.

As you move up in your career, your agenda must have certain fixed goals yet still remain flexible enough to accommodate change. Like any good strategy, you need a solid plan. The successful advancement plan has three parts: writing a mission statement, setting goals, and adopting the appropriate mind-set. Let's look at each one in detail.

Mission Possible: Mission Statement

Major corporations have mission statements—why not you?

Now, don't confuse your mission statement with a company's business plan. Somewhere between the delusions of senior management and the cold reality of the market lies a company's business plan. It has two major steps:

➤ Gathering information

➤ Ignoring it

Your *mission statement* is what you personally and professionally want to achieve with regard to office politics. Company business plans are rarely constrained by reality, much less common sense. As a result, company business plans contain irrational comparisons, bad alternatives that make everyone look good, and unrealistic revenue projections.

Your mission statement, in contrast, has a grip on reality. It makes sense and can help you. Here's a model mission statement to get you started: *I want to learn how to build powerful business relationships, network, and promote myself.*

Mission Statement

Write your mission statement here. (Stop trembling. This isn't being graded.)

_____

_____

_____

Win One for the Gipper

To meet your mission statement, you have to set specific goals. These goals should also be realistic, as in "to make vice-president by age 35" or "to become the market leader in fabric softener and satellite communications" rather than vague as in "to take over the world." Also avoid the unlikely and unrealistic, as in "to earn more money than Bill Gates." *No one* earns more money than Bill Gates.

While we're on money, don't think you're getting underpaid. Not at all! You just haven't considered all the elements of your virtual yearly compensation.

Your virtual yearly compensation is far more than the money you get after Uncle Sam and your pension plan. It includes the following components:

- ➤ bonus
- ➤ office coffee
- ➤ health plan
- ➤ personal phone calls
- ➤ stolen office supplies

- ➤ free photocopies
- ➤ sick and personal days
- ➤ surfing the Net
- ➤ frequent flier miles
- ➤ personal e-mail

See how well you're paid?

Mind Set

There's a lot to be said for positive thinking. The attitudes you assume to master personal growth and change can make or break your campaign. Here are some suggestions:

- ➤ Be positive.
- ➤ Remain flexible.
- ➤ Learn to focus.
- ➤ Make decisions.
- ➤ Be a team player.
- ➤ Never get caught stealing office supplies.

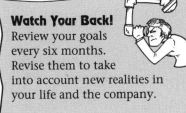

Watch Your Back!
Review your goals every six months. Revise them to take into account new realities in your life and the company.

The Least You Need to Know

- ➤ Like gravity, office politics are inescapable.
- ➤ Everyone can learn to master office politics, even if you can't balance your checkbook, use an ATM, or operate a Zamboni.
- ➤ You *must* have political and career goals to use your time efficiently, motivate yourself, and have objective standards for self-assessment.
- ➤ Select the political strategies that suit your personality and career goals.
- ➤ As you climb the corporate ladder, your agenda must have certain fixed goals yet still remain flexible enough to accommodate change.

Chapter 4

Like a Virgin

In This Chapter

➤ The importance of first impressions

➤ The consequence of meeting everyone, right from the get-go

➤ The business of coffee breaks

➤ Machiavellian methods and backstabbers

➤ Alliances and praise

Complete this sentence: A funeral is a good time to...

a. Remember the deceased and console loved ones.

b. Reflect upon the fleeting transience of earthly life.

c. Tell the joke about the guy who has Alzheimer's disease and cancer.

Everyone wants to be the life of the party, but humor is a funny thing: Sometimes it's amusing, and sometimes it's not. Making a good first impression on the job is a lot like humor: There's no middle ground between success and failure.

In this chapter, you'll learn how to get off on the right foot with a new job—so you don't end up without a leg to stand on.

First Day Jitters

So you have a new job. Goody for you. All sarcasm aside, it *is* good for you...if you listen to us. Let's start at the very beginning.

You know that first impressions matter. How you position yourself on the first day at a new company (or at a new job within the same company) is the way you'll be perceived for a long time. To avoid having to undertake a massive image-changing campaign, make sure your colleagues' first impression of you is a "value-added" one.

So let us show you how it's done.

Fly on the Wall

As you're making that crucial first impression, never say anything that could come back and bite you in the butt if it's taken out of context. For example, comments in an interview like "I'm just trying out my present job to see if I like the insurance field" can be used to show that you don't have a commitment to the company—which you probably don't, but that's beside the point.

This isn't to say that you can't manipulate your colleagues. For example, a little embellishment never hurts anything. Don't claim to be Michael Jordan (someone may ask you to sink a few baskets or look too closely at your sneakers—and then where would you be?) but don't be so quick to reject the chance for a little image enhancement.

Watch Your Back!

You know the handshake drill: grab, pump, drop. Make eye contact and smile. So far, so good, but not always. If you're a woman working with an Orthodox Jewish client, the handshake is taboo—as is any other body contact with men. That shouldn't stop you from introducing yourself and explaining your job, however.

Press the Flesh

Day 1: Your mission, should you choose to accept it, is to attempt to meet everyone in your department. It *is* essential that you walk around and meet everyone individually. Even though you run the risk of feeling like a politician glad-handing voters, we can promise you that you won't have to kiss any babies, pass out any bumper-stickers, or give any long-winded speeches. That's not to say you won't have those "election night" jitters, however.

Why is it so crucial that you make the rounds? Meeting everyone on the very first day

➤ Demonstrates that you're a friendly person

➤ Shows that you have an interest in becoming part of the team

➤ Highlights your political savvy

➤ Positions you as someone who takes charge

➤ Satisfies everyone's curiosity that you don't have two heads, rumors to the contrary

How can you meet everyone? One of the easiest ways is simply going from desk to desk, shaking hands, saying your name, and waiting to hear their name in return. For example, you might say, "Hi, I'm E. C. Duzit. I just started today as a systems analyst and I wanted to introduce myself."

Even though you won't remember everyone's name (and you're not expected to), introducing yourself shows that you're making the effort.

Break for Business

Sometime in the middle of the morning or afternoon, if someone asks you to take a brief break and join them for a cup of java, go. This is your chance to break into the informal political system that often dominates office politics. Unless you have been given express orders to the contrary or simply can't get away, it's essential for you to join the crowd on day one. If you don't, you're sending a clear message that you're not eager to meet everyone. This sets you back before you even get started.

Now, the people who tendered this first invitation might be genuinely nice folks whom you will enjoy working with. Fortunately, this is usually the case. However, they might also be weasels with an ulterior motive or two. Unfortunately, no one wears a sign that says, "I'm one of the nice guys" or "I'm just waiting to stab you in the back."

What's in it for the weasels? Here are a few of the most common ulterior motives you're likely to encounter:

➤ They're on the outs with your boss and anxious to curry favor with you.

➤ There's a long-standing office feud, and they want to get you on their side before the other camp grabs you. This happened to Laurie in her second job, and the situation was ugly enough to chase a bulldog off a meat wagon.

➤ They hear you're going to be powerful, and they want to get in good with you from the very beginning.

Corporate Mumbo-Jumbo
The trendy business term for a take-charge person, someone with leadership skills, is "proactive." It's an adjective, as in "a proactive manager."

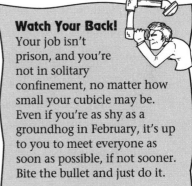

Watch Your Back!
Your job isn't prison, and you're not in solitary confinement, no matter how small your cubicle may be. Even if you're as shy as a groundhog in February, it's up to you to meet everyone as soon as possible, if not sooner. Bite the bullet and just do it.

➤ You might be a looker, and they might be interested in you from a less-than-professional standpoint. Laurie had this scenario, too (and at every possible opportunity, she reminds Bob how cute others found her).

At this point, there's no way you can discern anyone's motives. You certainly can't come right out and say, "So, what's your hidden agenda here?" Odds are, you probably don't know anyone else well enough to ask them to map out the new political minefield for you, either. So what to do? Try these ideas:

1. Be friendly. It costs nothing and doesn't hurt.

2. At first, give everyone the benefit of the doubt. Avoid prejudging people. Hey, you could end up working for them…or married to them.

3. Learn as much as you can by listening carefully to everyone, no matter where they appear to be on the pecking order.

4. Pay attention to nonverbal as well as verbal cues. For example, which people have their hands crossed across their chests? This is frequently a sign of blockage, as in "Keep your distance, pardner."

5. Say as little of substance as you can. Comment on how much you like the company, job, and people. Share some information about your background. For instance, you can explain where you went to school and what you studied or where you worked previously.

6. Don't offer any rash opinions about company policies. Remember, you don't know where the boss stands on multifaceted, nondisciplined, matrix-modeled untasked approaches to human integrational imperatives in a preholistic context.

Watch Your Back!
Feel free to talk about your previous position, if asked, but *never* trash your former job, employer, or colleagues—no matter how fervently you wish them all under the wheels of a bus. For all you know, a new colleague could (God forbid!) be friendly with a former nemesis of yours.

The key to success here is saying as little as you can while asking as many questions as possible. Not only does this make you seem interested, but it also gets you the information you need to figure out the political structure of the office.

Look for clues to the company's style and language. For instance, do the people in this company refer to their work as *jobs*, *tasks*, or *assignments*? Do they play Buzzword Bingo, flinging around quality vectors, paradigms, and motivational talks to put a fire in your belly? The sooner you walk the walk and talk the talk, the sooner you'll feel comfortable in the new environment—and be able to manipulate it to your advantage.

A Walk on the Wild Side

An acquaintance shared the following story with us. As you read it, see how you would have handled the situation:

> "The first day I started my new job, three colleagues invited me to have coffee with them. I was flattered to be included in the group so quickly, and we really hit it off. I felt that I was off to a great start because I was accepted by some nice people in the company. They told me all sorts of important information, too, especially stories about the boss, a real louse from the sound of it. The coffee break ran a little long, but I didn't think much of it because my new friends assured me that the rules were relaxed in this company.
>
> Well, we continued meeting for coffee breaks all week and boy, did I pick up the dirt. At the end of the week, my boss called me in and asked me why I was spending so much time with these people. I said, 'Well, they invited me.' My boss explained that they were all on probation for poor performance and work habits. Then I realized *why* my new 'friends' had been so nice to me; they were trying to use me to get even with the boss. I also realized that everyone else was keeping their distance from this crowd. Looking back, it all seemed so clear, but while it was happening, I felt special and flattered."

As "retrenching," "outsourcing," and "downsizing" become more and more common-place, workers who don't perform up to snuff are getting put on notice to clean up their acts. (More and more good workers are "reorganized" right out the door too. Especially the ones who don't understand how to use office politics to their benefit. But that's why *you* bought this book, isn't it?)

This can create factions, conspiracies, and cabals at all levels. What to do?

If the same people invite you to coffee the second day, just say no. *Never* let yourself be locked into one network when you're just starting a new job or position. Because you don't have a clue where the first group stands in the true scheme of things, the last thing you want to do is get sucked into their intrigues. You *must* get around.

If necessary, it's better to avoid schmoozing with anyone for a few days rather than getting aligned with a specific group before you've established the lay of the land. Take it as slow as continental drift.

Corporate Mumbo-Jumbo
In trendy business circles, actually getting to see someone super-important in person is now called having "face-time," as in "I got in some face-time with Mick E. Mouse yesterday."

I Get Around

As you ease into the job, you'll soon begin to see that the political situation is far more complicated than you likely assumed at first. Don't beat yourself up too badly about this because it takes a great deal of concentration, thought, and analysis to discover power blocs and vacuums.

At this stage, you should be starting to put the players in place.

How good are you about figuring out who stands where in the pecking order? Take this quiz to see. Put a check mark next to each technique you've used when you started a new job or position. Count each check mark as one point.

Job Techniques Quiz

❏   1. Watching carefully to see where each person fits in the informal power structure.

❏   2. Listening to see which bosses are deferred to by the masses.

❏   3. Figuring out which secretaries are truly powerful.

❏   4. Charting alliances among colleagues.

❏   5. Circulating around the office to increase your visibility.

❏   6. Making the scene at lunches and dinners with colleagues.

❏   7. Getting to the important weekend and evening office events.

❏   8. Making it easy for people to approach you.

❏   9. Identifying the people you might be able to trade favors or work with to both sides' mutual satisfaction and gain.

❏ 10. Making yourself generally useful and known as a team player.

Score Yourself

10 points	You Slick Willie, you.
7–9 points	You're *this* close. Stay with us.
4–6 points	How many roads must an employee walk down before you call him a cab? This is the cab.
0–3 points	Don't leave the room. You might end up with Timmy down the old mine shaft, but without Lassie to go for help.

The New Kid on the Block

As a new employee, you have a built-in advantage in your campaign to understand the company's office politics and culture. Because you're fresh meat, you might often be on the receiving end of your fellow employees' version of office reality. Some of these folks might be sincerely trying to give you the score; others might have another, less sincere agenda.

As the neophyte, you're a blank slate. Everyone wants to carve their impression on your tabula rasa. They're convinced that they will be able to influence you to see things through their eyes. We know better, don't we, kiddo?

Johnny B. Good

Now, listen up. Here's what you're going to do:

➤ Listen

➤ Take mental notes

➤ Be pleasant

➤ Never take sides

➤ Make up your own mind after considering what everyone has said, what you've seen, and what you've heard

Corporate Mumbo-Jumbo
To "work the room," you chat with everyone there, seeing and being seen. Masters of this art make it look casual, but don't be fooled: It's as carefully planned as any high-class seduction.

To put it another way, let's look back at a classic, Shakespeare's *Hamlet*. Old Willie was onto something, which explains why his plays are still fresh nearly 400 years after they were first penned. Here's the advice Polonius gave his son Laertes when Laertes was setting off for France:

> And these few precepts in thy memory
> Look thou character. Give thy thoughts no tongue,
> Nor any unproportioned though his act.
> Be thou familiar, but by no means vulgar.
> Those friends thou hast, and their adoption tried.
> Grapple them unto thy soul with hoops of steel;
> But do not dull thy palm with entertainment
> Of each new-hatched, unfledged comrade...
> Give every man thy ear, but few thy voice;
> Take each man's censure, but reserve thy judgment....
> This above all, to thine own self be true,
> And it must follow as the night the day
> Thou canst not then be false to any man.

In modern lingo, Polonius tells people in new situations to

1. Keep your mouth shut and think before you act.

2. Be friendly, but not vulgar.

3. Cherish your tried-and-true friends.

4. Don't be so quick to buddy up to new acquaintances.

5. Listen to everyone but reserve your judgment.

Watch Your Back!
Remember how your mother panicked when the kids were too quiet? It usually meant they were up to something dangerous. The same is true in office politics. Quiet people often deliberately stand back to see how a situation will pan out before they make a move. Because they listen more than they talk, they are sometimes at the center of power intrigues.

6. Most important of all, be true to yourself. If you follow your own code of ethics and morals, you can't be false to anyone.

Great advice for 16th century wage slaves, and equally good advice for Dilberts today. And you thought all Shakespeare did was mumble on about kings, queens, and melancholy Danes in Ye Olde English.

Hall Manners

And while we're on the issue of collegiality, let us clue you into hallway etiquette. The accepted rules of hallway etiquette only cover the first two times you run into the same person in the hall. After that, you're usually on your own. That's why you have *us*.

Our friend Amy shared this piece of advice with us:

I think the thing I frequently hear is "So and so is so unfriendly. He/She never says hello." The point is, of course, say hello first and greet everyone, from the mailroom person to the big boss. Just "hi," or "good morning," or whatever. Aside from just being polite, normal, socialized behavior, it gives you an edge as it makes you seem approachable and open, which generally works to your advantage. It's a simple thing I learned a long time ago and it's never failed me. You never know who you're eventually going to be working with, so presenting the best face possible is always a good rule of thumb. Plus, I just feel weird walking past people and acting like I don't see them.

Of course, if you really don't feel like talking to anyone and you have some papers in your hand, you can pretend to be (or actually be) looking over whatever is in your hand and not get accused of snubbing.

Good Buddies

As Barbra Streisand likes to warble, "People who need people are the luckiest people in the world." What she didn't mention is that they're also the smartest, as far as office politics are concerned. As your workload increases, you'll need friends and allies within the company—if you don't already need them. That's why it's so important to figure out who you can count on in a pinch.

If you've been following our advice, a few months into the job you should have a pretty clear idea of which people are powerful, which ones are powerless, and which ones are troublemakers. You should be able to discern who the bosses like and who has fallen from grace. But before you start getting involved in the fray, it's advisable to build some bridges by getting some allies. Here's how.

One of the best ways to build allies is by helping a colleague who's overwhelmed with work. Anticipate ways to be helpful rather than waiting to be asked. Of course, this means extra work for you, but it also means that you've got some credit in the "favor bank," that shadowy "one-hand-washes-the-other" network that makes the world go 'round on a business as well as personal level.

Here are some ways that we have helped our colleagues in the past. Each favor built good will and alliances. Read about our politically astute ideas, and then add four ways of your own that would work on your job right now:

1. Laurie: Took on a rush project to enable my editors and the production department to meet a promised deadline.

2. Bob: Arranged for a car service to take an employee home from the hospital. When she was feeling better, set up her home computer so she could work at home and recuperate at the same time.

3. Laurie: Picked up student term papers and delivered them to a colleague's house.

4. Bob: Caught what would have been a costly and embarrassing error in a colleague's proposal just prior to its presentation, enabling the presenter to correct it without anyone else knowing.

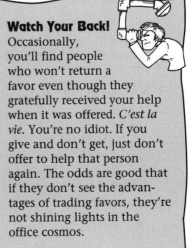

Watch Your Back!
Occasionally, you'll find people who won't return a favor even though they gratefully received your help when it was offered. *C'est la vie.* You're no idiot. If you give and don't get, just don't offer to help that person again. The odds are good that if they don't see the advantages of trading favors, they're not shining lights in the office cosmos.

5. _____

_____

6. _____

_____

7. _____

_____

8. _____

_____

Stack the Deck

Once you've got some alliances in place, it's time to start shimmying up the office grapevine. You can start by praising the help that others have given you. Why not just grab all the credit yourself? The same reason you don't take the biggest piece of cake. Your mama didn't raise no piggies.

You know that being gracious shows your good manners, which makes others admire your consideration.

In the same way, giving credit on the job makes you appear more powerful. Comedian Jerry Seinfeld applies this principle when he is quick to give his co-stars and collaborators the lion's share of credit for his show's success: "My real talent," he said in a *Time* magazine interview, "is in picking people" (January 12, 1998).

Since most workers feel they're not appreciated (and they usually aren't), giving credit is a win-win proposition. By giving credit—even for small favors—you get favorable recognition for yourself, your Quality Team, and your bosses.

Walk This Way

Protect Your Assets
Praise is like hot peppers—a little goes a long way. Keep it light, sincere, and specific. If you slather praise like special sauce on a Big Mac, you'll come across as a phony.

Give credit casually and naturally. Under no circumstances go running to the boss every five minutes with a "report" on a colleague's good deed of the day. Don't write it up for the company newsletter, either. And unless they've donated a kidney to a child from the Amazon rainforest, don't shout it from the rooftops.

Instead, use the office grapevine as a means to give credit. For example, when you're waiting your turn at the copying machine, you might say, "Chuck stayed late last night to help me organize the shipment. Wasn't that great of him?" You can bet your bippy that your "casual" remark will get back to Chuck, many times over. You can also be sure that it will pay rich dividends.

Don't Start No Mess, Won't Be No Mess

Tattle-tale, ginger ale, stick your head in a garbage pail.

Remember how much you hated the class tattle-tale? The kindergarten baby whose head you always wanted to stick into gravy? Well, even though you're long out of the land of Dick and Jane, these same malcontents are still around, only now they're full-sized, working in your office, and much harder to punch out.

Giving credit casually and sincerely builds goodwill. Telling tales destroys goodwill. It's one thing to point out an error to the person who made it. It's another to do it in a public forum or to the boss. And those few who run to the boss to tell their version of a fiasco so the blame will be cast on others rather than themselves won't find anybody crying if they're let go.

Even if these folks do great work, they'll be the first ones whose necks are on the chopping block when lay-off time comes. And everyone will be glad to see the last of them.

The Least You Need to Know

> ➤ Make a good first impression by meeting everyone in the office right away. Press the flesh.

> ➤ Schmooze with the crowd on Day 1, but don't get locked into the same scene.

> ➤ Mingle and work the room until you figure out the power blocs.

> ➤ Do favors to build alliances. Give credit where credit is due.

> ➤ A little sincere praise goes a long way; too much goes nowhere.

> ➤ Most important of all, be true to yourself.

Part 2
Empowerment Plays

In your opinion, the ideal pet is:

    a. A cat

    b. A dog

    c. A dog that eats cats

It's a dog-eat-cat world in the land of "Quality Vision," "Process Improvement," "Interdisciplinary Task Forces," "Decision-making Process, and "Excellence in Teaming." (That's the place we used to call "The Job.")

As you probably have discovered through painful first-hand experience, the goal of management is to pressure employees into thinking that extra work without extra pay, meaningless projects, and moronic self-appraisals are good for them. How do they do this? By the not-too-subtle application of power.

In this section, you'll discover why power is so important, how to get it, and how to use it to your advantage.

Chapter 5

Power Brokers

In This Chapter

➤ "Power" as it relates to business and office politics

➤ Different types of power

➤ The importance of being in command in all work situations

➤ Performance reviews and power

The boss liked to think of himself in presidential terms, going so far as adopting Harry S Truman's motto "The buck stops here!" and having it emblazoned on his office door.

To which one disgruntled worker added, "Which is why the rest of us are underpaid!"

In business as in life, there are many ways of looking at the same thing. In this chapter, you'll discover the importance of looking beneath the surface to discover the real power structure in your office. Why? Once you know who's *really* holding the strings, you can figure out how to pull them to your advantage.

More Powerful Than a Locomotive

Practically speaking, the most desired and useful objective in any job is *power*. If you have power, you can make things happen—or not happen. You can influence people—bosses, subordinates, peers—to do things your way. You can also try new ideas and get credit for the ones that work. Power enables you to:

➤ Direct your future

➤ Achieve goals

➤ Establish resources

➤ Laugh when someone with less power says "utilize clarification process" or "streamline processes to maximize empowerment." People with less or no power must nod soberly and pretend to understand.

➤ Exercise authority

➤ Maximize performance

➤ Say "No way" when someone with less power says "Guess what? You've been appointed to the Strategic Planning Team."

➤ Create new opportunities

➤ Help others

➤ Be fulfilled

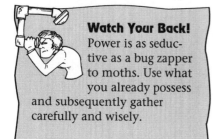

Watch Your Back!
Power is as seductive as a bug zapper to moths. Use what you already possess and subsequently gather carefully and wisely.

Protect Your Assets
The indirect use of power occurs when one person relies on the power of a second person to influence a third person. Got that? Now repeat after me: "Who's on first?"

➤ Have unlimited office supplies at your disposal with no questions asked and the ability to order a new lamp whenever you darn well please

Power is the prize, because money and influence follow it. People who have power move up rapidly. Therefore, it follows that their salaries rise as well. They get the good stuff: big houses, nice cars, and many flavors of overpriced designer coffee.

Now, there are some interesting and important exceptions to the power rule. For example, some administrative assistants, earning modest salaries, can make people who seem far more powerful tremble in their Gucci loafers. You might see a VP making $100,000+ a year kissing up to the mailroom manager, a guy making $20,000. Why the deference? The schlub has the power to get the Veep's job rushed through.

Several kinds of power exist. The specific type of power depends on its origin: the *organization* or the *person*. Organizations confer power, as they confer status and other tasty perks. People can also generate their own kinds of power in the workplace. Check out this powerful diagram:

People $\Rightarrow$ Power $\Leftarrow$ Organizations

Power to the People

The Company can give you many nice things, but the best and most useful is power. The three kinds of power that business can confer are *reward power*, *coercive power*, and *position power*.

➤ **Reward Power**

This power comes from the ability to provide something of value to someone else. For example, the boss exercises reward power by giving the peon a raise, an extra week of vacation, an office with a real window, or a chance to play hooky from the Management Practice Attainment Stage Seminar.

The short-hand version of reward power: "Do as I say if you want me to give you the things you want or value."

➤ **Coercive Power**

This power derives from the ability to punish or deprive someone of something of value. For instance, managers use coercive power when they discipline an insubordinate worker by placing him or her on probation, or even worse—making them attend the Management Practice Attainment Stage Seminar. In brief: "Do as I say if you want to avoid getting smacked upside your head, corporate-wise."

Watch Your Back!
Coercive power is efficient, but it doesn't build trust or commitment. That ol' brown-shirt fascist Mussolini used coercive power to get the trains to run on time, but look what happened to *him*.

➤ **Position Power**

This power comes from a person's role and the expectations associated with it. An executive director, for example, derives power from his or her title. Position power automatically confers compliance, usually without resentment. If you have less position power, this means you must take Systems Literacy Training to empower you to channel Multimedia Data Support Information Technology Training to the server (that is, you've got to go to that boring training class so you can slug away at your computer terminal in your little corner of the cubicle world because your boss says so).

Power from the People

The three main kinds of power that workers can generate by adroitly using their political skills are *power of position*, *power of influence*, and *power of scarcity*. Let's look at each of them in detail so you can decide which one or ones *you* want to achieve.

➤ **Power of Position**

This is the power that managers, directors, supervisors, and other hot shots have over the hoi polloi. It's based solely on their lofty perch on the organizational chart. If you have power of position, you get to make up the stupid buzzwords like "Diversify Next Generations Systems Upgrades" that make less powerful co-workers slam their heads against the wall in utter confusion. Sum it up as, "Do as I say because I have the right to tell you what to do."

➤ **Power of Influence**

This is the power that comes to workers with good "people skills" (a lot more on people skills later). Power of influence enables you to persuade people to do things you want done because they believe *they* will benefit as well. Sometimes, they do.

➤ **Power of Scarcity**

This is the power that secretaries, administrative assistants, and other members of the support staff wield. These people are powerful because they can extend or withhold vital services.

They are also powerful because they understand which jargon is meaningful that week and which is just designed to baffle the less powerful drones. That's because they're usually the ones typing up the buzzwords. One false keystroke, and *voila!* A new piece of meaningless language you have to learn.

In addition, many of these people are powerful because they've been with the company for a long time. Of course, this is not how the company handbook says the business should run. That's why you should trust us and not the handbook, even if it does use more fancy words you don't understand.

There are several kinds of informal power that are earned, not conferred. These are *expert power*, *friendship power*, and *presence power*.

Expert power is the power of respect gained as a result of what we know and what we can do. Laurie has this power as a result of having earned her Ph.D.; she is looked up to as an expert in her field and treated with considerable honor. She takes great solace in this on bad hair days. Bob has this power as the result of the innovations he has introduced in the company for which he works, which have then been adopted by the rest of the industry. And he wishes he had enough hair for a bad hair day.

Protect Your Assets

Presence power can help build expert power: People listen, in part, because you project an image of competence and self-confidence.

Friendship power, in contrast, is earned through trust. This usually comes only after years of association and can be easily destroyed. It also erodes easily if efforts are not made to sustain it. Like our front lawn, friendship power needs lots of attention and tender loving care.

Finally, *presence power* is the power of image—the way we project ourselves. You can build presence power by standing erect, making eye contact, dressing for success, and letting people know you're in the room. Laurie does this by assuming she owns the world, wearing overpriced but nonetheless gorgeous clothes, and doing the power walk. She can tell it works when she gets great seats at restaurants and free upgrades to first class on airplanes.

Top Dogs

Now, who has the power in the company for which you work? Figuring out who has the power can be as difficult as finding a parking space at the mall on Christmas Eve, fitting into your high school cheerleading uniform 10 years after the big game, or remembering where on earth you put your car keys.

Determining who has the power can be an especially difficult question to answer if you are new to the job. Perhaps you assumed that the people on the top of the company's flow chart are the movers and shakers. Never assume! Real power and someone's position on the organizational chart are not always the same. If anything, the chart usually tells you less about who has the power than a 15-minute coffee break with the secretary would.

To become savvy at office politics, you must first identify who has the power. You have to grasp the written—and unwritten—rules that govern who does what *with* and *to* whom in the office. How can you do this? Follow these steps.

Fly on the Wall

People with the power get to be on sexy projects. These are the desirable hot projects that get the big bucks and look great on your resumé. How can you tell the sexy projects from the cold ones? Think Sharon Stone or Mel Gibson on paper. Sexy projects often have the following buzz words somewhere in their descriptions: *multimedia, worldwide, advanced revenue, market, technology,* and *rapid.* Boring, flaccid projects often use these words: *accounting, operations, reduction, budget, quality,* and *analysis.* A sexy project is "Worldwide Advanced Revenue Multimedia Task Force on Technology." Add *palmtop, futuristic,* or *strategic* to the description, and you're on your way to ruling an empire.

Protect Your Assets
Try to get the most recent copy of the organizational chart that you can. Check the publication date in the company handbook; ask the Human Resources department or the administrative assistant who typed the chart when it was compiled.

Get Organized

Start by getting a copy of the company's organizational chart. You can often find it in the front office or in your company handbook. If not, you might have to ask your immediate supervisor for a copy. The company organizational chart will tell you the "official" power structure. This is rarely the same as the *real* power structure.

Following is a sample organizational chart. The one for your company should look similar to this model. If you cannot get the company's chart, complete our chart, using the names and responsibilities of each worker as your guide. It might not be completely correct, but it will give you a starting point.

Organizational Chart

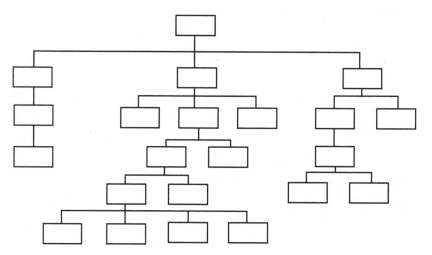

Get the Scoop

Now, find out who has the *real* influence in your place of work. Sorry, Charlie: This isn't as easy as it sounds. Variables include the meaning of specific job titles, the size of the company, and shifting responsibilities, to name just a few. But you have enough work to do, baby, so we're going to make it easier on you. Why not use the following worksheet to evaluate how much real power each person has in your company?

What happens if you work in the Worldwide Advanced Revenue Vision Quest Integral Rapid Imperative Technology Company along with 10,000 other under-paid menial assistants to the assistant? How many people should you evaluate in this case? It's plain that you can't consider all 10,000 souls. Instead, include anyone who could have any influence over you at all, anyone who could help your career, and anyone who could harm it. Better to include too many people than too few.

Directions: Answer each of the following questions. Use a separate sheet of paper for each person.

> **Protect Your Assets**
> The person to whom you report is very signifi-cant. If you report to an unimportant person, you are weakened by the relationship. Conversely, if you report to a boss who is very powerful in the pecking order, you have a much greater chance for advancement.

Power-Evaluation Worksheet

1. What is the person's title?

   _____

2. What do you think the title means within the company?
   Some titles, like "King," "Queen," or "Prince of Darkness" are easy to figure out. Others, like "Manager," "Supervisor," and "Director" are less clear cut.

   _____

   _____

3. To whom does this person report?

   _____

4. What is that person's position in the company?

   _____

5. Who reviews the person's decisions?

   _____

6. Who has veto power over the person's rulings?
   Knowing this can help you find the power vacuums. Otherwise, you might spend time impressing people who can't actually help you get ahead. You're better off spending some quality time with your remote control and sofa.

   _____

7. How many (if any) people report to this person?
   The body count matters. A corporate attorney who has two people reporting to her is less powerful than a plant manager who supervises 2,000 wage slaves. Even though the quality of the bodies is not equal, more *is* better in this instance.

   _____

8. What kind of people are they? For example, are they managers or serfs?

   _____

   _____

9. Is the person in a *line* or *staff* position?

   Line positions are income producing jobs, while *staff positions* are necessary jobs that nonetheless cost the company money. Generally, line positions are more powerful than staff positions.

   _____

10. How often has the person been promoted within this company?

    People in management tend to move around to acquire power, whereas people in staff acquire power by longevity.

    _____

11. What is this person's management style?

    There are many management styles; three of the most common are the *sales bosses* (who try to sell subordinates on what they want), the *social workers* (who constantly fret about employees' attitudes), and the *fire fighters* (who wait for minor problems to get worse so they can rush in and solve them heroically). If you can't put a name to the management style, just provide a description. And keep it clean; the kids might see this book.

    _____

    _____

12. How much do the person's decisions affect the overall success of the company?

    _____

    _____

13. Who consults this person on key decisions?

    Never underestimate the power of personal influence. At any level, someone who others consult *voluntarily* has power.

    _____

    _____

14. Who does this person play with? Who does this person have lunch with? Who does this person have drinks with after work? Who does this person play golf, tennis, and so on with on weekends?

    Networking matters. When four people plot the end of the world as we know it on a regular basis, they build rapport and a support system.

    _____

    _____

15. Put it altogether. How politically savvy is this person?

    _____

    _____

Get Crackin'

Draw your own organizational chart, using the company's chart as a starting point. Modify it to reflect what you have discovered about the real power structure in your company. The two charts might be very similar—or they might be very different indeed.

Remember, you can often get the inside skinny on the company power structure by breaking bread with colleagues and staff. Try eating breakfast and lunch with colleagues and having a chat here and there with staff. Just make sure you don't have any icky green things stuck in your teeth.

The Great Chain of Being

In the medieval and Renaissance world, everyone and everything had a fixed place in the cosmos, stretching from the lowliest creature in the natural world all the way up to the Big Fella in the sky. According to this "Great Chain of Being," everyone's place was as distinct as Don King's hair.

We could argue that the Great Chain of Being exists today in all companies, from the giants such as General Motors, Disney, and Time-Warner, all the way down to the little guys like Benny's Burger Haven, Trusses R Us, and Commemorative Plate Technology, Ltd.

Before you can even begin to deal with office politics, you have to figure out *who* within your company has the power. This will tell you which people can help and hurt your career. Check back to the power chart you've created.

Here's an easy and effective way to separate the super-powers from the mere mortals. Write the name of the most powerful person in the company in the center of the chart. Then write the names of the next most powerful people in the closest circle. Continue charting the power structure, working from the center of your corporate universe to the outer fringes of the power galaxy.

Protect Your Assets
Departments that generate income like Marketing and Sales usually have more power than personnel; manufacturing, which delivers a tangible product, is more powerful than accounting.

Watch Your Back!
Never work on your organizational chart at your desk or on your office computer. Take it home and leave it there. The last thing you want (well, maybe not the last thing, but pretty darn close) is to have someone find out that you're tracking the company's power hierarchy. You might as well put up a sign saying, "I'm moving full speed ahead and damn the torpedoes."

Watch Your Back!
As you get acclimated to the political climate in your office, make "subtle" your watchword. This is not the time for gangbuster tactics. Avoid questions such as "Is the boss really as stupid as he seems?"

Power Galaxy

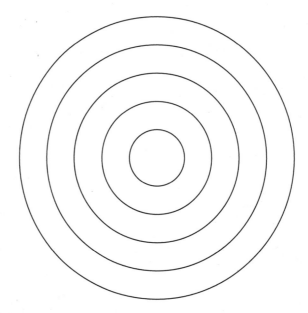

Performance Anxiety

That peculiar institution known as a "performance review" shows power at its most pernicious. In theory, the performance review is designed to be a positive interaction between a "coach" and an employee to achieve what's best for everyone. In actuality, it's more like playing poker and neither of you ever have to show your cards...with the only rule that the boss *always* holds the winning hand.

Because a performance review is nothing more than a thinly disguised power play, it is really designed to

➤ Inspire terror throughout the department

➤ Make you work like a one-armed paperhanger

➤ Amuse the other bosses

➤ Get you to eat a bug

➤ Justify your embarrassingly low salary

As you've no doubt noticed, we're concentrating on the negative performance reviews. If you have a great boss who sings your praises and gets you raises, you don't have to be concerned with this particular "game." We've been casting bosses in a bad light in this section to help you deal with the stinkers. In all cases, however, take performance reviews seriously because that's where your negotiation skills are going to be tested.

Unfortunately, as with the poker analogy, the boss always holds the winning hand. You can't change what he says, but fortunately, you can respond. Evaluation forms have a place for the employee to respond in writing. If yours doesn't, you can attach a page, but make sure to add a note like "Comments attached" to the line where you sign the form.

Your role is to leverage your power to squeeze as much money as you can from the company. Here's how.

Short-Sheeted

In this particular power *pas-de-deux*, your boss will try to maneuver you into admitting your shortcomings. Once your alleged flaws are in print, they are fodder for the power plays to come: You demand more money; your boss whines about your blots, blemishes, and boo-boos. Ergo: no bucks for you, buckaroo.

In order to burn you at the stake more efficiently, your boss will give you a Personal Evaluation Form to complete. A Personal Evaluation Form is like duct tape, one of the primal forces of the universe. As a result, it must be handled carefully, like a temperamental toddler.

Following is a sample Personal Evaluation Form. Fill it out now, based on your current performance.

Personal Evaluation Form

	Weaknesses			Strengths	
	1	2	3	4	5
Creativity	❑	❑	❑	❑	❑
Initiative	❑	❑	❑	❑	❑
Enthusiasm	❑	❑	❑	❑	❑
Leadership skills	❑	❑	❑	❑	❑
Communication skills	❑	❑	❑	❑	❑
Teamwork	❑	❑	❑	❑	❑
Strengths	❑	❑	❑	❑	❑
Quantity of work	❑	❑	❑	❑	❑
Quality of work	❑	❑	❑	❑	❑
Growth opportunities	❑	❑	❑	❑	❑
Personal grooming	❑	❑	❑	❑	❑
Plays nice with others	❑	❑	❑	❑	❑

Watch Your Back!
Remember that anything you put in writing can become part of your dreaded "permanent record." This gives people power over you that you definitely don't want them to have.

Ha! Gotcha! Under no circumstances should you have filled out the form honestly. If you have any control at all over written evaluations, remember that you're the greatest thing since spandex, Pez, and toaster pastries. Under no circumstances reveal any personal weaknesses in writing. Think of it as the Miranda warning: Any and all information you write on your Performance Evaluation can and will be used against you when it comes to raises and promotions. This is especially true of the "Growth Opportunities" section.

Blowing Your Own Horn

As part of your performance review, you'll have to document your accomplishments. Everything short of expelling gas in the middle of the boss's presentation can—and should—be spin-doctored into an accomplishment. Don't miss the chance to boast about your real accomplishments. But even the worst things you've done can be presented in a positive light.

Reality	Adjusted Reality
You lost big bucks on an important project.	"I took prompt cost-avoidance measures."
You did nothing for the recent assignment.	"I interfaced with the SDL unit to create FHGs for the LKK2 Task Force."
You took up space.	"A self-starter, I proactively reengineered my personal initiative during this fiscal year."
You procrastinated.	"I strategically repositioned my project in a lock-up session."

Get it?

Fly on the Wall

A "360-degree review" involves each employee being reviewed by subordinates, colleagues, and managers. There's a way to fix just about every corporate gimmick, and this fad is no exception. To rig this system, remind everyone involved that *you* are evaluating them as well. If you can make them believe *you* don't have to write yours until after you read theirs, you can really win big! This is power at its best.

The Least You Need to Know

➤ Your goal? To get power—all else follows.

➤ Business can confer *reward power*, *coercive power*, and *position power*.

➤ Employees can generate *power of position*, *power of influence*, and *power of scarcity*.

➤ *Expert power*, *friendship power*, and *presence power* are earned, not conferred.

➤ You can't use any political skills until you figure out who has the *real* power in your place of work.

➤ Performance reviews are no time for modesty or confessions. Remember: You're the greatest thing since the invention of phase-distortion graviton beam intermittent pulse multimedia technology.

Chapter 6

Master of Your Domain

In This Chapter

➤ Common political minefields

➤ How to take it all in before you speak

➤ Ways to get ahead on the job—fairly

➤ Down for the count: how to back-track out of an embarrassing situation

➤ Political strategies from the experts

Here are three rules to live by:

1. Your errors can be as noticeable (if not more) as your triumphs.

2. Experience is something you don't get until just after you need it.

3. People who hesitate are probably right—but not always!

Considering the potential fallout, no one wants to make a mistake when it comes to office politics. In this chapter, we'll show you ways to get the power you need through effective communication and decision-making. Once you master these skills, you can start using office politics to your advantage—with skill and confidence. No time to waste—wash out yesterday's socks, grab a snack, and prepare to discover how power makes you potent.

Having Your Cake and Eating It Too

It can be difficult for even the most skilled politician to act "correctly" in difficult or awkward situations. Following are some potential minefields. They're all common, unfortunately. Which ones have happened to you in the office?

➤ The "One sandwich short of a picnic" debacle: Having to support your boss when you know he's been a dope.

➤ The "If ignorance ever goes to $40 a barrel, I want drillin' rights on that man's head" syndrome: Being asked to support promotions for co-workers who you know can't possibly do the job.

➤ The "Eva Peron 'What I did for the people'" memorial award: Being made a scape-goat for a colleague's mistake.

➤ The "Let's put the genie back in the bottle" mess (also known as the "Don't go there" mess): Having a colleague share nasty gossip.

Protect Your Assets
Good communication can correct misunderstandings, but communication alone cannot change deep-seated feelings and long-held values. As a result, silence can sometimes be the most effective form of communication.

➤ The "Nosiest person since Mata Hari" situation: Having a friend and co-worker pressure you to share confidential information.

➤ The "Junior high all over again" flashback: Having someone else steal credit for your initiative, intelligence, or idea.

All together now: Yikes!

These political situations (and others like them) are tricky because they can harm you and others. They are political because they entail your making a decision that affects you and others.

A friend in publishing shared this story:

Protect Your Assets
Not all difficult office situations are political, and not all political situations are difficult. Nonetheless, even if it doesn't quack like a duck, assume that all office situations are political and difficult.

My ex-boss was a *complete* knucklehead. He was one of those people who just can't shut up no matter how much he embarrassed himself. Once we had an important meeting with our financial backers to present a new, young author and her book in hopes that they would fund the project. He started on a crazy monologue comparing the author to a "gangsta rapper." Here was this middle-aged, nerdy guy trying to act very, very cool and impress these big wigs, and it was just mortifying. They were staring at him in complete horror. I wanted to crawl under the table for being associated with him, but I felt obligated to keep a straight face, at the very least.

It's a true story. (We could make this stuff up?) Our friend found herself between a rock and a hard place here. Luckily, she chose the safest position, remaining impassive and waiting to see which way opinions went. After the meeting, if the boss asks "How do you think that went?" you might want to tell him what you really thought, but in front of the group, it's best to take the Switzerland approach.

The Cheese Stands Alone

You always want to make the best decision, no matter what situation presents itself.

"Best," however, is a relative term, like "liberal," "conservative," and "Quality Team Management." You deserve a break today, so we'll define a "best" decision as one in which everyone wins.

If that's not possible (and it rarely is), then we move to Plan B, the Big Picture. Often, looking at the Big Picture adjusts your focus and brings a much clearer understanding of your situation. At first, you may think there ain't nothin' in the middle of the road but yellow stripes and dead armadillos. But when you step back, you'll see the whole of your terrain.

We'll get into Big Picture situations a little later, but as a general rule of office politics, you can never go wrong by stepping back and assessing the problem before responding. In addition to giving you more information, looking at the situation from different angles buys you valuable time to get your brain in gear before you open your mouth. Although most businesses require quick decisions, it's brutally difficult to make the right decision under pressure. Successful business leaders use the following questions to help them make better decisions. Now, so can you.

1. How did the problem originate?
2. When did the problem originate?
3. Are you getting all the relevant facts, or do you need to investigate further?
4. How does the situation affect you? (Consider indirect as well as direct results.)
5. What actions could you take? How would each action affect you? How would each action affect others as well?
6. How do you feel about this situation? Are your feelings affecting your judgment?
7. What additional factor(s) (if any) should you consider as you make your decision?
8. What do you want to do about this situation—if anything?
9. Who will be affected by your decision?
10. What is the ideal outcome?
11. What is your final strategy? Why?

Watch Your Back!
Often, what happens to you is not as important as how you react to events—both positive and negative ones.

Don't Get Crushed in the Rumor Mill

Consider this situation:

Louis had been asked to join what we'll call the Big Shot Lunch Club, a group of the most important stockbrokers in his region. Louis listened patiently to the conversation for the first few weeks, but he began to feel out-gunned. Toying with his two-inch-thick sirloin steak one day, he thought, "It's time to let them know that I'm a player, too." So Mr. Too-Big-For-His-Britches chimed in with his own tales of corporate derring-do, including snippets of inside information, scraps of gossip, and morsels of innuendo.

Protect Your Assets
Before you criticize someone, you should walk a mile in his shoes. That way, when you criticize him, you're a mile away and have his shoes.

Unfortunately, Louis got a little carried away with himself and told the woman across the table that his next-door neighbor was a corporate recruiter. According to this neighborly corporate recruiter, there was going to be a massive shake-down in the top brokerage house in the area, where Louis works. "The new VP is going to bring in all his own people, since he's obsessed with power and control," Louis confided.

Who was the woman across from Loud Mouth Louie? You guessed it; none other than the new VP of the top brokerage house in the area. Oops!

Put yourself in the hot seat by answering the questions in the following worksheet.

Rumor Mill Worksheet

1. Who has the problem here: Louis, the new VP, or the neighbor?

   _____

2. Who made the first political boo-boo?

   _____

3. Who has the most to lose from this mess?

   _____

4. What should be done about this situation? Explain your answer.

   _____

   _____

   _____

5. Should Louis quit the lunch club? Why or why not?

_____

_____

_____

6. Do you think the neighbor's job is on the line?

_____

_____

_____

Not Waving, but Drowning

While there's no "right" answer here, here's our expert analysis. Compare your responses to ours.

1. They all do.

   ➤ The neighbor has the biggest problem because he violated his deal with the VP by spreading inside information. As an executive recruiter, the neighbor has a written or implied contract with the VP concerning the confidentiality of her new job.

   ➤ The VP also has a problem because now it's common knowledge that she's going to lay off people. This advance bad press makes it very difficult for her to come into the new job and be effective.

   ➤ Louis has a problem because he's a blabbermouth. But even though it seems that Louis is in the hottest water, he's actually the least affected. He's lost face; the others face potentially far more serious problems. In today's litigious society, the VP might even consider taking legal action against the corporate recruiter.

2. The neighbor made the first blunder by telling Louis confidential information.

3. The neighbor has the most to lose because he was hired by the new VP. The neighbor is bound by a corporate agreement; Louis is just a jerk.

4. The corporate recruiter has to do some serious back-peddling with the VP to smooth over the situation and prevent losing the account and perhaps even being sued. Louis can't do anything but tell the neighbor exactly what happened. Nothing would be served by Louis blubbering to the VP about what a jerk he is. The VP already knows.

5. Louis should not quit the lunch club; nothing is served by running away unless someone with a big gun is chasing you.

6. The neighbor's job is indeed on the line because he is the one who violated the trust.

Who's on First? What's on Second?

Before you're in too deep to get out, take a deep breath and try these steps:

1. Start by identifying your problem with the issue. Why are you likely to mess up in this setting? Perhaps you're feeling insecure and want to impress others; maybe you engage your mouth before putting your brain into gear.

2. Try to look at the situation from the other person's point of view. Best of all, consider multiple points of view.

Watch Your Back!
Never assume that you know all the facts. Even if you've been in on the situation since its inception, you could be missing a key bit of data.

3. If it's dangerous to talk to yourself, it's probably even dicier to listen. So before you say a word, ask a few trusted friends or relatives what they think of the situation. Get their input before you give yours.

4. Try not to pass judgment. After all, no one died and left you in charge (and even if they did, that doesn't give you the right to step on their shibboleths).

5. Protect yourself. Cover your flank, your butt, and any other exposed body part.

Damage Control

Okay, so you're in over your head, going down for the count. How can you reach shore in one piece? Truth be told, there are some days that you're doomed to sleep with the fishies. Just be glad you're not wearing cement overshoes as well. In these cases, the situation is so far gone that your only defense is silence. And lots of it.

Other times, however, you might be able to mop up the mess. Here are some ways:

Protect Your Assets
Admitting that you made a mistake is not the same as groveling. Say it and be done. Don't beat it—or yourself—to death. And once it's over, let it alone.

➤ Back-peddle by trying to correct yourself with a new statement.

➤ Let a smile be your umbrella, remain calm, and keep talking.

➤ Suck it in, admit you made a mistake, and apologize.

➤ Fake a heart attack, migraine, or recurrence of the killer mosquito bite you picked up in Aruba, or pray it's all a bad dream and that you'll wake up soon. Hey, stranger things have happened.

PC or Not PC

In some circles, *pc* (political correctness) has become a vaguely embarrassing personal foible, like a fondness for canned luncheon meat, "lite" music, or Dionne Warwick and her psychic friends. That's because some people make the mistake of thinking that being politically correct means doing only what is accepted by the majority. That's as simplistic as believing that men watch *Baywatch* to learn about water safety.

Political correctness is like good manners: It shows consideration for the next person's point-of-view, background, and feelings. The following true tale from the ledge shows a manager with a positive talent for being politically incorrect:

> A friend's doctor advised her to lose a few pounds and get more exercise. After she mentioned this to her boss, he e-mailed her a "motivational" image of a Playboy playmate with our friend's face and hair. A month later, she gave notice. He then e-mailed her an image of a pig with her face on it.

> Clearly, the boss has crossed the line here. Our friend should have spoken to the boss as soon as she received the first picture, telling him she did not appreciate it. If she didn't feel he addressed her concerns, her next option was the Human Resources department.

> After she gave notice, it did not matter that much to her that he sent a new picture. But she could have sent it along to HR. If nothing else, the boss would be warned against doing it to some future underling.

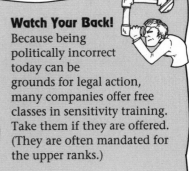

Watch Your Back!
Because being politically incorrect today can be grounds for legal action, many companies offer free classes in sensitivity training. Take them if they are offered. (They are often mandated for the upper ranks.)

If you have a hard time remaining politically correct in difficult situations or under circumstances you can't control, you are going to have to alter your thinking to survive in today's business world. More on this in Chapter 23, "Soldier of Fortune: Getting Promoted."

Taking Care of Business

At some point during your career, you're going to make a political faux pas. Learning from your (and other's) mistakes is important, but what else can you do to ease the weight of that political albatross? Plan ahead. The more you do to build political clout now will make things a lot easier for you later on when you step in it.

The best political strategists know that political power is something you build on from day one on the job. Here are their Top Ten Techniques for Moving On Up. Feel free to swipe them all and make them your own. (Hey, you might as well steal from the best.)

1. Take an active role in your own success.

   Look for projects that can increase your visibility, teach you new skills, and make a real contribution to the company's success.

2. Take educated risks that can pay off big.

   If you're offered the chance to make a speech in front of some key clients, grab it—even if you're quaking in your Hush Puppies. You'll do great! (More on public speaking and making presentations in the next chapter.)

3. Control your own destiny.

   Decide where you want to be and how you're going to get there. All jobs involve a series of choices. Make the choices that help you land in the position you enjoy.

4. Learn new skills and keep up to date on knowledge.

   Can't make a presentation with Microsoft PowerPoint? Unable to tell A+ from C++? Always RAM your ROM? Learn the new technology—and whatever else you need to make yourself a more valuable employee.

5. Embrace challenges; don't reject them.

   "Kiddo, we've selected you to head the Total Quality Paradigm Project. It's a major, high-visibility initiative," your boss says. Find out all you can about the project, and if it's right for your talents and interests, go for it. Don't be a wuss.

6. Compete fairly and ethically.

   Don't backstab, malign co-workers, spread gossip, or take credit for work that's not yours. Remember what you learned in the sandbox about playing nice.

7. Know how to enlist the aid of others.

   Working successfully in a group depends on being open about preferences, constraints, and skills, and then using creative problem-solving techniques. For example, one group member may prefer to outline the entire project all at once, while another likes to talk out ideas before writing. By being honest about your preferences, you make it possible for the group to find creative solutions that build on each person's strengths.

8. Use the rules to your advantage—and change the rules if necessary.

   A company's rules exist for many purposes. However, it might be time to change a rule to meet new needs. Don't be afraid to explore this option—but always do your homework first!

9. Bounce back from mistakes, rather than being defeated by set-backs.

   Bad things happen to good people. You might be demoted, downsized, or even fired from a job you love. Pick yourself up, brush yourself off, and get back into the game. Analyze what has happened and try to avoid falling into the same pit next time. How can you make yourself more valuable to your new employer?

10. Have a clear, strong personal agenda.

    Do you enjoy being the head weenie at the roast (management, that is) or prefer being staff? Do you work best in large groups, small groups, or on your own? Don't let your fate sneak up and bite you in the butt. Work out clear goals.

The Least You Need to Know

➤ Highly charged political situations require special handling. Start by stepping back and assessing the situation.

➤ Check the reaction of others to see if you've made a political faux pas. If so, try to fix it fast.

➤ Today's office politics demand political correctness.

➤ Plan ahead: Gather political points now so your errors won't seem so bad later.

Chapter 7

Meetings: The Work of Working

Some people are drawn to meetings as moths are drawn to porch lights. Others, who have not yet had their brains surgically removed, realize that meetings are nothing more than an excuse to avoid work. That's because rarely does anything productive happen when more than three people are in a room. And if anything productive *were* to occur in a meeting, it takes twice as long to accomplish it in a group than it would if one or two people were working on it. Proof? A camel is a horse designed by a committee.

In this chapter, you'll learn how to identify the different ways that people act in meetings. This can help you sort the powerful from the powerless. Then we'll show you how to deal with the mind-numbing boredom of meetings without letting on that you're wise to the truth. Finally, we'll even give you some ways to use meetings to your advantage.

Meeting of the Minds

An oxymoron is a self-contradictory saying, like "found missing" or "jumbo shrimp." Oxymorons liven up our lives by reminding us that we appreciate irony, mockery, and humor, while the rest of the world just doesn't get the joke.

Which of these phrases do you think is this most moronic oxymoron?

1. Safe sex
2. Airline food
3. Military intelligence
4. Alone together
5. Twelve-ounce pound cake
6. Definite maybe
7. Peace force
8. Business ethics
9. Advanced BASIC
10. Quick meeting

You can't have *military intelligence, peace force,* or *advanced BASIC.* In the same way, you can't have a *quick meeting.* Meetings can be useful, important, and even amusing—but if you want time to fly, try watching paint dry or linoleum curl. Don't even think of taking in a meeting or two.

By definition, meetings are dull. Actually, the word *meeting* comes from an Old English word that means "to bore you senseless and drain your life force, drop by drop." (Some sources claim the word *meeting* comes from a German word that means "ritual torture," but they have largely been discredited because some meetings do serve donuts.)

Corporate Mumbo-Jumbo

A *meeting* is a group of important individuals who alone can do nothing but who together can agree that nothing can be done.

Bob knows this first-hand because he has spent most of his corporate life in a meeting. The company calls each meeting a separate event, as in the "Tuesday Production Meeting" or the "Thursday Department Heads Meeting," but Bob knows the truth: He is doomed to spend his working days in one long meeting punctuated by quick meals and long train rides. The meetings Bob attends are so boring that several members of his staff devised a scale to measure the level of tedium.

Each day, one of Bob's employees would pass by the glass-walled conference room to take a reading on their "Boring Meeting Meter." They could tell how boring the meeting was by the angle at which Bob was reclining in his seat. "There were some weeks," one of

Bob's employees told me, "when he'd dipped below the level of the table." It was plain that Bob was not having fun.

That's because meetings are not designed for fun. If you're new to the wonderful world of work, you might mistakenly believe that meetings are a tedious, sadistic hell run by melon-head morons. Not so. Rather, meetings are a chance for everyone to play a role in the competition to Get Ahead on the Job. Here are the common roles people play at meetings:

1. Smarty-Pants
2. Help-Me-Hurt-You
3. Stress Puppies
4. Lost in Space
5. DOA

Anyone can play these roles, not just big bosses like Bob. Therefore, if you haven't honed your meeting role, this is your lucky day. Read on to pick the role that best suits your personality. (If you have already picked your part in the grand meeting scheme, you can instead decide which player you hate most so you can shoot paper clips in that direction during the next meeting. Hint: Aim for the cheek; it smarts.)

> **Watch Your Back!**
> Meetings are probably the greatest time-wasters in a worker's day. Lengthy telephone calls, not delegating appropriate tasks, and messy files can also fritter away precious time.

Smarty-Pants

Back in the first grade, someone told the Smarty-Pants that he or she had an astronomical IQ score. This was a big mistake, on the order of Watergate, Vietnam, and rice cakes. Shortly thereafter, the mother of Smarty-Pants fed her junior genius a steady diet of Shakespeare and wheat germ while the rest of us were watching *I Dream of Jeannie* and eating Hostess Twinkies. As a result, Smarty-Pants feels a compulsion to share his or her inexhaustible font of knowledge with one and all.

Are you stuck in meeting hell with a Smarty-Pants or two? Here's how you can find out. Put a check next to each line you've heard a co-worker utter during a meeting. Three or more, and you're dealing with a real Smarty-Pants.

> **Corporate Mumbo-Jumbo**
> An *idea hamster* is someone who always seems to have their idea generators running. The Smarty-Pants is clearly an idea hamster.

Smarty-Pants Worksheet

❏ 1. "If we lower costs and increase sales, we could make more money."

❏ 2. "We're bigger than the smaller companies in our industry."

❏ 3. "If fewer people worked on this project, we could save money on salaries."

❏ 4. "We are no longer supplying free soda because too many people are drinking it."

❏ 5. "Let's continue our policy of pursuing useless perfection."

❏ 6. "Never put off until tomorrow what you should have done yesterday."

❏ 7. "A penny saved is nothing in the real world."

❏ 8. "A journey of a thousand miles begins with a single step."

❏ 9. "If your e-mail doesn't work, please send an e-mail to Management Information Services to notify us."

❏ 10. "To err is human. Knowing the population of every town in the United States is not."

(Okay, so we made that last one up ourselves. Forgive us; together we've logged enough meeting time to justify earning a million frequent-meeting miles.)

Help-Me-Hurt-You

The "Help-Me-Hurt-You Colleague" sees this equation:

Meetings = Pain

That's because this good buddy sincerely believes that meetings should cause suffering, as in "I'm doing this for your own good" or "This hurts me more than it does you." To the "Help-Me-Hurt-You Colleague," a "good" meeting is like chewing on ground glass, jumping into a swimming pool filled with single-edge razor blades, or cleaning all the bathrooms in Grand Central Station with your tongue. This colleague's motto? "Sticks and stones may break my bones, but whips and chains excite me—especially at meetings."

Protect Your Assets
Important meetings involve money, personnel, money, vacations, money, promotions, and money. All other meetings are a waste of time.

How can you tell if you're dealing with a meeting sadist? If you can answer "yes" to any three of the following questions, you're doomed to endless interfacing with the Marquis of Meetings:

My Co-worker's Habits Worksheet

❏   1. Schedules meetings at 5:00 p.m. on Friday.

❏   2. Loves meetings that have no purpose.

❏   3. Serves coffee and then won't allow anyone to take a bathroom break.

❏   4. Asks pointed questions you have no reason to know the answer to.

❏   5. Allows everyone to babble on so the meeting never ends.

❏   6. Ends pointless all-day meetings with lines like, "We'll reconvene tomorrow morning bright and early."

Stress Puppies

Stress puppies feel much put upon by the demands of meetings, even clearly important ones. (Yes, there are a few important meetings, but only a few.) Even a meeting to allocate the bonus pool is greeted by "You mean we really have to talk about this? (sigh)" They also feel morally obligated to have you share their pain, so they complain, moan, grumble, and snivel until you're ready to shout, "Would you like some cheese with that whine?"

Common moans include:

➤ "Why me? It's always *me*."

➤ "Nobody told me we would have so many meetings."

➤ "Why do I always have to take minutes? Nobody else gets picked on like I do."

➤ "This coffee is so terrible. Why do they always serve such bad coffee at the meetings I have to go to?"

➤ "I have six people out sick today. I don't have time for a meeting."

➤ "You always schedule meetings at the worst possible time for *me*."

➤ "You can't imagine how these chairs make me suffer. I have a very sensitive rear end, you know."

➤ "No one ever understands me. They never listen to me."

Just think of these meetings as "Days of Whine and Poses."

Corporate Mumbo-Jumbo
A *stress puppy* is a person who thrives on being whiny and stressed out. Most of us feel they should be *uninstalled*—the latest euphemism for being fired.

Watch Your Back!
Do not make the mistake of trying to find meaning in the ramblings of the colleague lost in space. The comments have no meaning. There is no point. That's why they're lost in space. Instead, use this time to catch up on your sleep, trim your cuticles, or drop a line to dear Aunt Edna back in Glassy Point, Idaho.

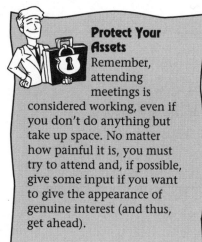

Protect Your Assets
Remember, attending meetings is considered working, even if you don't do anything but take up space. No matter how painful it is, you must try to attend and, if possible, give some input if you want to give the appearance of genuine interest (and thus, get ahead).

Lost in Space

These colleagues might have a point on top of their heads, but there certainly doesn't seem to be a point to what they're saying. Maybe their brains leaked out their ears; maybe all their synapses don't fire in a row. Whatever the reason for their ability to go off on a tangent, they do it with great zeal. As a result, they can make a long meeting interminable, an interminable meeting unendurable.

What can you do about long-winded Louie or Louise? Very little, once they get up a head of steam. If they're your rank or lower, you might be able to set up a temporary bulwark, but this is usually a finger-in-the-dike situation at best. As soon as this co-worker starts to ramble, break in with a comment along the lines of, "Well, that certainly was interesting, but let's now turn to the issue of Integrated Analysis Quality Online Multimedia Press applications." This is so baffling it can even stop a charging elephant dead in his tracks, felled by utter confusion.

DOA

These colleagues are the most intelligent of all the meeting attendees because they have simply given up any pretense of paying attention. Instead, they sleep, daydream, or just get some other work done. If you intend to play this role—and it has a lot going for it considering all the good stuff on late-night TV and the difficulty of programming a VCR—try these hints:

1. Dress well. Meeting props should look nice.

2. Never snore. It blows the illusion that you're really paying attention, even on a brain-dead level.

3. Every hour or so, look up and smile. Being polite can pay off big.

4. Never eat during a meeting. You could choke on a mini-Danish as you nod off.

5. Learn to use your arm to prop up your head. That way, your head won't fall on the table when you doze off. The *thud* could wake up other meeting attendees, and that is very rude.

Corporate Mumbo-Jumbo
Are you a SITCOM? That's the newest term for a Single Income, Two Children, Oppressive Mortgage worker.

Now, what to do if you're called on to comment on the proceedings thus far? Piece of cake. Just tap into the tricks you used in your college course on Advanced Differential Equations, as Dr. Humperdink droned on about vectors and angles. (And you thought that class was useless. See what good training it was for meetings?) Try these responses if someone is discourteous enough to wake you up and ask you a question before the meeting ends:

➤ "Mmmm" and a solemn nod.

➤ "Same ol', same ol.'"

➤ "Status unchanged."

➤ "Geez. You don't say."

➤ "I need a moment to consider that."

➤ "What can I tell ya?"

If all else fails and you can't think of a thing to say when they wake you up, admit you weren't listening—but only because you were thinking about the project you've been working on all week.

Strike a Pose

Knowing the stereotypical players at a meeting can help you get ahead because it reveals who has the power. The following chart can help you sort the winners and losers.

Protect Your Assets
The best way to save time is to look for ways to do things more efficiently. Changing how you handle an individual chore might not yield a lot of additional time, but there are ways to avoid wasting the precious moments you need. Start by making an appearance and then bowing out of unnecessary meetings early. How can you get away with this? Tell the person in charge that you have *another* meeting. Then, sneak back to your office, close the door, and do some real work.

Power Assessment Worksheet—Part 1

Behavior	Position	Power
1. Brought a sandwich from home	Support staff	None
2. Returns calls on cell phone	Middle manager	Some
	or	
	Awaiting a liver transplant	
3. Has no pen	CEO	All
4. Wearing argyle socks	Accounting VP	Some, but bad taste
5. Wearing a bow tie (either gender)	Legal staff	Some

Now, it's your turn. Fill in the second and third columns to sort the players in your meetings.

Power Assessment Worksheet—Part 2

Behavior	Position	Power
1. Runs screaming from the room if someone says "chainsaw consultant"	_____	_____
2. Giggles uncontrollably throughout the meeting	_____	_____
3. Speaks in a fake foreign accent	_____	_____
4. Carries (but does not drink) overly aromatic coffee from trendy coffee joint	_____	_____
5. Attentively writes and passes notes to others	_____	_____
6. Snores	_____	_____

Corporate Mumbo-Jumbo
A *chainsaw consultant* is an outside expert brought in to reduce the employee head count, leaving the top brass with clean hands.

Protect Your Assets
If you're running the meeting, you can set the style. The most effective style: Keep the meeting short. Keep the list of attendees short. Keep the agenda short. But don't *wear* shorts, even if it is a dress-down Friday in August.

Speak Now, or Forever Fall to Pieces

One afternoon as usual, the Roman emperor Nero went to the arena to see the lions do lunch with the Christians. The determined animals were munching away with their usual gusto until one Christian spoke to a lion, who listened attentively and then trotted away with its tail tucked between its legs. The same fellow continued to speak to lion after lion. Each one hurried away, as meek as it had been ferocious a few minutes before. Finally, Nero could no longer take the suspense. He had the Christian brought to him. Standing the smiling fellow in front of his throne, Nero said, "If you tell me what you said to the lions, I'll set you free."

The Christian replied, "I told them, 'The lion who wins this contest has to get up and say a few words to the audience.'"

If the king of the beasts is afraid of speaking in public, what does this say about the rest of us? We might have nothing to fear but fear itself, but according to a poll in the *New York Times*, our greatest fear is speaking in front of people.

According to this poll, stage fright beat out fear of heights, financial problems, deep water, illness, death, flying, loneliness, dogs, and even fear of icky bugs.

Maybe your problem with meetings is not one of boredom (not always, anyway). Maybe you feel you really want to make a contribution during the meetings you go to—or even are frequently asked to do so. But the idea of opening your yap and speaking in front of people (even if you *do* see these folks every day) terrifies you. Time to work on your public speaking skills, kiddo.

Nightmare on Wall Street

For years, our friend Gail worked as an engineer for a large aerospace company on the West Coast. She had just been assigned to a very important new project and promoted to senior engineer. The annual company conference was her first chance to give a professional presentation. Although nearly immobilized by fear, Gail did not dare back out or let her terror render her powerless. Instead, she began her campaign. Here's what she did:

1. Asked for help from two of the best and most admired speakers in the company.
2. Signed up for evening classes in public speaking and presentation skills.
3. Got help for her slide presentation from a designer in the graphic arts department (and gave him credit at the conference).
4. Let her boss know how valuable everyone had been in helping her.

Her slides were sensational, her presentation most professional, and her boss was quite pleased (and convinced that he had indeed made the right move in promoting her). The results of the story:

➤ Gail turned a potentially disastrous situation into a great personal success.
➤ She created power for herself by positioning herself to succeed.
➤ She used colleagues as resources, building relationships and allies.
➤ She overcame her fear and learned vital public presentation skills.
➤ She negotiated skillfully.
➤ She gave due credit graciously.

> **Watch Your Back!**
> In most instances, verbal channels of communication are better than written channels for group decision making because they allow misunderstandings to be corrected much more quickly. Verbal communication also seems more personal, another great way to build alliances and power within companies.

> **Corporate Mumbo-Jumbo**
> A *conference* is a meeting that takes place at a location other than your office (quite often at a resort), to which people come from many locations and, usually, many companies. Unlike at a regular meeting, most people want to attend conferences and find ways to duck out of them. These savvy attendees come back nicely tanned.

Not all meeting stories end happily ever after, but there *are* usually ways to turn potential disasters into success (or at least learn from your mistakes). Trial and error is often a big part of the learning process, especially where office politics are concerned.

The Goose That Laid the Rotten Egg

So you want to know how can you tell if you said the wrong thing during your little soliloquy at a Very Important Meeting and stepped in it? Here are some hints:

1. The room becomes very quiet and everyone is looking at you. It's the big chill.

2. Your colleague leans over and hisses in your ear, "What *were* you thinking?"

3. Someone in the room suggests that it's time for a break.

4. People cough, squirm in their seats, and blush.

5. Your boss asks to see you after the meeting.

6. Everyone laughs...but you weren't trying to be funny.

7. A colleague changes the subject—very quickly.

8. Everyone looks away and pretends to be taking notes, finding lint on their jackets, or searching for flying saucers out the window.

Working the Room

To help ourselves in business, we often have to turn to others. This helps us establish power. And what better place to turn to others than at a meeting?

We asked some of our colleagues what good things they could say about the meetings they attend. Here's what they offered:

1. "Ours is a fairly large company. The weekly meeting is the only time I get to see some people."

2. "The five minutes before the meeting begins gives me some face-time with the big boss. I use it for casual chat about our kids, giving him another way to remember who I am."

3. "Once a month I represent our department at a scheduling meeting. It gives me a chance to network with the department heads."

Watch Your Back!
According to conservative estimates, over five million speeches are delivered in the United States every year. Out of all these speeches, about one million are delivered by business people for business people. What does this mean for you? Well, first, the odds are quite good that you're going to have to deliver a whole stack of speeches during your career.

Protect Your Assets
Being a good public speaker makes you visible in business and gives you an edge. Effective speakers have knowledge, self-confidence, enthusiasm, preparation, and a valid message.

4. "I can see who actually has some clout and who is just a big mouth."

5. "They usually have fruit and pastries."

Kiss Up

Okay, so you take meetings seriously, have no fear of speaking up, and even wear your best power suit when you know you have one coming up. You see meetings as a chance to get in some serious face-time with the big shots. This is assuming, of course, that some big shot is attending the meeting and actually staying awake during it.

If this is the case, far be it for us to rain on your parade. If you really want to create a positive impression, here's how you can do it:

1. Stay awake.

   This seems self-evident, but it *is* really important.

2. Ask smart questions.

   Smart questions show that you are really awake, even though your eyes are closed and you are breathing deeply. What's a smart question? It's a question you already know the answer to that prompts an influential person to say what he or she really wants to say. Smart questions pave the way for the head honcho to get to the main point. Be aware that everyone will shoot you for being such a suck-up, however.

3. Allow others to talk.

   Yes, we know you won the Parent-Teacher Inter-scholastic Dingbat Award in third grade. We know you proactively prioritized the quality mission objectives. We even know you can walk and chew gum at the same time. Because we know all that, you can take a breath and let someone else talk. Jabbermouths are obnoxious, even though they *do* let everyone else off the hook.

4. Take notes.

   Keeping your own set of minutes can help you pay attention through the meeting, but even if you're really writing your guest list to this weekend's barbecue or a plan to blow up the cube farm, it looks good if you put pen to paper during a meeting (or at least *bring* pen and paper to the meeting). And who knows—maybe you'll actually hear something that you will want to write down. Stranger things have happened.

Corporate Mumbo-Jumbo
A *cube farm* is an office filled with cubicles.

Watch Your Back!
After you finish running a meeting, protect yourself by putting every decision in writing and informing all participants—and keeping a copy for yourself.

5. Appear intelligent.

    This is the hardest one of all, because after 15 minutes in a meeting, everyone is an idiot. That's because meetings create a vacuum, sucking all the intelligence from a room. Do the best you can; we understand. And remember: Appearance is reality.

The Least You Need to Know

➤ Meetings are rarely productive and usually boring.

➤ People often play specific roles in meetings, including the smarty-pants, stress puppies, DOAs, and those lost in space.

➤ Hone your public speaking skills; they'll come in handy when your boss wants to know what *you* think (it does happen!).

➤ Analyzing how people act at meetings can tell you their level of power.

➤ Staying awake at a meeting can give you a distinct advantage over your sleeping colleagues.

➤ Asking intelligent questions, allowing others to talk, taking notes, and appearing smart are also effective political strategies for putting one over on your dozing co-workers.

Chapter 8

The Rules of Acquisition

In This Chapter

➤ Why appearances matter

➤ The importance of a real office

➤ Embellishments: location, windows, doors, furniture, and carpets

➤ The anti-office: Cubicle Hell, Office Lite, and the Non-Office

➤ Presentations: how to give yourself the professional edge

➤ Perks and how to get them

In *My Fair Lady*, Eliza Doolittle knew exactly what she wanted:

> All I want is a room somewhere
> Far away from the cold night air.

What about you? Well, we know what you want when it comes to your career: You want to get ahead in the office. Otherwise, you wouldn't have shelled out your hard-earned bucks for this book.

Increasingly, appearance is reality. You know all the clichés: Clothes make the man (and woman); what you see is what you get; it's what's up front that counts.

Maybe you can't judge a book by its cover, but in the cutthroat world of office politics, the *illusion* of success can often help create the *reality* of success. That's because we do judge someone's success and power by the outward signs: what they wear, where they sit, and how the whole package is presented.

In this chapter, we're going to teach you an excellent way to get ahead in the corporate world: get the trappings of success. You'll learn that there's power in position and possessions. Read on to find out how to get what you deserve—or make the most of what you have.

> **Watch Your Back!**
> Under no circumstances do you want an office in the boondocks, or God forbid, in outer Fuhgeddaboudit. Unless, of course, your alternate choice is a cubicle in those places.

> **Protect Your Assets**
> In many companies, secretaries have power in part because they manage the traffic in and out of the Head Honcho's office. They have the power to wave you in—or keep you out. Often, stewards derive power in the same way, because they go in and out of the boss's office often enough to get the inside skinny on everyone.

Space, the Final Frontier

You know the three rules of real estate: location, location, location. The same rules apply to jockeying for an office. First, you want an office as close to the source of power as you can get. This means that your office should be belly-to-belly with the boss—or as close as you can get. Let's look more closely at the geography of power by studying the world center of power: the Oval Office of the White House.

For staffers at the White House, proximity to the president is everything. For example, former White House chief of staff George Stephanopoulos used to occupy the prime power office, just steps from the Oval Office. Because George was never far from the action, he saw it all. This is real, serious power.

The same holds true for you, lowly peon though you may be at the present. The closer you are to the power center—usually the office of the president/CEO/manager/director/ boss person—the more power you have.

>
> **Fly on the Wall**
>
> If you get an office located in a corner of the building, you know you've arrived. That's because corner offices are the most prestigious ones. Here's why:
>
> ➤ They're bigger than most other offices.
>
> ➤ They have twice as many windows as non-corner offices.
>
> ➤ There are very few of them.

Size Does Matter

G. K. Chesterton and several other famous writers were asked what one book they would take with them if they were stranded on a desert island. *"The Complete Works of Shakespeare,"* answered one writer. "I'd choose *The Bible*, instead," said another. When Chesterton was asked what book he would select, the famous English man of letters replied, "I would choose *Thomas's Guide to Practical Shipbuilding*."

Like Mr. Chesterton, you're a sensible person. You never play "fetch" with a pit bull, and you always wait an hour after a meal to go swimming. You lather, rinse, repeat. We'll bet you even floss twice a day. You know that regardless of what you have been told, size matters. The bigger, the better—at least when it comes to offices.

Corporate Mumbo-Jumbo Cubicles are offices created with temporary walls usually furnished with standard prefab fixtures. They are also called "pods" or "work spaces."

Here are the office perks that distinguish you as a mover and a shaker:

➤ Windows

➤ A door

➤ Real furniture (that is, matching guest chairs, sofas, end tables)

➤ A plant or two (living plants score higher than plastic ones, but, of course, you need real sunlight streaming through a window or two to keep them alive)

➤ Carpeting

And most important of all, you want real walls. Without real walls around your office, you're doomed to life on the cube farm.

Cube Farm

Now, there's nothing really wrong with a cubicle in the abstract. There's nothing wrong with freeze-dried luncheon meat, either, but would you really want to eat it? Why are cubicles so bad? Because they serve as a constant reminder of your lowly status in the corporate order. They mark you as a peon, a menial, a wage slave, and serf—in short, a person woefully without power. (Remember, power is what you want when it comes to the workaday world and office politics.) You can't take it with you, but you sure can enjoy it while you've got it.

Lest we depress you unnecessarily, cubicles *do* have some noteworthy advantages. Here are the most important ones:

1. An open top

   This is a great feature because it enables you to enjoy all the surrounding noise. And, for some reason, people talking nearby don't think you can hear them. Keep an ear open; you never know what you can learn.

Protect Your Assets

Unless your salary is published (as is done in government employment and unionized jobs such as teaching), you might be better off taking a little less in salary for a little more in visible benefits: an office (or a bigger office), a parking space, or rights to the corporate dining room. By making you more visible, these perks can help you leap to a better job.

Corporate Mumbo-Jumbo

Prairie dogging describes what happens when something exciting happens in a cube farm, and people's heads pop up over the walls to see what's going on.

2. Compact size

   If you're a pack-rat by nature, you'll never have to worry about anyone at work finding out. You'll have nowhere to stash stuff and will be forced to take it all home.

3. Solid walls

   They eliminate annoying drafts from windows. And they're better than nothing. Imagine having only the back of the guy in front of you to tack memos to.

4. Impermanence

   As a result, you don't get bored sitting in the same place for months at a time. On a whim, the bosses can rearrange the entire work area.

5. Neutral colors

   Dishwater gray and washed-out blue don't clash with your business suits.

You Snooze, You Lose

When it comes to being at a disadvantage as far as office politics go, what's worse than a cubicle? Could anything be worse than a cubicle? Fortunately, modern corporations have thought of everything when it comes to saving money and robbing you of your dignity. The newest way to strip you of your last shred of belonging is the concept of *hoteling*.

Hoteling is a system in which cubicles are assigned to employees as they show up each day. No one gets a permanent "office," such as it is. Instead, it's first come, first served.

Office Lite

There is also the concept of telecommuting. If you can do most of your work via telephone and computer, you can do it as easily from home as you can in a cubicle. While telecommuting keeps you from interacting with anybody else, it does have its upside. You can work in your pajamas and you don't have to attend any meetings.

And what's the logical outcome of all this? No office at all. Some day, you could be keyboarding from your bed, sending faxes while ordering a Big Mac at the drive-in window, and e-mailing while waiting for your kids to come out of the school building.

The problem with this? Out of sight, out of mind. Virtual offices have all the disadvantages of telecommuting with none of the advantages. They're isolating and lonely. Because you're not in the office, you can't use office politics to your advantage. Without a permanent work space, you can't build up alliances, network, or get in on the action. You're frozen out of the action in office Siberia.

In addition to robbing employees of the chance to work the room and work their way to the top, hoteling and telecommuting make it that much easier to downsize and rightsize the work force. Because these office arrangements eliminate all physical evidence of the employee's association with the company, the employee doesn't even have to clean out a desk when the ax falls. With hoteling, every employee has one foot out the door at any given moment; with virtual offices, you're already out the door, and they just have to change the locks.

The message? You're nothing more than a cog in a wheel. Because you don't even rate an office, why should we care about giving you perks, pensions, and power? That's why you want a real office, or at least a real cubicle.

The Best Seat in the House

What's Laurel without Hardy? Fred without Ginger? The President's staff without subpoenas? And what's an office without furniture? An empty shell, a mere husk of a status symbol.

Furniture matters...a lot. You want proof? Consider this: If you get fired, your furniture stays behind. *It* still has a job. Ergo, when it comes to offices, your desk and chair are more important than you are.

As a result, it's not surprising that furniture equals status. There are times when a cigar is just a cigar, but office furniture is rarely what it appears to be. If you have a $1,125 Aeron ergonomically correct chair with knee tilt, lumbar support, and adjustable armrests, the message is, "Kneel at my feet and worship me. I am important."

Here's a quick guide to office furniture.

1. Your chair. After all, you'll be spending some serious quality time together. No matter what type of chair you get, be sure that it has armrests. Otherwise, it will be very hard for you to nap safely in your chair without falling on the floor.

Protect Your Assets
To get the best naps at work, pull a document up on your computer screen, put your back to the aisle, balance your arms on your armrests, and saw some wood. Of course, this could have a serious effect on your chances of being promoted.

2. Workstations: A "workstation" is a multilevel desk, with an adjustable surface for work events. At the very least, your workstation should be adjustable; at best, it should be expensive, sleek, and sexy.

3. Other fixtures: The more room you have, the more you need to fill it up. A guest chair implies that other people need to speak to you in your workspace. Two guest chairs mean you have important information to share regularly. Got room for a little table or small filing cabinet? Find one and put some important-looking papers or books on top, along with a candy dish or tasteful tissue box.

Fly on the Wall

News flash: Impressive office furniture is only available at senior management levels. (This is not to say you can't swipe someone's nifty chair. Just don't get caught.)

Making the Most of What You've Got

Sometimes, there's not a lot you can do about the space available to you within your company. If they don't have large offices or matching chairs, you'll never have either, period.

Because you're probably not senior management yet, what you'll get for a "chair" is a leftover piece of lawn furniture or a rickety stool; but thanks to our survey, at least you'll know what kind of seat you should strive for. Your workstation will probably be a big ol' board that stretches the length of your cubicle and keeps the Rolodex from falling into your lap.

But that's okay. In these cases, what matters is what you make of what you have. Although the type of work you do truly does matter, it's only a component of a package. You have to present the proper image, or you might not be taken seriously at all.

Although where you sit (and whether where you sit has a window or not) definitely is a factor, the following elements are also crucial to your success:

➤ How you dress

➤ How you present yourself

➤ How well organized you are (or appear to be)

➤ How well you observe the conventions of the business world, such as being on time

Let's look at each one of these factors in detail.

1. **Dress for Success, Not Excess**

   If you dress like a schlump, you'll get treated like a schlump (unless you're in a super high-tech job, which is a different realm altogether). On the same theme, if you dress like a college student, you'll be treated like a college student, no matter where you sit. Get where we're going with this? Your clothing, posture, and overall "look" matters—a great deal. Lots more on this in Chapter 18, "Culture Club."

2. **Image Is Reality**

   If you present yourself too casually to the wrong people, you won't seem serious. Nor will you be taken seriously. Watch your use of slang, regional words, and profanity if you want to present a professional image. And ditch the gum, heavy cologne, and mile-high hair.

   Additionally, you have to take note of your environment and act accordingly. Someone working in a bank position on Wall Street or in a law firm will have different issues than someone in publishing or graphic design, for example. The former will have a much more serious demeanor than the latter.

3. **Getting It Together**

   If you look like a slob and your office or cube looks like a bomb went off in it, no one will want to rely on you. From appearances, they'll think that you can't be trusted with anything important. Their fear? A key document will get buried in the time capsule you call a desk, and no one will ever see it again. And odds are, they have a point.

   Neatness counts. And ditch the bizarre photos, too. A nicely-framed photo of your family or significant other is most appropriate, but no one wants to see a candid of your pooch dressed as the Easter Bunny or your canary decked out as a pirate. Ditto on your genuine Star Trek phaser, your artful display of Barbie dolls, and your collection of soda can flip-tops. We actually know people who display all this kitsch in their cubes. Tacky.

4. **Time Flies When You're Having Fun**

   If you're late for work every day (or even once a week), it won't matter if you do a bang-up job. All that your supervisor and colleagues will notice is the time you're wasting—and they're wasting waiting for you or covering for you.

   Observe the conventions of time as well as space. If you work from 8:00 to 5:00, work from 8:00 to 5:00, not 8:30 to 4:45. And if you want to make a really good impression, get to work a little early and stay a little late. If you hang around the office until 10:00 p.m., people will think you don't have a life (and you couldn't possibly fit one in), but punching out on the dot creates the impression that you won't go that extra inch for the firm.

All these issues add to the overall perception you convey at work. They're each integral to moving up in business, no matter what business it is. Politically, they show you're a savvy, committed worker.

That Extra Edge

A very young, beautiful woman sat down at a wedding reception with her much older husband. The woman sitting next to her stared at the gorgeous diamond ring the young woman was wearing. "Why, that is the most beautiful diamond I have ever seen," she said.

"This is a famous diamond," the young woman responded. "It's known as the Plotkin diamond. There is even a curse associated with it."

"How romantic," the other woman commented. "What is the curse?"

"Mr. Plotkin."

Life is full of trade-offs. You give a little, you get a little, as this story illustrates. This is especially true when it comes to office perks.

Your business *perks* (perquisites) signal your status in the corporation. They're a visible indication of your value and status. Some perks are worth real money; others have enormous psychological currency. In either case, perks help you establish your hegemony in the scheme of things.

Here are some of the most valuable perks available in corporate America:

➤ A contract

Because corporate America offers as much security as a berth on the *Titanic*, a contract is a very good thing. Even if you do get the ax, a contract guarantees you a pay-off. Unfortunately, contracts are usually only given to senior people.

➤ A travel and entertainment budget (usually called a "T&E" budget)

This is money you can use to entertain clients, seal key deals, and attend out-of-state meetings. So what if the summer meetings are in Death Valley and the winter ones are in Siberia? You want *everything*?

T&E money pays for "working lunches," dinners, snacks, and drinks with clients. It lets you charm customers ringside and courtside. On the more practical side, it gives you car fare to get home if you work late. Hey, Big Spender, we're talking to *you*.

Watch Your Back!
While we're on the issue of T&E budgets, a word of advice. When using the company's money to pay for a meal, don't order the most expensive items on the menu, such as caviar, lobster, or anything on the endangered species list. On the other hand, feeding yourself from the "99¢ Special" list is just wasting good perks.

➤ Health care

Health care is another one of those perks that workers of previous generations accepted as their birthright, along with a lifetime guarantee of employment and a car that cost less than a house.

Not any more. Increasingly, more and more companies are making their employees foot all or part of the bill for medical care (not to mention the cost of dental care, vision care, prescription drugs, plus copayments and deductibles). Whether you spend pre-tax or post-tax money, you're still shelling the money out of your pocket. As a result, having a good health plan has become a high-prestige item. Current law requires companies with over three employees to offer the same plan to everyone. But if the cost is the same for you and the person making four times your salary, who do you think takes the bigger hit?

➤ Life insurance

Okay, so it's not sexy, but your heirs will think the good thoughts if you cash out early and leave a big pile of chips for them to spend in Aruba or on the mortgage. Like health care, life insurance was one of those expected benefits a generation ago, buried in the fine print. Now it's a perk.

➤ Retirement package/pension

Unfortunately, pensions are no longer standard—gone the way of two pairs of pants with a suit or steak knives with a fill-up at the gas station. Today, pensions are as scarce as a taxi cab in the rain. The latest in retirement packages is a "we-all-chip-in-so-no-one-gets-hurt" deal. You pay a certain amount toward your 401K plan, and the company chips in a certain amount, usually a matching contribution. Often, the company's share is in company stock. Of course, the company gets to hold your money and use it for their own evil ends, unless you have the temerity to retire and ask for it back.

Protect Your Assets

PPO? HMO? POS? Today, health plans have more initials than a bowl of alphabet soup. If you're in the fortunate position of bargaining for a health plan, look before you leap. Check out the health plans' ratings in *Consumer Reports* before you make your selection. For more advice, you can also contact Health Care Financing Administration (6325 Security Blvd., Baltimore, MD 21207) or Group Health Association of American (1129 20th St. NW, Suite 6000, Washington, DC 20036-3403).

Watch Your Back!

If you don't have a company pension or 401K plan (and even if you do), check with your tax preparer or financial advisor about some of the new retirement vehicles available, such as Keogh plans and the new Roth IRA. Be careful, however, because all of these nifty plans have very specific income guidelines.

➤ Stock options

Such a sweet deal! Traditionally available only to the highest mucky-mucks, stock options are increasingly being offered to everyday wage slaves. That's because they cost the company very little and generate great good will. Get in on this if you can.

➤ Vacation time

Find out what's standard in your company. Two weeks? Three weeks? Four weeks? Often, vacation time is computed on a sliding scale, depending on how long you've been with the company. There's no play with vacation time on government jobs and in education, but it *is* a negotiable perk in many private companies.

➤ Tuition assistance and merit awards

Because a college education at a private university now costs the GNP of a small banana republic, this is a serious perk. Fortunately, it's often available at all levels of employment rather than being something reserved solely for upper management. Many companies sponsor awards for employees and their family members based on grade-point average. It's to your advantage to unearth the forms if your firm is one of these.

Protect Your Assets
If your company offers tuition assistance, *grab it!* You can never go wrong with additional training, especially if it's free. So what if you're exhausted at the end of a long day at work? Scarf down some sugar and caffeine and crack the books. You'll thank us later for this hint.

➤ Executive dining room

Many companies have an executive dining room. Not only does access to the executive dining room show your power within the company, but the food is usually excellent and the surroundings sumptuous.

➤ Cell phones, beepers, and so on

These are cheap but potent symbols of power. They say, "The bearer is so important that they can't be out of earshot for a moment." Either that, or they say you're running an escort service.

➤ Upgrades on travel

First class is a thing of beauty, but in a pinch, business class is also quite fine. One trip in the front of the plane, and you'll never be comfortable in steerage again.

➤ Car allowance

With cars costing more than our houses, this is a perk worth negotiation.

➤ Corporate charge cards

Many companies give employees who travel charge cards to use for hotel bills and incidentals. This carries status, but file your expense reports promptly, or you'll just be floating the company a series of ongoing interest-free loans. Also, don't use this card for personal purchases; card activity is usually monitored. You don't want the CFO to know you've been calling those 900-numbers, do you?

➤ Product discounts

Many firms offer executives and even the hoi polloi a rake-off on their products. This is fine only if you use their products, of course. How much grout cleaner, rug shampoo, and nuclear waste does one family need? As a result, you might choose to work for a company whose products you need and actually like.

Watch Your Back!
Be sure your credit rating is clean if you're offered a corporate credit card. You'll lose face if you're not eligible for credit because you buy more shoes than Imelda Marcos and never remember to pay that pesky bill.

➤ Access to the health club/exercise room

A sweet perk, but who has the time to pump iron and develop washboard abs? Nevertheless, just show up anyway so everyone will know you have the key.

➤ Parking space

In some companies, a parking spot is a given, like an office used to be. In other companies, a parking spot is a hot perk. Of course, the closer the parking spot is to the door, the better it is. Naturally, a parking spot with your name and title stenciled on it is *sizzlin'*.

➤ The executive washroom (if there is one!)

A friend related this tale: "After confronting my boss, I finally got his grudging permission to use the executive washroom during working hours. 'But,' he warned, 'don't make a habit of it.'"

➤ Exit package

Parting is such sweet sorrow, but it's a whole lot sweeter with a so-called "golden parachute." If you were given a contract and didn't think to negotiate this up front, retain a skilled labor lawyer to help you get what you deserve should you and the company part ways prematurely.

➤ Office supply subsidy

All the paper clips, pencils, note pads, and tape you can steal, um, accidentally put in your briefcase and take home. (Not to mention long-distance phone calls, photo-copying, and manila envelopes.)

Top of Your Game

You get the perks you want through *persuasion*. Your success depends on building a common ground, supplying logical reasons, and showing how your boss will benefit from giving you what you want. To be effective, you must understand your boss's biases, objections, and needs.

Bosses are highly sensitive to manipulation, so no matter how much you disagree with your superiors, respect their intelligence (or give the illusion of doing so). Try to understand why they believe or do something and why they might resist your demands. If you can understand your bosses' positions, you'll be more likely to get what you want—and you won't alienate your bosses by talking down to them.

Remember, everything but death and taxes is negotiable—and we know people who have successfully negotiated their tax bills. (There are very few substantiated cases of people negotiating their way out of death.) So no matter what "facts" you get on the grapevine about "No one ever gets three weeks' vacation" or "They never give mid-year promotions *here*," decide what you want and then go for it. And here's how *not* to do it.

Make an Offer They Can't Refuse

Yes, your offer *can* be refused, and probably *will be* if you use threats. Not only do threats make you look like a big baby, but even more important, they rarely work. Here's why:

➤ Threats have a way of blowing up in your face.

   If you threaten to quit if you don't get what you want, you're likely to find yourself calling the headhunter, reading the want ads, and pounding the pavement.

➤ Threats don't produce permanent change.

   You might be able to threaten your way into a big corner office for the moment, but you'll be unlikely to keep it for long.

➤ Threats create tension.

   People who feel threatened put their energies into ego rather than giving you what you want.

➤ Threats create enemies.

   Yes, your boss may be a cement-head. But threatening your boss into giving you what you want—even if you "win"—will result in your paying for your "victory" down the line. You're not likely to get this boss's cooperation and support during the next battle.

And here's how *to* do it.

In the Know

So how can you develop a persuasive strategy by using office politics to your advantage? Walk this way:

➤ Start small.

When you face resistance, you won't get everything you want at once. Ask for one step that will move you toward your larger goal. For example, if you want a corner office, start with a move from the cubicle to an office with real, solid walls.

➤ Try to find a win-win situation.

Management will be far more likely to give you the perks you want if they can see some advantages for themselves. So point out why you should get what you want. If necessary, modify your original request to respond to changed circumstances. For example, you might say, "With a T&E account, I could bring in some big business from the ABC Corporation—where my brother-in-law is a buyer..."

➤ Make your case from management's point of view.

Show why giving you what you deserve will help the bottom line, making *the company* look good.

➤ Find out why management won't give you what you want.

At first, don't even try to persuade. Just try to understand.

➤ Find a way to let management save face.

Don't force the boss to admit he's a lying weasel. (No boss ever will.) Weasels tend to bite if you back them into a corner. Instead, try to hammer out a mutually agreeable situation.

> **Protect Your Assets**
> Is there strength in numbers? Not when it comes to perks! Remember: You're not negotiating a union contract. You only want benefits for yourself. The only time to even mention another employee is if he or she is already getting a perk you want. Use this information as leverage.

It might take you some time to get the perks you want. You'll need the patience of a pine tree and the doggedness of a field general. Don't give up. Hey, it took engineers 22 years to design the zipper.

The Least You Need to Know

➤ In the cutthroat world of contemporary business, the *illusion* of success can often help create the *reality* of success.

➤ The size and location of your office help determine your status within the company.

➤ Present yourself as a professional, and you're much more likely to be perceived as one.

➤ Impressive furniture and perks such as a contract, a travel and entertainment budget, and stock options also mark you as a force to be reckoned with.

➤ You get the perks you want through *persuasion,* not threats.

➤ Start small and set up a win-win situation.

Chapter 9

Loose Lips Sink Ships...and Careers

In This Chapter

➤ The value of office gossip

➤ Two kinds of office gossip

➤ Ways to gather office gossip

➤ E-mail and office gossip

➤ The rules of Netiquette

Mr. and Ms. Office Manners (that's us!) were recently asked this question:

Question: When you are being introduced, is it all right to say, "I've heard a lot about you?"

Answer: It depends on what you've heard.

Speedy Gonzalez is fast. The Starship Enterprise is faster. Gossip, however, is fastest of all. *Nothing* in the universe travels faster than gossip. In this chapter, we'll give you some savvy tips on how to handle office gossip—and show you how to use it to your advantage.

I Heard It Through the Grapevine

Question: I have always wanted to have my family history traced, but I can't afford to spend a lot of money to do it. Any suggestions?

Answer: Yes. Run for public office. Before you know it, the whole world will know *all* the dirt.

In the past, office gossip was thought to be the province of small-minded workers who had nothing better to do with their time. A closer look at office gossip, however, reveals that it serves several important work purposes. Office gossip does the following:

➤ Builds peer relationships.

➤ Is a socializing force.

➤ Serves as the lifeblood of personal relationships in an office.

➤ Improves morale by spicing up the day. It may even make some highly repetitive jobs bearable.

Watch Your Back!
If you get caught up in petty gossip and rumor-mongering, you could seriously damage your professional reputation. Never reveal confidential information and avoid confirming or denying any rumor.

➤ Is a humanizing factor in an otherwise increasingly technological and depersonalized workplace.

➤ Helps workers get ahead by allowing them to build on important news.

While you don't want to be the office tattle-tale, no one can be powerful—or even moderately successful—on the job without accessing the office grapevine. If you have always believed that office gossip is as tacky as Liberace and as worthless as New Kids on the Block eight-track tapes, it's time to change your tune. That's because the office grapevine is the lifeblood of the informal news system in any office. Knowledge equals power.

I Told Two Friends and They Told Two Friends...

There are two kinds of office gossip: *personal gossip* and *professional gossip*. There's quite a difference between them in both import and importance.

➤ *Personal gossip* is who's doing the hokey-pokey with whom, who eats spray cheeze right out of the can, and who's just gotten a Golden Retriever the size of a pony.

➤ *Professional gossip* covers such topics as the business, competitors, and the economy as a whole (as well as which individuals in your field are as popular as a Fig Newton and which ones are as forlorn as Wayne Newton—or vice versa.)

Listen to all of it, but let the personal gossip pass in one ear and out the other. Professional gossip, however, is very important. Pay attention and keep track of it because that's one of the ways you'll become skilled in office politics.

In our experience, office gossip is about 80 percent accurate. That's because news is exchanged by people who are long-standing members of primary information groups. These groups tend to be very stable because the members like and trust each other. As such, they function as support systems.

Pssst...

How can you get the scoop on what's really going on in your office and industry? To get information, you have to give information. If you only collect gossip, your sources of information will dry up quickly.

Furthermore, don't go using your powers for evil. Co-workers will be unwilling to share information with you if they think you'll use it for something underhanded. Make absolutely sure that you never betray someone's confidence, or you'll lose them as both friends and information sources.

Fly on the Wall

A famous story about office gossip gone astray concerns the unlucky manager whose mouth ran away with him. Called to take on a special assignment, he was told he got the job because the executive normally responsible had been called away for a few days.

The manager said that he'd be glad to help because he knew his colleague's absence was occasioned by a court summons—apparently a well-guarded secret until that moment. The slip became a huge issue as efforts were made to find the leak. It wasn't so terrible that the naive manager revealed secret information. The real danger was the collapse of security, with several trusted employees trapped in the wreckage.

In the early stages of your endeavors, you're probably going to rely on a random selection of co-workers who have shown a proclivity to gossip. No one of them will know the whole story, so it's your job to piece together the gleanings into a logical whole.

Be patient. As you move up the ranks, however gradually, gossip will come to you more readily, carried by people who want to curry favor with you. The turning point will likely come when you acquire your own administrative assistant or secretary who can become a valuable fount of gossip (with proper training). Now you'll no longer have to bother gathering everyday gossip yourself. This will leave you plenty of time to seek out higher-level gossip.

On the Inside Track

People will gossip about anything; that's just human nature. But as you trade professional gossip, be aware that some tidbits are more valuable than others when it comes to advancing your career. Here's the gossip hit parade, from most to least valuable.

1. Job changes, including resignations, firings, demotions, layoffs, and special assignments

2. Mergers and acquisitions

3. Hostile takeovers

4. Romances

See the pattern? Gossip about the job is more important than personal information (even though the latter is usually a whole lot more fun). That's because job-related news gets you where you want to go—up the corporate ladder. So these juicy morsels will get you more useful office information in return.

Actress Minnie Driver got in dutch with the crew of her latest movie when she gossiped about them to the press. "When I got back to the set," she said, "it was like being ostracized at school. I've got a big mouth, and I paid for it. That stuff goes around and is added to your reputation. It was a mistake." (*GQ*, January 1998)

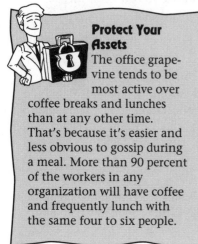

Protect Your Assets
The office grapevine tends to be most active over coffee breaks and lunches than at any other time. That's because it's easier and less obvious to gossip during a meal. More than 90 percent of the workers in any organization will have coffee and frequently lunch with the same four to six people.

The people you work with are just that: the people you work with. They are not your friends. They may be your allies, mentors, accessories-after-the-fact, accomplices, even your cellmates. Do not make the mistake of assuming they are your friends. So think before you share any comments, suggestions, and gossip. *Always* assume that what you say will get around.

Your goal? You want to develop the ability to absorb tons of valuable office gossip but rarely act on it. Listen to all the gossip floating around to develop a complete mental dossier. Then use what you learn to fully understand the overt and hidden structure with the company. More on this in Chapters 20, "Interoffice Romance: Your Cube or Mine?," and 21, "Crossing the Line."

The Naughty Bits

A word on gossip about office romances and other delicate subjects: Some people believe this gossip to be extremely valuable because it allows them to catch their colleagues with their pants down, so to speak. This is undeniably true.

However, in earlier chapters, you've learned that you can play the game of office politics any way you like, but when push comes to shove, you're still going to have to face yourself in the morning. Mornings are tough enough without dealing with all that guilt and shame of having betrayed a co-worker with smarmy gossip. Because there's so much "clean" gossip to deal with in any office, why bother with the tacky stuff? Just say no.

Byte Me

Just as computers have replaced typewriters, electronic mail (e-mail) is rapidly taking the place of printed letters and memos in many companies. Increasingly, e-mail is becoming a universal medium of business and personal communication—and a rich source of office gossip.

E-mail, like super-premium ice cream and spandex, is a double-edged sword. If used wisely, e-mail can be a valuable tool to advance your career. If used stupidly, e-mail can make it even easier for you to shoot yourself in the foot. Here's why:

Corporate Mumbo-Jumbo
Electronic mail (e-mail) refers to messages sent electronically from one computer to another.

:-)	:-(
E-mail is fast; messages are transmitted almost instantaneously.	You can write (and send) a message often without thinking. This encourages bad gossip.
E-mail is cheap. Once the company connects to a network, e-mail is low-cost or even free.	This encourages people to e-mail messages that are better left unsaid.
You can e-mail numerous people at once.	Numerous people know instantaneously when you "say" something stupid.
E-mail is convenient. You can write and send e-mail any time you want. You can whip off a message at 3:00 in the morning.	And we're all at our best at 3:00 in the morning.
E-mail is more casual than snail mail.	There's a lot to be said for professional distance between colleagues.

Sloppy Copies

Question: I cant spell worth a dam. I hope your going too tell me watt to do?

Answer: Get out the dictionary and use that spell checker! Sloppy spelling in a purely written forum sends out the same silent messages that soiled clothing would when addressing an audience.

Many of today's offices have dress-down Fridays, when employees can doff their blazers for sweatshirts. While this *does* save on dry-cleaning expenses, dress-down days present a strong temptation to let it *all* hang out. This is rarely a pretty sight.

The same is true of e-mail. Neither a bloated butt nor some offensive e-mail is a pretty sight. The former is ugly enough to chase a pit bull off a meat wagon, but the latter can wreck careers.

Because e-mail is a more casual form of communication than a memo or letter, many workers treat e-mail like speech. Speech is speech. E-mail is writing.

Communicating by e-mail is no different from writing on your company letterhead. A business communication is business, period. As a result, a certain degree of formality is required. Just because e-mail tends to be more immediate and personable, it can't be casual. Business e-mail *must* be businesslike. You'll be judged by the quality of your writing, so spelling and grammar do count.

All forms of business communication you send reflect on you, affecting your chances for advancement. Sending e-mail riddled with misspellings is the same as wearing a shirt spattered with catsup. Sloppy e-mail gets tongues wagging about the writer's literal failings.

Watch Your Back!

All e-mail sent from the office—both personal and business—is the property of the company. Personal e-mail sent from a company computer can and will be used against you in a court of law. Also, unlike speech, e-mail is permanent. Even if you don't send the message and even if you erase it, the corporate computer geeks can retrieve it from your computer's hard drive or the central "post office" and use it against you.

Protect Your Assets

If you're spending a lot of time on the Net and you're shaky in these areas, it's worth brushing up on them. There are plenty of books available. We highly recommend *The Complete Idiot's Guide to Grammar and Usage.*

Sentence and Sensibility

When you send e-mail, know what you're talking about and make sense. This is also a good rule to follow every time you open your mouth, especially where gossip is concerned.

Pay attention to the content of your writing. When you see yourself writing "It's my understanding that" or "I believe it's the case," ask yourself whether you really want to post this note before checking your facts. On the Net, bad information propagates like Tribbles.

In addition, make sure your notes are clear and logical. It's possible to write a paragraph that contains no errors in grammar or spelling but still makes no sense whatsoever. This is most likely to happen when you're trying to impress someone by using a lot of long words that you don't really understand yourself. Trust us: No one worth impressing will be impressed if they can't understand your message. It's better to keep it simple.

Capital Punishment

Business communication requires proper use of written language, including the proper use of capital letters. Some offices permit—even encourage—all lowercase for internal memos. This is rude and slovenly when used in intercompany communications. Would you write a letter on company letterhead using all lowercase? We hope not!

In addition, typing in ALL CAPITALS is the e-mail equivalent of shouting. Capitalize a word for emphasis, but otherwise keep that Caps Lock key on the *off* position.

Here are some additional guidelines:

➤ *Internet* is a generic term, not a proper noun. Use lowercase and capitalize only at the beginning of a sentence.

➤ *Intranet* is a common noun. Capitalize *intranet* at the beginning of a sentence and when the word has been particularized, as in "the IBM Intranet" but not "IBM's intranet."

➤ *World Wide Web* should be capitalized. Ditto with the initials *WWW* (World Wide Web). They are not separated by periods.

➤ *E-mail* is written with a lowercase *e*, except at the beginning of a sentence, and the word is hyphenated.

➤ *On-line* is hyphenated. However, *Online* is commonly used in trade names (for example, America Online), in which case it should be written as the trade name dictates, usually not hyphenated and capitalized.

➤ *First names and titles.* If your correspondent uses your first name, then by all means use his or hers. But should you be the first to do so? Many people do not want such immediate informality in a business situation, especially in the international arena. Business people in many countries find the friendly nature of Americans, for example, overbearing. For international e-mail, err on the side of caution and write formally or send your first message without salutation. Stay away from "Dear Friend" or "Hi Neighbor."

➤ *Age and rank.* Consider age and rank if it can be discerned from the correspondence. Outside

Corporate Mumbo-Jumbo
Sometimes I think e-mail is like the Hotel California: You can check out any time you want, but you can never leave. Folks who have spent too much time on-line invented the following smiley faces to convey a light tone for informal communications. Read these sideways:

:-)	basic happy smiley face
;-)	winking smiley face
:-(	sad face
:-D	laughing face
:-X	lips are sealed face
:-C	really bummed
:-/	skeptical
%-)	bleary-eyed

North America, people in a position of authority and people of mature years expect a certain deference from their juniors.

➤ *The Message.* E-mail is often brief. This is desirable, but business messages will usually be longer than personal notes. It is important, also, to communicate: Don't kill understanding with brevity. You're not paying for e-mail by the word, after all.

➤ *Replies.* You will often be replying to only part of the received message. Maintain the thread, by all means, but save space by returning only the part of the message to which you are replying.

➤ *Smileys.* Don't use "smileys" (also known as emoticons: :-) ;-) :-/ and so on) in business correspondence. These are fine for personal notes but are inappropriate for business use.

Protect Your Assets
When you send e-mail, say where you obtained the e-mail address of the person to whom you are writing. Or mention the Web page name or URL if you e-mailed from a Web page. Many business people have more than one page on the Internet, and knowing from where or why they are being contacted is helpful. It might even get you a more meaningful reply.

Corporate Mumbo-Jumbo
Netiquette is etiquette for cyberspace.

Netiquette

Question: What sort of tone should I take in my e-mail?

Answer: Doing business over the Internet is a new phenomenon. Associated protocol is being created now, and you can contribute to the rule-making process. Nonetheless, some people have already managed to leave their mark in cyberspace as rude boors. How can you avoid joining their ranks? Learn Netiquette.

Netiquette is network etiquette, the dos and don'ts of on-line communication. Netiquette covers both common courtesy on-line and the informal "rules of the road" of cyberspace.

Netiquette follows the basic rule of etiquette: Show consideration for the other party. If you will just stop and think how the other person is likely to receive your communication, you will go a long way toward preventing misunderstandings and not giving offense. Ask yourself, "How would I feel in these circumstances if I received this message?"

Here are the top three rules of Netiquette:

Rule 1   Don't make yourself look like a jerk.

Rule 2   Don't flame.

Rule 3   Don't spam.

Let's look at each rule in detail.

Rule 1: Don't Make Yourself Look Like a Jerk

You wouldn't tug on Superman's cape, go 12 rounds with Mike Tyson, or try ballet dancing with a sumo wrestler. Neither would you spread vicious rumors about a colleague live and in person. So why would you act like a cement-head when you send e-mail?

You have to be even more careful when you send e-mail than when you trade gossip in person. That's because you never know who's going to read the memo. Our colleague Gary Krebs, the brilliant executive editor of the *Idiot's Guide* series, passed along this hint: Always assume that everyone in the company is going to read any e-mail you send—even if you just send it to one person.

Think carefully before you send any e-mail; often, you're better off not putting anything in writing and especially not posting it on the Net.

Rule 2: Don't Flame

Flaming is what people do when they express strong opinions and language without holding back any emotion. It's the kind of message that makes people respond, "Oh, come on. Tell us how you *really* feel." Tact is not its objective.

Does Netiquette forbid flaming? Not at all. Flames can be lots of fun, both to write and to read. And the recipients of flames sometimes deserve the heat.

But never, never, never flame when it comes to business.

Rule 3: Don't Spam

Spam is unsolicited e-mail, the junk mail of the Internet. *Spamming* is sending the same message to hundreds or thousands of e-mail addresses in the hope of hitting a few interested people. It displays extreme selfishness and total disregard for the zillions of people who are annoyed and inconvenienced by it.

Just as junk postal mail is annoying and wasteful, junk e-mail is more so. But with snail mail, you can throw the envelope away unread. With junk e-mail, you often have to read it to find that you didn't want to. It is therefore time wasting, inconsiderate, and very bad Netiquette.

Protect Your Assets
If you decide to inform someone of a mistake they've made on-line, point it out politely, and preferably by private e-mail rather than in public. Give people the benefit of the doubt; assume they just don't know any better. And never be arrogant or self-righteous about it.

Watch Your Back!
Although the law regarding e-mail and the right of privacy is still developing, at this time company managers have the legal right to enter an employee's e-mail and review, copy, or delete any messages.

Corporate Mambo-Jumbo
Spamming is sending the same message to hundreds or thousands of people, without considering the relevance. If you spam, you'll be considered rude and thoughtless.

Watch Your Back!
A particularly detestable aspect of *spamming* is the advent of chain-letter e-mail—those mean little letters that promise "good luck if you send this letter to 10 people you know," or bad luck if you don't. No one likes getting these via snail mail: It's even more infuriating to get them on your e-mail at work. Keep your superstitions to yourself and spare your co-workers the displeasure of receiving one of these nasty little buggers. And if your company is one of the many that bans such e-mail, sending it would bring you a lot more bad luck than not sending it!

Watch Your Back!
Always use a title in the "subject" area that tells the recipient what you are offering. "Low Cost Long Distance" or "Want to Patch that Bald Spot?" will win more customers than "Hi, There!" or "An Important Message." Messages that arrive with no indication of source and no subject are very likely to be treated as junk mail.

But direct mail does work. How can you satisfy the need to get new customers, which by definition must be strangers to your business, and at the same time be polite? Remember our first rule: Show consideration for the other party.

Any business solicitation can be condensed to one line. It is unnecessary, counterproductive, and rude to send 20 pages of details before confirming that the recipient is interested.

1. Only send one-line solicitations, followed by "E-mail for details." Here's an example:

   We are Individual Dignity Enhancement, Ltd. We are developing a list of contacts in Armpit, Idaho. Please e-mail if you would like to exchange details.

   E. Beaver (eager@beaver.dam)

2. Use proper bulk e-mail software that suppresses the list of names or…

3. Put the list of e-mail addresses in "bcc" ("blind carbon copies") to protect the privacy of your audience. "cc" lets all recipients see the full list of addresses. Apart from the privacy angle, it's frustrating to receive a one-line message preceded by five pages of e-mail addresses.

4. Put your own e-mail address at the top of the list, as a quality check, so you can see what everyone else is receiving.

5. End with your full name.

Hooked—Line and Sinker

Like Chunky-Monkey ice cream, e-mail can be addictive. After all, both offer instant gratification, and e-mail isn't even fattening. How can you tell when you've been trapped in the web? Perhaps you start tilting your head sideways to smile. And that's just the beginning.

You know you're an e-mail addict when:

1. Your cat has its own home page.

2. Your phone bill comes to your doorstep in a box.

3. You tell the cab driver you live at "http://1000.edison.garden/house/brick.html."

4. You get a tattoo that reads "This body best viewed with Netscape Navigator 1.1 or higher."

5. You spend half the plane trip with your laptop on your lap and your child in the overhead compartment.

6. You start using smileys in snail mail.

7. Your hard drive crashes. You haven't logged in for two hours. You start to twitch. You pick up the phone and manually dial your ISP's access number. You try to hum to communicate with the modem...and you succeed.

8. You refer to going to the bathroom as "downloading."

9. You can't call your mother; she doesn't have a modem.

10. You move into a new house and decide to Netscape before you landscape.

Corporate Mumbo-Jumbo
CLM (Career-Limiting Move) is a trendy new term for a type of gossip that harms your career. A CLM is an ill-advised activity, such as sending a complaining e-mail memo to your boss and then copying it to your boss's boss.

The Least You Need to Know

➤ You can't be successful on the job without being part of the office grapevine. Key into professional gossip and ignore personal gossip.

➤ Develop alliances to get the gossip. It's a give-and-take relationship.

➤ Nowadays, much gossip is transmitted via e-mail. You can't win it if you're not in it.

➤ When you send e-mail, watch your logic and writing skills. Maintain business formality.

➤ Follow the rules of Netiquette: Don't make yourself look like a jerk, don't flame, and don't spam.

➤ A computer is an electronic device that will never replace office workers until it learns how to spread gossip and laugh at the boss's jokes.

Part 3
Dealing with the Suits and Ties

Bosses fall into several basic categories:

1. *The* classic *boss says: "Get me some coffee or I'll slay your entire family."*

2. *The* self-deprecating *boss says, "I am unworthy to breathe the air you have exhaled."*

3. *The* cheerleader *boss says, "Okay everyone, let's make a human pyramid to sell those office supplies!"*

4. *The* big brain *boss says, "Let's keep searching for excellence in the quality chaos."*

5. *The* fugitive *boss says, "I'm off again to do really important things where you can't reach me."*

6. *The* self-starter *boss says, "Invent some objectives and write your own performance review."*

As this list shows, being a boss doesn't make you a leader any more than going to the garage makes you a car.

Bosses are among the most difficult people in the world to change. They probably got to the corner office by behaving in the same way that's driving you 'round the bend. Nonetheless, there are ways you can deal with difficult supervisors, managers, and other suits and ties. That's what this section is all about.

Chapter 10

Great Lies of Management

> **In This Chapter**
>
> ➤ The Peter Principle and your boss
>
> ➤ The key management falsehoods
>
> ➤ A few more fibs
>
> ➤ Some methods to deal with these lies

Here are the Top Ten biggest lies of all time:

10. The check is in the mail.

9. I gave at the office.

8. I'm from your government, and I am here to help you.

7. Don't worry, he's never bitten anyone.

6. ...then take a left. You can't miss it.

5. Drinking? Why, no, officer.

4. I never inhaled.

3. I never watch television except for PBS.

2. Don't worry, I can go another 20 miles when the gauge is on empty.

And the biggest lie of all time?

1. You can trust your boss to do what's best for your career.

Now it's time to learn how to deal with the front office. First, you'll discover that you're not crazy when it comes to assessing management: More bosses than you think are unable to do their jobs as well as they should. There are a lot of different reasons for this, but in many cases, your boss might just be in the wrong job. Your supervisor might be perfectly competent, brilliant even, in the right job. Unfortunately, too many people in management are in the wrong job. Who deals with the mess? We're looking at *you*.

Then we'll show you how misplaced managers deal with their ineptitude. It isn't going to be pretty, but you'll thank us in the morning.

The Peter Principle (or That's Why My Boss Is Such a Dork)

We got the following gem from a close buddy. It's a clear case of the *Peter Principle* at work.

> Happy with my preparation for international travel, I told my boss, "I've just completed my visa application." He said, "I prefer American Express for international travel."

The Peter Principle says that everyone eventually rises to their level of incompetence.

Fly on the Wall

The concept of the Peter Principle comes from Lawrence J. Peter's book *The Peter Principle*.

Watch Your Back!
Remember, your position exists in the corporate structure solely to make your boss look good. If you don't fulfill that Prime Directive of Corporate Life, plan on taking a *very* early retirement.

Nearly every boss knows this principle, but few think that it applies to *them*. According to this scientific principle, all stupid executives will rise in a company, but executives who are *exceedingly* stupid often reach their level of incompetence faster than they should. But not all promotions are in anyone's best interest—least of all your boss's.

A promotion that isn't suited to someone's talents and abilities only speeds up the Peter Principle. This often happens to super salespeople, for example. They are so productive that management feels compelled to promote them. The result is usually disastrous. The worker bee accepts the promotion even though he or she has no interest in managing people (or any talent for the task). The result? Everyone ends up suffering.

For example, Babe Ruth, one of the greatest baseball players of all time, was a horrendous manager. Just because you excel at your job doesn't mean you can direct anyone else on how to do it.

The following quiz proves our point. We've compiled five stories of moronic managers. To test your level of tolerance for incompetent management, how many of these could you cope with?

Coping Quiz

❏ 1. **Boss A** heard there was an opening for a plant manager in our South American facility. To better prepare for the position, Boss A decided to attend Spanish classes on the company's time and at their expense. The only problem? The plant is in Brazil where they speak Portuguese, not Spanish.

❏ 2. **Boss B** called and informed an employee that their e-mail system was down. The boss said, "I was going to e-mail you to let you know your check was in, but the system is down and no mail is getting through. Could you come in and fix this problem? I want to send you that message as soon as possible."

❏ 3. **Boss C** wanted to send a fax to the head office but was afraid someone else would read it besides the president. So Boss C put the message in an envelope before faxing it.

❏ 4. **Boss D** asked each manager to prepare detailed building and capital improvement "wish lists" to plan their facility's budget. Two weeks later, Boss D said, "Oh, your wish lists are just that; don't expect anything you requested to actually get done. It was just an exercise."

❏ 5. **Boss E** returned a modem to the computer store. The excuse? "The lights on the front kept flickering."

Score Yourself

0–2	Okay, your tolerance level needs some raising until *you* become a boss.
3–4	You're a graduate of the "grin-and-bear-it" school, aren't you?
5	Get on the phone to the Vatican and apply for sainthood.

Read My Lips

Because management is sometimes made up of people who have climbed the ladder through personal and corporate incompetence, they're backed into a corner when it comes time to do their jobs. Sometimes they get bewildered just trying to string together a few rational sentences. As a result, they feel they have to lie.

Protect Your Assets

If you wish, number these lies from 1 to 5. That way, instead of having to recite the entire sentence to explain how you've been mistreated, you can simply say, "I've gotten #4 again" or "He told us #2, and we all ambled back to our cubicles and chuckled."

For your convenience, we have compiled the Top Five Management Lies of all time. How many of these have you heard?

➤ "I reward risk-takers."

➤ "I value my employees."

➤ "Good performance will be rewarded."

➤ "Training is very important to me."

➤ "We're reorganizing to serve you better."

We know you're not a newcomer to the corporate badlands, but you might still have some shred of hope that the boss is on your side. The following section will stomp it out.

"I reward risk-takers."

"Take risks," unsophisticated guides to office politics exhort. "Be proactive, daring, and bold," they chant. And while you're at it, slam your hand in your desk drawer a few times (unless you have a workstation without a drawer, of course. Then just pound your head against the wall. Wait a minute; you're in a cubicle with soft walls. What the heck. Just take a risk and shoot your chances for promotion once and for all.)

Here's what a colleague told us about his attempt to be a proactive risk-taker:

> I submitted a suggestion to my boss that would save the company millions. After two weeks of silence, I went to my boss to get feedback. My boss said, "Oh, I threw your suggestion away. Only managers can make suggestions."

Of course you should take risks to get ahead. But be aware that risks can cost you big time when it comes to office politics. Why?

➤ Co-workers might feel threatened.

If your risk pays off, your colleagues are apt to think you're too big for your britches. And odds are, you will be. When you outshine your fellow grunts, they're virtually guaranteed to resent you. Look what happened to Galileo, Joan of Arc, and Magellan. See them getting invited to the A-list parties?

➤ People who take risks and succeed make their boss look bad.

Unless you're savvy enough to share the credit with your boss (or let you boss seize it), your risk-taking is going to look like a bold attempt to get your boss's job. Which is, of course, exactly what you're trying to do, because your momma didn't raise no fools.

➤ Most risks fail.

If you fall on your face, your boss is surely going to throw you to the sharks, because you've cost the department time and money—as well as making your boss look like a jerk for backing you. Even worse, you could get assigned to a Quality Team. But on the plus side, you'll get the pity vote from your fellow co-workers.

> **Watch Your Back!**
> Don't be surprised if management rewards the mediocre worker rather than the shooting star. Mediocrity isn't a threat to anyone.

"I value my employees."

What do the following four stories have in common?

➤ After several strong sales months, the company decided to print employee appreciation T-shirts. They went on sale the following Monday.

➤ I was suffering from the flu, but I came to work to meet a deadline. After I finished the task, I asked my boss if I could go home. It was obvious that I was very sick. The boss said, "No. If you couldn't work, why did you come in?"

➤ It was Friday afternoon, and we were having a terrible time with a new program. My first vacation in two years was about to start, and I had to catch a flight. When I reminded my boss that I had a plane to catch and couldn't work through the night, I was told, "Don't worry. Your vacation doesn't start until Monday."

➤ When I'm not at my desk, my boss answers my phone to see if I get personal calls.

Now, how do we reconcile the statement "I value my employees" with the harsh reality of the workplace? We can't. In nearly all companies, employees are about as valued as bunions. Employees are a necessity, like furniture, and so in the corporate balance sheet, you rank right up there with your desk, workstation, and cubicle—until one of you becomes obsolete.

What *do* companies value? Money. Profits. Capital.

Don't delude yourself that you're one in a million, the cog that drives the engine, the key to the kingdom. You're only as valuable as your use for the moment, as the following story illustrates:

I accepted a position as Service Manager of a fitness equipment company. I was supposed to earn a salary plus commission.

It was slow going at first, but soon I was churning out the work and making money. Then the bonus checks started to shrink. When I investigated, I found that the sales department was charging all their expenses against my department to keep their

Protect Your Assets

It's not always easy to distinguish between a manager's outright lie and an everyday blockheaded comment. How can you tell the difference? If your manager is willing to put the promise in writing, you're dealing with a jerk. If not, you're dealing with a liar.

Corporate Mambo-Jumbo

A *performance review* is a newly discovered level of hell. In theory, it's an opportunity for positive interaction between a "coach" (boss) and employee to achieve maximum performance. In reality, it's one more way to deny an employee a fair raise by coercing a signed confession of your crimes against productivity. More on this devious method of torture later.

bonuses higher. My bosses said they were "part of the team" and this practice was okay.

The delivery department got wind of the sales department's practice, and they started charging delivery expenses to the service department. I complained to the store manager about the improper charges.

The next month, I got no check at all. I learned from accounting that my bosses had charged all their expenses to my accounts.

I found a job with a better accounting system.

"Good performance will be rewarded."

Yes, and you'll lose those extra 10 pounds, no one can tell that you're using hair in a can, and iguana really tastes like chicken.

In life, no good deed goes unpunished. This is especially true when it comes to dealing with management. You can often build up favors with co-workers (and well you should), but don't count on it with management. Is it really likely that management is going to proclaim, "Forget our gargantuan year-end bonuses. How could we have been so selfish? Let's give all our money to our employees."

And after you get put through a Performance Review that requires you to do everything but dance barefoot in a campfire and catch a bullet with your teeth, your (microscopic) raise will be the same whether you're Mother Teresa or the Son of Sam.

Want some proof that rewards in the business world have little to do with sterling performance? Try these on for size:

➤ In one company, the employees were divided into four work teams, each with eight members. The teams entered a sales competition, the first prize being eight baseball tickets. Our friends' team won. Their boss went to the next eight baseball games alone.

➤ The workers in a company were recently told that no pay raises would be awarded this year. At first, everyone took it in stride. Then they learned that managers eligible for bonuses could expect a 150 percent increase.

116

➤ Work at a company was never getting finished on time. Missed deadlines became a way of life. What did the company do? They started awarding big buck bonuses to employees whose work was done on schedule. Ergo, people were rewarded for simply doing the job they had been hired to do.

Watch Your Back!
If you are behind schedule, you must be goofing off. If you are on schedule, then your plan was not aggressive enough. And you want a pat on the back, too?

"Training is very important to me."

Just for fun, let's say that company profits are down this year. Is it more likely that

a. Management will leave the training budget untouched and thus save money by delaying the launch of a new product.

or

b. Management will raid the training budget, launch the project, and pay megabucks to consultants to fix the mess at the back end—after they have collected their glory, raises, and bonuses.

When budgets get tight, money set aside for training vanishes faster than hair gel at a convention of Elvis impersonators. Here's a case in point:

I work for a big management consultancy partnership. We pride ourselves in the quality of our internal training programs. However, once these programs started costing too much, a senior manager suggested we make the "Team-Building Exercise" an "Individual Self-Help Study Course."

"We're reorganizing to serve you better."

Is it really likely that this latest reorganization—in contrast to all the other reorganizations that have come before it—will turn your company into a Center for Excellence? Is the company running in the red because the organizational chart isn't backward compatible? Isn't your time better spent rearranging the deck chairs on the *Titanic* than juggling the corporate structure?

Or could it be that management doesn't have the slightest idea how to fix the problem? Because they don't have the budget to hire additional help (or someone who can actually save the project), they'll shuffle and befuddle the current staff to give the illusion of progress.

Here are two examples of theory put into practice:

➤ After downsizing, there was a headcount freeze and a noticeable reduction in our output. To rectify this, we hired twice as many temporary employees. This action was approved by corporate because temporary employees are *not* included in the corporate headcount under the reorganized plan.

➤ Our company was running into financial difficulties, and my boss asked me to work for half of my salary. I said, "Well, I can work half the time for half the pay." The boss said, "Oh, no. You usually work 80 hours a week with 40 hours of unpaid overtime. Now I want to pay for just half of the first 40."

Truthfully Challenged

Management can be a devious bunch. In their defense, they often don't have a choice. After all, they're usually hanging on by the fingernails themselves. As a result, the higher-ups have more than five lies to protect their bacon by keeping you guessing. This gives them some moral wiggleroom when things get tight.

For example, let's say you hear some rumors about impending layoffs. You decide to check out these rumors with management. Bad move. Is the boss really likely to say, "Yes, kid, your job is on the line. As a matter of fact, so's mine. Let's run for the hills." Not bloody likely.

Fly on the Wall

Yes, the American economy is on an upswing right now, but according to the *New York Times*, real wages have fallen from a 1979 average of $24,000 for a high-school graduate to a 1995 average of $18,000. According to a number of studies, workers have a third less time for leisure and family activities than they did in 1969. Further, every year, nearly half of all workers witness layoffs in their own workplace. As a result, 40 percent of workers say their employers expect them to work an unreasonable number of overtime hours.

What you're likely to get is something along these lines:

You: "Boss, rumor has it that deranged squirrels from Planet X are going to swallow up our company in their relentless drive to conquer the universe."

Boss: "Not to worry. It's business as usual right now. But maybe you should store some acorns in your desk."

You: "Well, I certainly feel better now."

Here are seven more prevarications you can expect to encounter in the workaday world:

➤ "My door is always open."

➤ "I never shoot the messenger."

➤ "You could earn more money with these changes."

➤ "Your comments are important to me."

➤ "Your future is bright with me."

➤ "I'm watching out for you."

➤ "It ain't broke, so we have no plans to fix it."

Let's see how these affect your daily life and long-term future.

"My door is always open."

Choose a or b:

a. Your boss welcomes a steady stream of whiners who complain about things that can't be changed.

b. Your boss tries to intimidate people from coming into the office in a vain attempt to get some work done.

This is a no-brainer, pal. We all know that bosses love to be distracted from their work by malcontents and malingerers. After all, what's more fun than listening to an hour of aimless venting? (Listening to two hours of aimless venting?)

How do bosses discourage employees from entering their inner sanctums?

➤ They discourage people who believe this lie by assigning extra work to anyone who ventures in.

➤ They intimidate you by explaining how you're going to be the human charcoal at the next reorganizational barbecue.

➤ They tell rambling stories about status reports, market segmentation, and utilizing bottom-line revenues.

➤ They doze off when you reach the point about last week's meeting of the Oversight Committee.

➤ They pretend to be wax statues.

➤ They close their doors and lock them.

➤ They do other work while pretending to listen to you.

"I never shoot the messenger."

Three guys were about to be shot in a prison camp. The first one thought, "If I could just find a distraction, maybe I could escape."

Just then, the squad leader said, "Ready, aim..." The first prisoner shouted, "Tornado!" The members of the firing squad looked around, and the prisoner ran away.

The second prisoner decided to try the same thing. The squad leader said, "Ready, aim..." The second guy yelled, "Flood!" Sure enough, the members of the firing squad looked around, and the prisoner ran away.

Watch Your Back!
A memorandum is usually written not to inform the reader but to protect the writer.

The third guy thought, "Hey, we're on to something here." But when the leader yelled "Ready, aim...," the third guy yelled "Fire!"

Your goal when it comes to dealing with management? Always be a moving target. Never stand still. It just makes it easier to get hit. Anyone foolish enough to stand in the firing line is going to get it right between the eyes.

"You could earn more money with these changes."

Yes, and if pigs had wings, they could fly. Is it really likely that the company is suddenly going to change its entire compensation plan to give you the money you deserve? Or is it more likely that the changes are designed to make it impossible for anyone without a Ph.D. from the London School of Economics to figure exactly how you're getting cheated now?

Here's what management will tell you: "The company has been re-engineered, and you have been functionally re-aligned and placed in management optimization groups."

Here's what it means: "You work more hours with fewer people for less pay."

"Your comments are important to me."

Here's the employee input equation:

Employee comments = More work = Not good

Most managers would rather rip out their intestines with a fork than deal with employee suggestions. That's because employee suggestions rarely make managers look good. After all, if the suggestions are really valid, why didn't the managers think of them in the first place?

Odds are, your boss will listen politely to your suggestion, nod, and do exactly what he or she planned in the first place, as the following story illustrates:

"After letting my boss know that I thought the new tech support applicant was over-qualified and would be bored in the position he was being offered, the boss said, "That's what everyone else said, but I'm going to hire him anyway.""

Brutally honest bosses might say: "I'm sorry if I ever gave you the impression your input would have any effect on my final decision" as they override the decision of a task force they created.

The manager is faced with a dilemma. If the manager goes with your idea and it flops, it's the manager's butt on the line with the bigger bosses. Of course, if it works, you won't get credit for it anyway—so which scenario do you prefer?

Here's a peach of an example that shows the incentive for employee input:

One of the employees in my department resigned. Instead of filling the position at $30,000 per year, I suggested an alternative incentive plan. Each month, the most productive worker in my department could earn a $1,000 bonus if the department's monthly goals were met.

The boss reviewed my proposal and rejected it—including the $18,000 annual savings. The boss said, "What if this worked? Everyone in the company would want to work for you."

"Your future is bright with me."

Yes, business is rosy, but according to the U.S. Department of Labor, from now until the year 2025, college graduates will outnumber jobs available to them by 20 percent each year.

Former State Senator Bill Bradley said, "Economic anxiety eats away at people who work in America."

Besides, is it likely that your boss is the reincarnation of Nostradamus, able to predict the future? Remember, this is the same person who, when told that the new computer had a Pentium chip, replied "I'm in no rush. I'd rather wait and get a computer without chips, dings, or gashes."

Protect Your Assets
The riskiest industries (in order of risk) are coal mining, miscellaneous business services, holding companies, fishing, and apparel manufacturing. So don't start a freelance business involving coal mining for fish in designer jeans.

Save Yourself

Now that you understand that managers are forced to lie to their employees to save their necks, you can listen with a slightly more cynical attitude to their assurances. Thanks to us, you'll never again believe "Our people are the best" or "We'll review your performance in six months." You know that management regards most employees as mere road kill; you understand that your manager expects to get a new job in six months and never have to deal with you again.

So when your manager dishes out one of the 10 classic lies, you should...

1. Consider the source: What is your relationship to the manager? Is it your mother— or just another in an endless series of revolving managers? Why on earth would you believe this person?

2. Consider the situation: What does your manager have to gain by lying? By telling the truth?

3. Consider the consequences: What can happen if what your manager says is true? If it's not?

4. Consider the past: Have you heard this line before? Or one like it? What did it mean then?

5. Consider the effect on you: What can you gain from this? Or lose?

The Least You Need to Know

➤ The Peter Principle states that everyone eventually rises to their level of incompetence.

➤ A promotion that isn't suited to someone's talents and abilities only speeds up the Peter Principle.

➤ Managers lie to cover their incompetence.

➤ The Top Ten lies are "I reward risk-takers," "I value my employees," "Good performance will be rewarded," "Training is very important to me," "We're reorganizing to serve you better," "My door is always open," "I never shoot the messenger," "You could earn more money with these changes," "Your comments are important to me," and "Your future is bright with me."

➤ Carefully evaluate everything your managers say. Odds are, every third word is correct.

Chapter 11

My Way or the Highway

In This Chapter

➤ The characteristics of a toxic boss

➤ How they make your life miserable

➤ Ways to deal with a sadistic superior

➤ Political savvy that can help you save yourself

A friend told his boss, "Rome wasn't built in a day."

The boss replied, "I wasn't in charge of that job."

In this chapter, you'll learn how to deal with the toxic boss who pushes you beyond your limits, challenges your authority, and scrutinizes every aspect of your performance. Totally ruthless, this boss rules by intimidation and fear. But don't shake in your Florsheims or Ferragamos: We'll teach you how to use office politics to manage the cutthroat boss who wants nothing more than to chew you up and spit you out.

In Your Face

Exhibit A: Clueless Boss

My boss fired a sales person the day after she closed a $70,000 sale. A few days later, the boss asked me why company morale was so low.

Exhibit B: Sadistic Boss

After an hour of furious debate, I finally understood the point my boss was trying to make. At the moment I expressed my agreement with his position, he said viciously, "It's too late to agree with me now because I've changed my mind. And if you don't like it, I'm going to make your life at work miserable. You know I can do it, too."

How can we explain the fact that your boss seems to be deliberately trying to make your life hell? There's the endless screaming, sabotage, and snooping. There's punishment and retribution. And let's not forget the fear of reengineering, downsizing, and rightsizing. How can we explain your feelings that your boss is out to get you?

The answer: You're not an idiot. Your boss really *is* out to get you. That's because your boss is a micromanaging Machiavellian monster. You have a boss from hell.

Fly on the Wall

A now-famous executive was working with his supervisor to prepare for a big meeting with the head of their division. The executive and his wife were expecting their first child at the time.

Their son was born two months premature, the weekend before the big meeting. On Monday, the new papa came to work to tie up loose ends and to tell his boss about his son's critical life situation.

The boss said, "Don't let your personal life interfere with your job. It can only hurt you, professionally. I knew I'd have to take charge of this myself to get it done right. I can't expect *you* to come through for me."

In previous chapters, you learned about the Peter Principle, the concept that people invariably rise to their level of incompetence. What happens when the merely incompetent become actively vicious? Are you working for a lion who has tasted blood? Take the following quiz to find out. Check the correct answer for each question.

Sadistic Superior Quiz

Yes	No	
❏	❏	1. Does your boss always look for a scapegoat? Is it usually you?
❏	❏	2. Does your boss feel compelled to explain in great detail why "profit" is the difference between income and expense, making you feel like an idiot?

Yes	No	
❏	❏	3. Does your boss live by this creed: Once is happenstance. Twice is coincidence. The third time is enemy action…and your boss is usually out to get you?
❏	❏	4. Does your boss think employees should schedule funerals only during holidays?
❏	❏	5. Does your boss have difficulty telling the difference between screaming and communication?
❏	❏	6. Does your boss believe that he or she can do everything better than you can—or anyone else in the department, for that matter? If you provide facts to prove that you're correct, your boss will shrug and say, "That wasn't what I said."
❏	❏	7. Does your boss want everything done *yesterday*—and then criticize you because it isn't done "right"?
❏	❏	8. Does your boss rifle through your desk, try to read your e-mail, and listen in on your phone calls?
❏	❏	9. Does your boss go over and over your work, finding "mistakes" like upside-down periods?
❏	❏	10. Does your boss get a noticeable kick out of being called "boss"?

Score Your Boss

8–10 Yes's	Who stole the strawberries?
5–7 Yes's	Only thing missing from your office is the goose-step.
2–4 Yes's	As a self-made man or woman, your boss is more of a warning than an example.
0–1 Yes's	You've got the good boss. Your boss does what God would have done if He had the facts.

Watch Your Back!
To make things even worse for you, micromanaging bosses will usually take the credit for anything you do that's right—and blame you for everything that goes wrong. To combat this, keep a careful record of events, including official documents such as receipts, telephone logs, and e-mail.

The Toxic Boss

No one can make your life more miserable than your boss can. And your boss can do it in so many ways, from trying to control your every move to simply being inept.

Like Michael Jackson's nose, abusive bosses come in all shapes, sizes, and colors. They can be high-school dropouts, or they can hold advanced degrees from prestigious institutions. The micromanager can present a good appearance to those who don't have the misfortune of working for them. They usually come across as

➤ Intelligent

➤ In charge

➤ Decision-makers

➤ Proactive

Unfortunately, there's no demographic profile of a boss likely to go ballistic and make your life hellish. However, there are some qualities these toxic bosses have in common.

These kinds of bosses are often

➤ Controlling

➤ Haughty and conceited

➤ Inconsiderate

➤ Aggressive

➤ Hostile; they often push your buttons deliberately

➤ Convinced of their own superiority

➤ Insulting; they often call you names

➤ Emotional blackmailers

Protect Your Assets

Paradoxically, abusive bosses might also have an inflated, unrealistic view of themselves and their capabilities. They start believing their own press clippings and so think they deserve special treatment.

Toxic bosses tend to lack self-respect. Many have worked for equally abusive bosses in their past; they may even have been abused as children. They are people who believe that because *they* don't deserve dignity and respect, no one else does, either. Even on the rare occasions when what passes for praise crosses their lips, it's usually condescending enough to be taken as an insult. For example, "You know, Deb, you really can do good work when you put your mind to it."

The following example shows a toxic boss in action.

How Not to Win Friends and Influence People

Jim was an achiever from birth. According to his doting parents, he walked, talked, and reconfigured hard drives before he was a year old; by the age of five, he was solving quadratic equations, writing the Great American novel, and doing the Samba on ice skates. He was always the first one done with every assignment in school; he always had the highest grades, of course. His drive to excel helped him earn an MBA from an Ivy League school and an armload of accolades and achievements.

Corporate Mumbo-Jumbo
An *ego wall* is the boss's wall of honors, awards, diplomas, and certificates.

He brought the same intense work habits to his first job as a regional operations manager for a national car rental company. He loved the job because it allowed him to show that he—and only he—knew how to get things done right.

At his first regional meeting, Jim asked each of his 10 managers to present a 10-minute overview of what their divisions had done in the previous year and what their plans were for improving their performance in the coming year.

None of the managers had ever received any formal training in making presentations, and Jim didn't provide any guidelines, either. As a result, the presentations were adequate but not inspiring. They were missing the bells and whistles that Jim had learned in his tony MBA program.

When everyone had finished their dog-and-pony shows, Jim got up and screamed, "I have never seen anything so unprofessional. I gave better speeches in junior high school. I don't know what your previous boss told you, but from now on, I expect quality work. No manager in my division is going to make me look bad with this kind of amateur-hour trash. If you can't take a simple assignment like this seriously, how can I trust your commitments to the really important aspects of your job?"

As you might have guessed, Jim's bellowing criticism didn't go over well. Jim was about as popular as fire-proof matches. "Mark my words," said Lisa, one of the managers. "One day he'll get his."

Watch Your Back!
When people are belittled or de-graded, they find ways to retaliate or sabotage other people's efforts. In more cases than not, what goes around, comes around. We know revenge feels *sooo* good, but remember that it's a dish best served cold.

Over the next few months, Jim rode his managers hard. He drilled them, screamed at them, and humiliated them. He peered over their shoulders and mercilessly wrote and rewrote their presentations. Not surprisingly, the next round of presentations *was* far better. Lisa's speech was especially outstanding.

Sure enough, about a month later, Lisa took a job with another firm. She walked out on Jim during Thanks-giving week, one of the busiest times in the car rental business.

Status Quo

How can such a cutthroat, abusive boss as Jim survive? How can any screaming, sadistic boss last until it's time for the gold watch and the big retirement party?

Time for a reality check. In corporate America, if the work gets done, there's little likelihood that upper management will notice (or even care) that the boss is shoving little bitty pieces of bamboo up everyone's fingernails. As long as the money keeps rolling in and no current federal laws against harassment are being broken, your boss can continue to scream. In fact, management might even encourage such abusive behavior, under the theory that "If it ain't broke, don't fix it."

The Sounds of Silence

Furthermore, most employees are inclined to suffer in silence when they work for a tyrant. After all, their livelihood depends on this individual. If you complain, you're likely to get targeted as a troublemaker. There are even some poor souls who believe that it's their fault the boss is a maniac. After all, if they were better employees, the boss wouldn't get so provoked. But we don't want to go *there*. That's TV movie-of-the-week territory.

Stop, Drop, and Roll

How can you deal with this type of behavior? You can always use the method recommended by pyrotechnic experts when you're on fire: stop, drop, and roll. Or you can try our ideas. Here are some suggestions that have worked for us:

1. Wait.

   Don't even attempt to reason with these kinds of bosses until they have blown off steam. Save your breath to cool your porridge.

2. Listen.

   Listen until they run out of things to say. As you listen, you'll gain their confidence. Use this to position yourself to propose a solution.

3. Analyze the situation.

   Try to discover the real reasons behind the attack and the boss's motivation for acting so unreasonably.

4. Jump in.

   When the boss begins to wind down, jump in with an assertion of the needs to be met in this situation.

5. Stay firm.

   Try not to let your boss interrupt, but as you're confronting this type of boss, never say: "I'm not finished (or through) yet." That opens the door for your boss to say, "Oh, yes you are" and boot you out the door. If the boss does interrupt, return to Step 2.

6. Don't counterattack.

   This only causes toxic bosses to escalate as they feel more threatened and hostile. Instead, respond actively and enthusiastically.

7. Use "I."

   Avoid the word "you," which sounds like a counterattack. Talk about the situation in the first person, instead.

8. Stay on topic.

   Address their concerns directly, or they might erupt again. The attacker's intent is to throw you off course so you are an easier target. Stick to your personal and professional goals but don't feel compelled to announce your agenda.

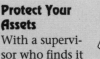

Protect Your Assets

With a supervisor who finds it easier to criticize than praise yet clings to you like a cheap suit, set up meetings at least twice a year to discuss your strengths and weaknesses. At the end of every project, solicit feedback.

9. Suggest a schedule for feedback.

   Tell your boss that you want to relieve any anxiety he or she might have about whether the job is getting done correctly. Establish times when the boss can check on your progress. Suggest meetings for a few minutes at the start or finish of each day. Or you can submit a written weekly progress report.

10. Grin and bear it.

    If the screaming boss is someone who trains or promotes you, you can always try to develop a thicker skin. You can sometimes move your career along briskly by sticking with a lunatic for a while.

    Furthermore, it might actually be worth it to take the abuse if you're making megabucks. This sounds callous, but many workers are motivated by the new Golden Rule: The one with the gold rules.

11. Take a time-out.

    If you're dealing with a boss who can break the sound barrier without a microphone, politely tell him or her that you can't respond when you're being screamed at and that you'll return when he or she has calmed down.

12. Remain confident.

    The bully boss enjoys seeing your fear. Close off your vulnerable spots and stay self-assured.

13. Establish allies.

    Your defense is always stronger if you are a welcome member of a team and a valued peer.

14. Get help.

    If all else fails, remember that you do not have to take abusive behavior from your boss. Seek help through your union or human resources department. If necessary, you might have to consult an attorney and seek a legal solution.

Corporate Mumbo-Jumbo
Management: The art of stepping on your employees' toes without messing up their shine.

15. Hit the high road.

    If your boss merely micromanages you and insults you without giving you the experience you need to get ahead, why stick around any longer than you need to? Get to know managers in related departments who, over time, can help you move out.

The Big Chill

A friend of mine recently wrote a justification to buy a new PC. It had to be approved by the manager. Unhappy with my friend's writing style, the manager rewrote the justification to show her how it should be done. After it was finally written properly, the boss turned it down. There went *that* promotion.

Watch Your Back!
Remember: Attackers are not in control in the first place. You don't want to contribute to their fire or play by their rules by becoming equally irrational.

Never lose control. Whenever you face a toxic boss (or any other seemingly impossible political situation in the office), remain in control of your emotions. Go home and yell at the TV, kick a stuffed dog, even throw some (cheap) crockery, but in the office, stay stony. You have every right to be angry and even outraged at a vicious attack, but losing control and striking back will never improve your situation in a business setting.

Try these ideas:

➤ Establish some distance by trying to see the situation as an outsider might. Does your boss act up only at certain times such as pressure situations? Is the anger work-related or habitual? If you can identify certain types of situations that provoke your boss's wrath, you might be able to stay out of the firing line.

➤ Play by the rules. Don't set yourself up for abuse by cutting corners, cheating, or lying.

➤ Evaluate your own feelings and needs. What is the nature of the behavior that bothers you? Each boss must be evaluated individually—as must each worker.

Welcome to the Outer Limits

Your boss controls the horizontal and the vertical. Do not attempt to adjust your set. Welcome to the Outer Limits of your job.

Another way a toxic boss can make your life miserable is by creating unacceptable work conditions. This political strategy is often used by bosses who want to get someone to leave the company.

For example, your boss can make you travel 20 days out of 30, knowing that you would rather not leave town when your children are young. Your boss might force you to work out of three different branch offices or exclude you from key activities such as staff meetings.

Managers might also want to dump employees because they are perceived as a threat. Bosses are more likely to be worried that an underling is trying to oust when they have doubts about their own abilities. Such employees are seen as rivals because they act like opponents—deliberately or accidentally—working to upstage their managers. But unlike a turf war between colleagues, a fight between manager and subordinate isn't an even match; the manager has the power and wins most of the time. In this situation, it is incumbent for the employee to convince the boss that they're on the same team. (Of course, this is somewhat hypocritical if you really *are* trying to grab the boss's job.)

Chances are that conditions will not change as long as your boss is determined to get rid of you. What can you do? Start by opening up communications to make sure that you are right in assuming that your boss is out to get you. See if you can figure out why you're the target. If you are indeed in the firing range, you have only three choices:

1. Start with the company's Personnel Office or Human Resources department to see what protection the company offers you, if any.

2. If you are a member of a union, you can seek help from them. You might also consider hiring a lawyer.

3. Position yourself for another job in the same company or change companies completely. This is not throwing in the towel. In this situation, it's being realistic.

Protect Your Assets
The anti-discrimination laws have opened up many new areas of protection for employees caught in the cross fire of office politics. For example, you might be sheltered as part of a "protected class." More on this to come.

Watch Your Back!
If you're unhappy with your boss, have a short temper, and like a drink every now and again, you might want to take a pass on office parties. Even though we believe that it's vital to socialize with your co-workers and bosses, we also believe that it's vital not to get soused and decide that it's time to level with the boss—in front of the entire company.

The Least You Need to Know

➤ There are many different types of abusive bosses, but they can all make your life miserable.

➤ Wait, listen, and analyze the situation before you jump in.

➤ Stay firm, don't counterattack, and focus on the situation at hand.

➤ Take a time-out, remain confident, and establish allies.

➤ If all else fails, bail out. Life is too short to suffer. Remember, you're the master of your fate.

Riddle Me This

Do you feel left out in the cold because you have no idea what your boss wants? Do you rarely get clear instructions from your supervisor? Then this chapter is for you. Find out how to use your political skills to deal with a boss whose motto is "I shouldn't have to tell you what to expect."

What Color Is the Sky on Your Planet?

You know that the dynamics between boss and employee can be dicey. In theory, the relationship *should* be symbiotic: Managers set the goals, and staffers implement them. Both groups support each other because they need each other to succeed.

Reality, however, doesn't always work so neatly. What happens if you can't figure out what your boss is talking about?

An acquaintance shared this tale from the ledge:

> I was hired as a language instructor at a vocational training institute. At the time, the school was on probation with the local governing board of education. Our graduates were not finding jobs.
>
> Because I had prior experience in employment staffing, my supervisor asked me to help. I rose to the challenge. I rolled up my shirt sleeves and went to work. I created a job search program. I taught students how to write resumés, how to interview, and how to keep jobs. I found companies who liked our graduates and would hire them. The job statistics went up dramatically, and the school was removed from probation.
>
> After all this, I didn't get a raise. I was furious. I said to my supervisor, "You wanted results, and I got them. What more could you ask of me?"
>
> My supervisor replied, "Yes, the students got jobs, but did they get careers?"

Huh?

The *puzzler* is a boss who sends conflicting messages and withholds information you need to do your job. This type of boss also

➤ States goals in abstract terms. The terms are never quantitative or definitive.

➤ Changes his or her mind more often than Madonna changes her image.

➤ Gives conflicting signals.

➤ Rarely sets standards by which you can judge your achievements.

➤ Fails to provide clear performance evaluations.

➤ Is often unwilling to put anything in writing and usually can't write clearly anyway.

➤ Is often most concerned with saving his or her fanny rather than accomplishing meaningful work or shepherding your career.

➤ Does not pass on feedback from higher-ups.

➤ Responds to disagreements among subordinates by ignoring them, asking people to play nice, or smoothing over differences

➤ Rarely wants to hear bad news.

Strictly speaking, a wishy-washy boss is not a difficult person because he or she might not have any personality or attitude problems. They are normally very nice people in the abstract—but terrible bosses. They can make life astonishingly difficult for you because you can't find a way around their inability to make a decision.

Here are some examples of puzzling bosses. See if your boss would act this way:

➤ Instructions from the boss: "We have four 15-inch computer monitors in storage. I want you to get the biggest one and put it in my office."

➤ Replying to my questions about advancement, the boss said, "Your future isn't what it used to be."

➤ The boss told an employee that she was unfit, incompetent, and untrained and that she didn't belong in the department at all. The boss then looked at the employee anxiously and said, "But we can talk about it, if you like."

➤ After a year's hard work, an employee did not receive a raise. The boss said, "Your work is important, but not valuable."

➤ Comment from the boss: "What this department lacks is leadership."

Watch Your Back!
Sometimes, bosses are unwilling to make decisions because they don't understand the job and are afraid to admit it. They can get hostile if forced into a corner. Don't openly challenge these types of bosses if you value your job.

Fly on the Wall

The difference between success and failure in business is often the ability to communicate clearly and effectively. Business leader Lee Iacocca achieved success because of communication skills. He saved the Chrysler Corporation by using his talent as a communicator to win the backing of the President, Congress, and Americans in the largest corporate bailout in our history. Even Iacocca credits his success to his ability to communicate: "I've seen a lot of guys who are smarter than I am and a lot who know more about cars. And yet I've left most of them in the smoke. Why?…You've got to know how to talk to them, plain and simple."

Come Again?

The wishy-washy boss is an expert at saying things that seem to have meaning but upon closer examination are as empty as a Spice Girl's head. As a result, you have no idea what the boss wants. In effect, you're getting a lot of words but no meaning. Try it yourself.

Match each of these puzzler boss comments to its meaning. Write the letter of the correct answer in the space provided.

Wishy-Washy Comments Quiz

	Dialogue	Meaning
___	1. "Employees are our most important asset."	A. Nothing
___	2. "Our strategy is to improve long-term profitability."	B. Nothing
___	3. "We are studying the key issues so we can prepare a plan."	C. Nothing
___	4. "It just makes good sense to put all your eggs in one basket, but not always."	D. Nothing
___	5. "I want to thank every one of you for having extinguished yourselves during this meeting."	E. Nothing

Break the Code

A linguistics professor was lecturing to his class one day. "In English," he said, "a double negative forms a positive. In some languages, though, such as Russian, a double negative is still a negative. However, there is no language wherein a double positive can form a negative."

A voice from the back of the room piped up, "Yeah, right."

Like all unsatisfactory bosses, puzzler bosses think they are very busy people. As a result, they can't be bothered wasting time clarifying directions. A positive statement, a negative statement, a double negative: It's all the same to them. It's *your* job to figure out what they mean and what they want. You have to use your own best judgment to decode their nonstatements.

Unfortunately, you usually can't figure out what a "puzzler" boss wants from you. Even the boss's handwriting is unclear. For example, the memo might say, "The clients must be *killed* at once." On the other hand, it might really say, "The clients must be *billed* at once." Who can tell? Certainly not you, unless your undergraduate degree is in cryptography. Where *is* that Rosetta Stone when we need it?

Say What?

The "oblivious" boss is a variation on the puzzler boss. The oblivious manager seems to be perpetually out to lunch—even at 9:00 a.m. This type of supervisor manages to zone out when anyone mentions a problem, dilemma, or issue that has even the most remote chance of becoming unpleasant. In addition, this type of boss

➤ Doesn't care about the opinions of others.

➤ Is rarely approachable.

➤ Tries hard to avoid confrontation.

➤ Cuts off your ideas in mid-sentence.

➤ Doesn't understand that communication is a two-way process.

➤ Appears to listen attentively as you patiently explain something and then says, "Give it to me in a layperson's terms."

➤ Sees most complaints as a waste of time.

➤ For the sake of being liked, will often tolerate mediocre performance or unacceptable behavior—or simply ignore it.

➤ Appears blissfully unaware of reality.

Take this simple quiz to see if you're working for an oblivious boss. Write *true* or *false* for each statement.

Oblivious Boss Quiz

True	False	
❏	❏	1. How do you make the boss's eyes twinkle? Shine a flashlight in his or her ear.
❏	❏	2. Why did the boss scale the chain-link fence? To see what was on the other side.
❏	❏	3. Why did the boss keep a coat hanger in the back seat? In case the keys got locked in the car.
❏	❏	4. Why did the boss get so excited after finishing the jigsaw puzzle in only six months? Because on the box it said "from 2 to 4 years."
❏	❏	5. How do you confuse your boss? Ask him or her to alphabetize a bag of M&Ms.
❏	❏	6. What did the boss say after looking into a box of Cheerios? "Oh, look! Donut seeds!"
❏	❏	7. Why can't bosses put in light bulbs? They keep breaking them with the hammers.
❏	❏	8. Why did the boss have tire tread marks on his or her back? From crawling across the street when the sign said "Don't Walk."

Score Your Boss

7–8 correct	X-ray the boss's head, and you'd find nothing.
5–6 correct	One sandwich short of a picnic.
3–4 correct	Not the sharpest knife in the drawer.
0–2 correct	Absent minded, not AWOL.

Mea culpa; we did fudge a little. Bet you confused an oblivious boss with a stupid one. However, it is an understandable mistake. Even the most brilliant, oblivious boss seems like a nitwit. That's because these types of bosses are so unwilling to clue in that they seem clueless.

If It Ain't Broke, Don't Fix It

Another subdivision of the wishy-washy "puzzler" boss is the *wussy* boss. These wimpy souls are nonassertive, even with subordinates. They avoid all high-risk actions, even if there's a strong possibility of high gain. They check with supervisors for authorization to begin projects, for approval of work done to date, and for permission to continue.

Protect Your Assets
How can you tell if you're dealing with an oblivious boss? These bosses try to turn a deaf ear. Listen for this excuse: "I don't have time right now; please make an appointment."

This type of boss also

➤ Says little at meetings.

➤ Phrases even assertions as questions.

➤ Apologizes for ideas.

➤ Tends to downplay praise.

Wimpy bosses are so annoying they can even make you yearn for wishy-washy puzzlers.

Singing the Blues

Puzzler bosses are especially frustrating because they don't seem to mean you any harm. Nonetheless, working for them is like trying to stay afloat on quicksand; the harder you try to understand, the deeper you seem to sink. Here's a story we got from a friend in sales:

> A software salesman was cooling his heels in the outer office of the president of a major computer company. Just as he was about to be granted an audience, an old gypsy woman was ushered in ahead of him.
>
> "What's she doing here?" complained the salesman.
>
> "Oh," replied the secretary, "The boss only brings her in for the really important decisions."

Okay, so you know what you're dealing with: a weak-willed, wishy-washy boss. They have trouble deciding what to order for lunch, much less how to deal with employees, projects, deadlines, conflicts, and turf battles.

Read on to find out what you should and should not do to get ahead with this type of boss. See how you can use your political skills to make sense of the puzzler.

Steer Clear

Before we discuss what you *should* do to cope with an ineffectual boss, let's show you what you *shouldn't* do. When you deal with an indecisive boss, don't

➤ Second-guess your boss's wishes. You'll rarely guess correctly—if indeed there *is* a correct answer. And even if you do hit the jackpot, your boss won't confirm or deny your guess.

➤ Try talking louder or faster. The boss isn't deaf or slow—just uninterested in communication.

➤ Assume the boss just doesn't care. On one hand, the puzzler boss *might* be insensitive or cold. On the other hand, the puzzler boss might not be sensitive and warm. Who can tell? All you know is that the boss doesn't seem to listen and won't take action.

➤ Ask your co-workers what they think your boss wants you to do. What makes you think they have any idea? They don't read minds any better than you do. Besides, a less-than-scrupulous co-worker could use the opportunity to burn you.

➤ Pester, annoy, nag, or badger your boss. Harping on the issue won't get you anywhere with a wishy-washy boss.

➤ Confront the boss without having a *really* solid remedy—solid as in prestressed concrete or Roseanne.

➤ Publicly complain or insult the boss.

➤ Assume that as time passes, the boss's expectations will get clearer. They won't.

➤ Make unilateral decisions for your boss. Your lifesaving efforts won't be noticed. If they are, we guarantee they won't be appreciated. No Medal of Honor for you in this situation, bubba.

➤ Become indecisive yourself. This is not an "If you can't beat 'em, join 'em" situation.

Watch Your Back!
Don't apologize for taking the boss's time or preface your discussion with comments such as "You're probably busy now but..." You have nothing to apologize for; it's the boss's job to communicate and make decisions. Starting off with an excuse just makes you look weak and indecisive. In the end, this behavior just gives the boss another reason to stay indecisive.

Walk This Way

Here's what you can do to get the directions you deserve from a fence-straddling boss:

1. First, find out if other people have the same problems with the boss. Ask one or two colleagues, "I wish I had clearer directions from the boss. Do you ever feel that way?" If they have no such difficulty, it's time to clear out the earwax. You may be *hearing* but not *listening*.

Protect Your Assets
Fatigue, boredom, and external distractions can also make it difficult for you to focus on your boss's words.

Watch Your Back!
If the boss has nothing to gain by giving you more specific directions (or any direction, for that matter), you can push until the cows come home, but you're not going to get the direction you want. Without sufficient motivation, a wishy-washy boss isn't going to change.

Protect Your Assets
An indecisive boss can drive you 'round the bend (if you let it affect you), but there's also a real up side to working for a waffler: A weak boss leaves you a lot of room to take the initiative. You might have to run the show, but you will have a chance to shine. (This is also true of a boss with a drug or alcohol problem. You know the type; they get lost after lunch.)

It's especially important to listen to wishy-washy bosses because they are often very hard to read. How many of these listening faults can we pin on you?

➤ *Pseudo-listening* occurs when you go through the motions of listening. You look like you're listening, but your mind is a thousand miles away.

➤ *Selective listening* occurs when you listen to only those parts of the message that directly concern you. For example, during a meeting with your boss, you might let your mind drift away until you hear your name or some information that is directly relevant to your concerns. You'll get more action from a boss who's unwilling to give directions if you listen to the whole message.

➤ *Self-centered listening* takes place when you mentally rehearse your answer while the person is still speaking. As a result, you're focusing on your own response rather than the boss's words. Correct this situation by letting your boss finish speaking before you start to frame your response.

2. Ask yourself, "Why isn't the boss more clear with me?" Carefully analyze the boss's fears, concerns, and needs. Figure out what's really going on here.

3. Determine what the boss stands to gain by being more specific with you. Would the company make more income? Would the business reduce expenses? Would there be better customer service? Find the right button and push it.

4. Schedule a meeting with the boss to get some specific direction. You can say, "I'm concerned about what goals you have set for me. Could you please clarify them?"

5. Listen to your boss's response to see if you can figure out why you're not getting any guidance. Carefully consider the situation from all sides.

6. Don't keep pushing until you drive your boss to the edge. The squeaking wheel gets annoying. If you can't get the help you need, try the next two suggestions.

7. Put it in writing. One way to pin down a wishy-washy manager is to write a memo outlining what you think (or want to think) he or she wants from you—and then have your boss sign off on it.

8. Build alliances with other bosses, because your boss will never give you the guidance you need to get ahead.

The Least You Need to Know

➤ *Puzzler* bosses send confusing messages and withhold information you need to do your job. They might change their minds often, fail to pass on feedback from higher-ups, and ignore shoddy work and conflicts.

➤ A variation on this theme is the "oblivious boss," who ignores problems and tries to avoid confrontation.

➤ The wussy boss is nonassertive and avoids all possible risk.

➤ Never second-guess a wishy-washy boss's wishes, hit up co-workers for clarification, or publicly complain.

➤ Instead, meet with the boss to get direction, get your boss to put your goals in writing, and build alliances with other bosses.

Chapter 13

When Winners Work for Losers

In This Chapter

➤ What workers want from bosses and their jobs

➤ Bosses who grumble and gripe

➤ Bosses who play favorites

➤ Gender issues

➤ Self-sabotage

A juggler, driving to his next performance, was stopped by the police. "What are those knives doing in your car?" asked the officer.

"I juggle them in my act."

"Oh yeah?" says the cop. "Let's see you do it."

So the juggler started tossing and juggling the knives.

A guy driving by saw this and said, "Wow, am I glad I quit drinking. Look at the test they're making you do now!"

Seem like the hurdles are getting higher and higher every day? Just can't figure out a way to make the boss happy? Perhaps you haven't figured out what type of boss you have. Only then can you use office politics to your best advantage.

Watch Your Back!
If you commute just 20 minutes one way to work, five days a week, by the end of the year you could be spending over 160 hours commuting.

In the previous chapters, you learned how to deal with the cruel, toxic boss, and the puzzler boss (along with the variations: "oblivious boss" and "wussy boss").

In this chapter, we'll show you how to deal with perpetually dissatisfied bosses and bosses who play favorites. You'll hone your political skills to overcome these hazards and get ahead on the job. Along the way, we'll explore and explode some myths about working for a female boss. We'll also see if it's really your boss—or you—who's making your life a Dilbert hell.

I Can't Get No Satisfaction

What do workers want? Based on a survey by the Gallup organization, the most critical factors bearing on employee satisfaction and job performance are the following six factors.

Workers want

1. To know that their jobs are important.

2. The chance every day to use their best skills and training to the utmost.

3. Materials and equipment to do their jobs properly.

4. Their jobs and concerns taken seriously.

5. Supervisors who care about them as people.

6. Bosses who give them opportunities to learn and grow.

But with a perpetually dissatisfied boss, it's hard to get an accurate meter reading, much less any job satisfaction. That's because nothing you do seems right.

Are you working for a grumbler? Put a check next to each statement that describes your boss.

Grumbly Boss Quiz

❏ 1. Complains about everyone's performance—and everything else as well, from food to the weather.

❏ 2. Reports the employees' shortcomings as reasons for his or her own failures.

❏ 3. Often claims that you're not giving "110 percent."

❏ 4. Worries about what can go wrong without thinking about potential gains.

❏ 5. Tends to be highly critical. Has "Every morning is the dawn of a new error" tattooed where the sun don't shine.

❏ 6. Looks for the worst—and seems to find it.

❏   **7.**   Resists change.

❏   **8.**   Brings bad news with glee.

❏   **9.**   Nit-picks at your behavior.

❏   **10.**   Loves to say, "I told you so."

❏   **Bonus:** Greets every problem with the lament, "Why is this happening to *me*?"

Score the Boss

8–10 correct	Keep counting…only 3,597 days to retirement.
5–7 correct	With this boss, you'll never forget that "work" is a four-letter word.
3–4 correct	War might be hell, but with your boss, work ain't no stroll in the park.
0–2 correct	Can we have your job? Please?

Would You Like Some Cheese with that Whine?

You just can't please some folks, no matter what you do. Ain't it just the way? Working for a boss who complains is about as hard as pleasing a teething toddler or a tyrannical prima donna. We can't help you with the toddler (a trust fund?) or the prima donna (top billing?), but we *can* help you deal with a boss who grumbles and groans.

Here's what *not* to do if your boss gripes. Don't

➤ Lose your temper. It won't accomplish anything—and can even make matters worse.

➤ Automatically attribute malice. Often, the boss's complaints, worries, and criticisms aren't personal attacks—even if they seem that way.

➤ Assume there's no merit to the complaint. Even the Boss Who Cried Wolf was right once.

➤ Let the boss's negativity get to you.

Turning Whine into Water

Now that you know what *not* to do if your boss continually complains, it's time to look at what you *can* do:

Watch Your Back!
If you see the glass as half full, you're likely to have even more trouble with a boss who sees it as half empty. Positive-thinking employees find it especially difficult to deal with bosses who gripe. Keep this in mind if your boss likes to vent more often than Mount Saint Helens.

Protect Your Assets
Most bosses who continually complain don't intend to rain on your parade. Rather, these people often can't help themselves. If it's any consolation, they often wreak even more damage on their own lives than they do on yours.

➤ Listen carefully to see if the boss's complaints do indeed have merit.

➤ If they do, take appropriate action.

➤ If they don't, be positive, not argumentative. Don't rise to the bait. Do what you have to do to keep your job, but be careful not to become the fall guy for your boss.

➤ Stay focused and realistic. Don't buy into your boss's warped world view.

➤ When there's a critical decision to be made at work, try to make the decision without involving your boss the complainer. Although end-runs around your boss are tricky plays, with a complainer boss you stand an equal chance of having him or her complain that you did something or *didn't* do it.

Playing Favorites

I got the following amazing story from a close friend:

> After two and one-half years of college, I quit and got a job at a major retailer. I quickly learned the ropes; within the span of eight months, I began training the newly hired managers. I repeatedly asked to enter the management training program, because I already knew how to run the store and had proven myself as an outstanding employee.
>
> My district manager repeatedly denied my requests—while hiring management trainees with no retail experience or degrees in related subjects. I finally confronted my boss when a fellow associate was promoted after being with the company for only three weeks. The boss replied, "I just liked him better."

Favoritism on the job is a fact of life, like hair loss, cellulite, and summer reruns. Yes, it's unfair, but so is the fact that kids *don't* go to school year 'round.

Nonetheless, you don't have to sit back and take it. We'll show you how to use your political skills to deal with a boss who plays favorites.

Watch Your Back!
Favoritism takes a potentially explosive turn when it is sexually or racially motivated. You may have to consult a labor lawyer or your union if you find yourself in this situation.

Mom Always Liked You Better

First of all, how can you tell you're dealing with a boss who responds to employees according to personal preference, rather than on merit? Here's how.

These types of bosses

➤ Give the plum assignments to their darlings.

➤ Love employees who flatter, don't rock the boat, and bring good news.

➤ Often discriminate on the basis of gender, race, age, appearance, or social class.

➤ Frequently hold up the work of their pets as examples.

Teacher's Pet

> I was hired as a third-shift security officer in a local chemical plant. The company was losing supplies, and they wanted me to investigate. After just two weeks, I informed the Plant Manager that the foreman on third shift was carrying the goods off the rear loading dock. He said, "My brother?"

Sometimes, there's nothing you can do to combat favoritism on the job—especially when it's nepotism (giving preferential treatment to relatives).

Corporate Mumbo-Jumbo
Nepotism is showing favoritism on the basis of family relationships, especially in business and politics.

The telephone was 51 years old before one was installed on the desk of the President of the United States. Leonardo da Vinci spent 12 years painting the Mona Lisa's lips. Rome wasn't built in a day. Some things take time. Fortunately, dealing with a boss who plays favorites is easier than you might think, nepotism aside. Start by learning what *not* to do if you find yourself in this situation.

Don't

➤ Focus your anger at the pets. They haven't created the situation; the boss has.

➤ Allow your concern with inequitable treatment affect your performance on the job. Even if your work isn't being appreciated by the boss, continue to do your best.

Protect Your Assets
Reality check: Everyone wants to be the boss's pet. Any employee with a grain of sense is trying to get into the boss's good graces.

➤ Be imbecillic enough to think that anyone will appreciate your pointing the situation out. If you do explain the situation to the boss, you'll likely get, "I reward those employees who are most loyal to me and the company. And that ain't you."

➤ Delude yourself into believing that the pets want to lose their most favored nation status.

Balance of Power

Now that you know what *not* to do when your boss blatantly favors other employees over you, here's what you *should* do.

Protect Your Assets

If you still aren't comfortable with the reality of the workplace, you might want to consider striking out on your own. You might want to give this some serious thought. Why not check *The Complete Idiot's Guide to Making Money in Freelancing* to see if you might be better suited to being your own boss.

Watch Your Back!

If you believe co-workers are getting extra pay or benefits, you might be staring a discrimination case in the face. Consider contacting your local Affirmative Action or EEOC office.

First and most important, think hard. Are you contributing to the situation by refusing to play office politics out of a misguided sense of moral indignation? You know the drill: "I'm too good (righteous, talented, holier-than-thou) to stoop to currying favor with the boss."

Then try these ideas:

➤ Consider what is motivating the boss to play favorites. Perhaps the pets are doing better work and so deserve the preferential treatment they're receiving.

➤ Seek out chances to be involved in projects that will raise your profile. Look for projects whose successes will be highly visible. Get known outside your department as a rising star.

➤ Find a mentor who can help you become one of the elite.

➤ Look for ways to cause your boss to favor *you*.

➤ Lay your cards on the table. Tell your boss, "I want to improve my performance in this department and gain more recognition from you as one of the indispensable employees. I want to look good for both of us."

Gender Bender

In February 1996, when *Working Woman* magazine published its annual list of the 20 highest-paid female executives, number 20 made $833,350 in salary, bonuses, and stock options. The next year, the magic number was $1.33 million; in 1998, a woman executive would have to pocket at least $1.8 million to make the list. That's a 166 percent increase in two years. (Stop crying; you're getting the page all wet. Face it: Life isn't fair. If it was, you'd be bringing home the bacon, and someone else would be frying it up in a pan.

Who were the 10 highest paid female executives in 1998? The envelope, please. Here's hoping *your* name made the cut.

Number	Executive	Company	Total Yearly Compensation
1	Linda Wachner	Warnaco Group	$10.27 million
2	Jeannette Meier	Sterling Software	$10.06 million
3	Jill Barad	Mattel	$6.62 million
4	Ngaire Cuneo	Conseco	$6.51 million

Number	Executive	Company	Total Yearly Compensation
5	Janice Roberts	3COM	$5.81 million
6	Carol Bartz	Autodesk	$5.51 million
7	Marion Sandler	Golden West Financial	$4.47 million
8	Dorrit Bern	Charming Shoppes	$3.6 million
9	Amy Lipton	CUC International	$3.46 million
10	Rosemarie Greco	CoreStates Financial	$3.36 million

Source: Working Woman, *February, 1998*

Fly on the Wall

In 1998, 10 American CEOs earned more than $20 million; another 60 got more than $10 million. Executives in Japan earn 16 to 25 times the pay of the average worker; American CEOs, in contrast, can earn 200 times more. So who's been naughty, and who's been nice?

Jerry Sanders, CEO of Advanced Micro Devices, gave himself $50 million in stock options in 1998—without noticeably improving his company. Carol Bartz makes 237 percent more than the market average in her industry. Marion Sandler, however, is running a huge company with an outstanding performance. According to market analyst Graef Crystal, Sandler should be making about $6 million more to equal industry standards. (*Working Woman*, February, 1998)

The Other Differences Between Men and Women

We've heard all about how men are from Mars and women are from Venus. There are some undeniable differences between men and women. For example, you would never hear a man say:

➤ "Here, honey, you use the remote."

➤ "Ooh, Antonio Banderas *and* Brad Pitt? Wow! That's one movie I just gotta see!"

➤ "I put the seat down for you."

➤ "Why don't you go to the mall with me and help me pick out a pair of shoes for work?"

➤ "Hey, let me hold your purse while you try that on."

➤ "You're right, I *do* need to get some new T-shirts."

Watch Your Back!
Chew on this as you skim the want ads and consider your next position, girlfriend: Even though the earning gap between men and women is narrowing, women still earn only 75 cents for every dollar earned by men.

Protect Your Assets
According to the *1998 World Almanac*, the six most lucrative occupations for women are lawyer, physician, engineer, physical therapist, computer systems analyst, and scientist. There are fewer than 50,000 women employed in each of these fields.

And we'll bet that you'd *never* hear a woman say:

➤ "Can we simply not talk to each other tonight? I'd rather just watch TV."

➤ "Aww, don't stop for directions. I'm sure you'll be able to figure out how to get there."

➤ "I put the seat up for you."

➤ "Honey, does this outfit make my butt look too small?"

➤ "And for our honeymoon, we're going fishing in Alaska! I just love to clean those salmon."

➤ "I just love that manly way you belch."

Of course, these statements are stereotypes, but you'd be astonished how many people believe them—especially when it comes to working for a female boss. (Okay, maybe you won't be surprised, but work with us here for awhile.)

In the good old days, when only pirates and people of the female persuasion wore earrings, bosses were men. But that's okay, because all managers, supervisors, and bosses in companies were men. Women were secretaries.

You've come a long way, baby. Women have made substantial progress in obtaining jobs in virtually all managerial and professional specialty occupations. In 1985, they held 43 percent (11 million) of these high-paying jobs; a decade later, they held 48 percent (16.9 million).

Check out these facts:

➤ Women accounted for 59 percent of the labor-force growth between 1985 and 1995.

➤ Of the 103 million women 16 years old or older in the United States, 61 million were working in 1998.

➤ By the year 2005, women are projected to make up 48 percent of the labor force.

➤ Of the approximately 69 million families in the U.S. in 1998, about 12 million (18 percent) are headed by women. In Hispanic families, the number is 24 percent; in African American families, it's 46 percent. Women aren't working for the fun of it.

The Queen of Mean

Before you make any judgments about your boss on the basis of his or her gender, take this simple test to see what preconceived notions you have about working for a woman.

In the boxes we've thoughtfully provided, check True if you think the statement is True or False if you think the statement is false.

Preconceptions Quiz

True	False	
❏	❏	1. Women managers are more fair than male managers.
❏	❏	2. Wasn't Attila the Hun a woman? If not, he should have been.
❏	❏	3. Women managers, unlike male managers, try to help subordinates. They're naturally kinder and gentler than male bosses.
❏	❏	4. Don't expect any help from a female boss, especially if she's an old crone and you're a pretty piece of eye candy.
❏	❏	5. Women managers are generally more productive than male managers.
❏	❏	6. Women managers are generally less productive than male managers, because they're busy fighting turf wars and getting hissy over real or perceived slights.
❏	❏	7. Women managers are less likely than male managers to expect subordinates to flatter them.
❏	❏	8. You have a female boss? Better not forget flowers, stuffed teddy bears, and other signs of appreciation.
❏	❏	9. Women bosses expect less work from an employee than a male would on the same job. That's because they don't want to rock the boat.
❏	❏	10. Women managers feel compelled to be perfect in every way. That means they want perfect subordinates. Duck and cover.

Score Yourself

Every answer is false. Stop yelping.

There *are* differences between male and female bosses. There are also differences between male bosses. And differences between female bosses. That's because there are differences between people.

Our proof? Career Strategies, a career consulting firm in Wilmette, Illinois, surveyed a large group of men and women who worked for bosses of the opposite sex. The results? What male workers identified as weaknesses and strengths in female bosses were identical to what female workers identified as weaknesses and strengths in their male bosses.

Watch Your Back!
Women are still over-represented in relatively low-playing jobs. More than 40 percent of all female workers (about 25 million women) are employed in sales, technical, and administrative support positions.

Ergo: Neither faults nor virtues on the job are sex linked.

Here's our advice: *Every boss, whether male or female, should be treated as a boss first and a man or woman second.*

So throw out the sexist stereotypes. They're as bogus as a Milli Vanilli record. You'll get lousy male bosses and you'll get lousy female ones. You'll get great male ones and great female ones. It's not gender, peaches, it's your boss's personality and your political savvy that determine if your professional interaction is explosive or easygoing.

Shoot Yourself in the Foot

Yes, sweetums, there are some pretty dreadful bosses in the workaday world. Odds are, if you think your boss is an ogre, he or she probably is. But you might also be sabotaging yourself.

Self-sabotage exists in varying degrees. At one end of the scale, we have workers ruled by self-pity, procrastination, and astonishing bad judgment. You can time their explosions, like Old Faithful's eruptions.

Then come the self-saboteurs who blow infrequently, like bicycle tires. Stress usually causes them to lose control and do something astonishingly stupid, like take unauthorized vacation time, leak confidential trade secrets, or get soused on company time.

At the far end come the workers who are prone to self-destruction, but who realize their problems and make a concentrated effort to avoid shooting themselves in the foot.

Is there a saboteur in you? See how many of the following inner fears have trapped you at work.

1. Fear of failure

   Failure can become a self-fulfilling prophecy. Believe you'll gum up the works and you probably will.

2. Fear of confrontation

   No one wants to be the bad guy, especially in front of co-workers. But an unwillingness to confront or even acknowledge issues can prevent you from resolving important issues.

3. Low self-esteem

   It's become fashionable to blame everything from job failure to bad taste in clothes on low self-confidence, but a weak self-image can hinder your chances of getting ahead on the job. This is not an excuse to strip, paint yourself blue, and beat a drum in the woods, however. There's no excuse for *that.*

4. Exaggerated self-esteem

   On the other end of the scale, we have egomania—a blatant, over-inflated sense of personal worth. No one is indispensable, not even the 10 people with the secret formula for Coca-Cola.

5. Victimization

   Having an exaggerated sense that everything is your fault is the politically correct stance of the '90s, as fashionable as double lattes and multigrain muffins. It's also a great way to lose your job and alienate co-workers. No one's going to pin Vietnam on you (unless you're LBJ), but there *is* the matter of Chia Pets. Suck in your gut and just take it on the chin.

6. Blaming

   An inability to accept blame is as dangerous as a willingness to shoulder the entire burden.

7. Letting it all hang out

   Work is work, and home is home. Divulging too much personal information can lead to gossip and the belief that you're a motor-mouth. It can also set you up for being sabotaged by others.

8. Procrastination

   Putting off important tasks usually means you're afraid to fail.

Protect Your Assets
No self-destructive behavior will ever be changed overnight. It takes time to reinforce appropriate responses. It's also important to develop realistic expectations with colleagues. They're not going to change overnight, either.

The Least You Need to Know

➤ Workers want bosses who give them opportunities to learn and grow.

➤ To get ahead with bosses who complain, evaluate the messages, take appropriate action, and stay focused and realistic.

➤ To deal with bosses who play favorites, don't focus your anger at the pets or allow the unfair situation to harm your work.

➤ Be sure you're not contributing to the situation by refusing to play office politics.

➤ You can also seek out chances to be involved in projects that will raise your profile.

➤ Every boss, whether male or female, should be treated as a boss first and a man or woman second.

➤ Don't sabotage yourself.

Part 4
Games People Play

Many pharmaceutical firms supply drugstores with order forms listing products and their costs. When one company neglected to do this despite repeated requests, an employee attached this note to an order: "Your computer and I have been having communication problems. If you no longer supply order forms, please let us know...that is, if you still employ real people."

With the next delivery there was this note: "Enclosed please find six order forms. Please forgive the delay. Yes, we still employ people. Therein lies the problem."

Signed, "IBM 402."

Co-workers. Can't live with 'em, can't live without 'em. (Actually we can, but we'll never have the chance, so why should we toy with your emotions?) In this section, you'll learn how the evolution of idiots affects you at work. We'll also teach you how to keep your sanity when all others have lost theirs.

The Backstabbers

In This Chapter

➤ Spotting backstabbers

➤ Different types of backstabbers

➤ Ways to deal with backstabbers

➤ Protect yourself

Some folks have the smarts to do well in the working world, but they use their wits to undermine others. These are the office "backstabbers," people who just can't be trusted.

They're like the love child of a pair of Albanian werewolves—totally without mercy.

In this chapter, we'll explain this kind of treachery in detail. Then we'll give you specific techniques for dealing with colleagues who just don't know how to play nice.

Covering Your Tracks

It's Monday, and you're just not in the mood for work. Maybe your kid had a fever all weekend, and sleep is but a distant memory. Perhaps the bus system is on strike, and it took you an extra hour to get to work. Did you rip your jacket, lose your wallet, or forget your lunch? Whatever the reason for your black cloud, the last thing you need today is Tony the Toad, the office backstabber.

"I just can't get that report in for the big meeting today," he whines. "And, oh, did I forget to tell you that the vice-president is going to be at the meeting?" We call such behavior "Department of Transportation Tricks," because your co-worker is throwing up roadblocks to slow your work up and undermine your career. These devious colleagues stall on tasks that affect your work. Why? Because they're evil little vermin. They also want to prevent you from getting your work done in a timely manner so you look incompetent, and they look great when they come in and "save the day."

Watch Your Back!
Remember: Even wimps are strong enough to carry a grudge—especially wimps with power over you.

Corporate Mumbo-Jumbo
Backstabbers are colleagues who try to ruin another colleague's reputation for their own gain. Their actions are usually deliberate and premeditated. Don't confuse backstabbers with the normal gossiping and jockeying for position.

As competition increases, so does bad office behavior. Usually people are driven to underhanded tactics by fear of competition or a feeling that they're not getting what they deserve at work. Because everyone feels disgruntled at one point or the other, backstabbers in the office tend to be as common as ants at a picnic.

You can find them at all levels of the job. A backstabber can be a competitive peer, an ambitious subordinate, or even a jealous supervisor. Unfortunately, efficient employees pose a threat to the less productive ones, giving the latter group a sweet incentive to back-stab.

Backstabbers will use any available vehicle to hatch their devious plots: They spread their venom via e-mail, in office memos, or, more often, through a series of shared secrets and betrayals.

Spotting a Stabber

It can be difficult to know if that shiv is sliding between your shoulders. Like a stealth bomber or advancing middle-age, backstabbers sneak up quietly, often catching you completely by surprise. To your face, a backstabber might appear to be your biggest fan. How can you tell if you're about to get gored or if you're already bleeding and just haven't checked the mirror yet? Use the following checklist to see if you're in danger from a backstabber.

Backstabber Checklist

❑　1.　Is your work as good as always, but suddenly nothing you do can satisfy?
❑　2.　Are you suddenly excluded from meetings?
❑　3.　Do colleagues stop asking for your input?

❑ **4.** Do important memos, papers, and e-mails never make their way to your in-box?

❑ **5.** Is a colleague being overly nice to only you for no apparent reason?

❑ **6.** Does the conversation stop suddenly when you enter a room?

If you feel unhappy or threatened at work, follow your instincts. It could be that a colleague is deliberately trying to undermine you professionally. Unfortunately, by the time most people see the glint of the blade, it's too late. The worst thing you can do is to assume that you'll never be the victim of a backstabber.

An Ounce of Prevention

Recognize that some backstabbers aren't really aware that they're doing damage. They believe that because they're really committed to the company, they are obligated to point out a colleague's shortcomings in a brutally honest way. Instead of offering constructive criticism ("To improve sales, why don't you…"), they focus on the negative and undercut your chances of succeeding.

Whatever a backstabber's motives, if you're wise (and we know you are), you'll take steps to protect yourself against underhanded co-workers as soon as you start a new job. Here are two actions to take immediately:

➤ Make a favorable impression on your co-workers and supervisors from the very start (go back to Chapter 4, "Like a Virgin," for tips on building a good rep from Day 1).

➤ Establish allies from Day 1. If you do, colleagues will be more likely to come to your defense if backstabbers move into action. If you haven't built up a network, you're likely to end up like the cheese, standing all alone. Figure on spending 20 to 30 percent of your time above what's necessary to get the job done schmoozing.

Watch Your Back!
Backstabbers frequently lack the guts to fight openly and use devious methods to undermine you. In addition to lying, they often attribute their devious motives to others, as in "Guess what so-and-so is saying about you!"

Field of Schemes

Mario knows the boss is really proud of his new marketing plan—and the plan is a real loser. He also knows the boss hates any criticism of his ideas. David, new on the job, thinks Mario is his friend. David and Mario recently had this exchange over the paper shredder:

Protect Your Assets

No matter what type of smarmy co-worker you're stuck with, *always* keep the line of communication open with your boss. This is the best way to prevent anyone at work from sabotaging you by making you look bad, taking credit for your accomplishments, or otherwise making your life miserable.

Watch Your Back!

Never retaliate with the same dirty tricks. This is about as smart as going into a biker bar on a moped. First, this strategy rarely works. Second, it just makes you look as bad as your sneaky co-worker. Third, the really sneaky ones will have devised a way to hoist you on your own petard.

Mario: It's a shame the boss's new marketing plan is such a turkey."

David: "Well, I happen to have come up with a great way to improve his plan."

Mario: "I suggest that you present it to the boss as soon as possible. I know that she is always willing to hear ideas."

Yes, and if pigs had wings, they could fly. You weren't born yesterday—even if David was. Mario is giving *false support* to undermine David's career. This is a common way that unethical colleagues try to subvert each other. By seeming to be on your side, they subtly use you to achieve their own aims. "It's all fun and games," they might protest, but sooner or later, someone loses a promotion, raise—or even a career.

The Devil Made Me Do It

How can you protect yourself against this kind of backstabbing sabotage? What you'd *really* like to do is smack your obnoxious colleague upside his head with our book. This is not a good idea. Even though this is a very well made book (we have a great team in Indianapolis to thank for this), you still might damage the binding with a stray body blow.

Instead, always think about a "friendly suggestion" from a co-worker before you take it. Carefully investigate before you act on anyone's advice, especially advice from a co-worker who seems too willing to act as your advocate. Here's a handy worksheet you can use to assess the situation. Fill in the blanks to connect the dots.

Situation Assessment Worksheet

1. *Why* is this person helping me?

   _____

   _____

2. What does he or she have to gain from going to bat for me?

   _____

   _____

3. What have our past dealings been like?

_____

_____

4. How do others feel about this so-called "friend"?

_____

_____

5. What's the inside skinny from the grapevine on this situation?

_____

_____

6. Is there a third party I can safely talk to about this?

_____

_____

I Hope You Won't Take This Personally

It's high noon at the OK Corral, pardner. Time to shoot it out. The mistake we make with these devious colleagues is not confronting them because we don't want a scene. Even if it doesn't repair all the harm, having a meeting can help you contain the damage.

Further, confrontation surprises the offender, who expects that you haven't heard about the treachery, and if you have, you wouldn't dare say anything. Before you act, though, take a minute. Never assume that the gossip is true. Always allow yourself at least a day or two to check out the facts and cool off.

So set up a meeting. This strengthens your case and increases the other person's understanding of the impact of his or her unacceptable behavior. At the very least, it lets your unscrupulous colleague know you're wise to his or her tricks. Here's how to do it:

1. Arrange a private meeting with the person who is undermining you.
2. If you suspect the meeting will be unpleasant or the person continues to undermine you, have someone from Personnel, Human Resources, or your union also attend to serve as a witness.
3. Think carefully before going to your supervisor about a backstabber; the action can backfire because it suggests that you're not competent to deal with the situation yourself.
4. Be sure to bring in the boss when backstabbing becomes threatening. Unwanted sexual advances or constant public humiliation should be reported to the boss.
5. Avoid sarcasm and moralizing. It feels good, but it won't get you what you want. Try something along these lines, "I've heard you don't think I'm paying enough

attention to the E-ZDuzIt account. I want to talk so we can correct the problem. Can you tell me more?"

6. Insist on the behavior you want. For example, you can say, "Next time, I expect that you'll let me know exactly how you feel *before* you go to anyone else."

Protect Your Assets
Don't worry too much about a backstabber's excuses because they really don't matter. Most backstabbers will scramble to excuse their behavior or foist the blame on someone else. What you're really doing by calling the meeting is sending a signal that their behavior isn't acceptable. You're marking your ground and showing that you can't be taken advantage of.

7. Try not to accuse, even if you know the person *is* guilty of stepping over the line. Instead of saying, "This person is a sleazeball," describe what he or she did and let others come to that conclusion.

8. Focus on how the backstabber's behavior is hurting the department. Your boss will be more likely to view you as a team player than a tattletale.

9. Never let backstabbers know that you have been hurt by their actions. That only encourages more of the same behavior because it gives them the satisfaction they crave.

10. Avoid finality, as in "I'll never trust you again, you snake's belly."

Hashing it out with a backstabber is often enough to stop the behavior. That's because backstabbers hate to be found out. Most of all, they fear being ostracized by others in the office.

The Blame Game

Along with false support, many backstabbers try to discredit their colleagues. To do so, they spread damaging statements about you, questions concerning your ability to do the work, or false concerns about you. Here are two examples of this type of backstabbing:

➤ A colleague might give you a "friendly warning" that the boss is going call later because you seem tense and out of sorts. The colleague has told the boss that you've complained of a hangover every day this week.

➤ A colleague might call your ideas "stupid," "worthless," or "ridiculous" in front of your co-workers. "You never do anything right," is another common method to ridicule a colleague and set up a fall guy. Or the colleague might focus attention on a minor detail, such as a spelling error, to discredit a beneficial proposal.

This devious political tactic injures you just enough that you'll take your own fall. How? This type of backstabber constantly undermines and destroys your self confidence with put-downs, negative comments, and outright lies. You feel worthless, which can lead to the point of being unproductive. It also heightens the attention others pay to your work; in effect, the backstabber will have everybody looking for your missteps.

Fortunately, there are effective ways to combat this menace. Here are some of the most effective strategies:

1. Stay positive and believe in yourself. If you don't, who will?

2. Practice self-promotion. Toot your own horn; make sure your boss knows your accomplishments. This way, if someone later tries to take credit for your hard work, the facts will already be out in the open. Of course, you should be subtle when crowing about your accomplishments so you don't look like such a flagrant braggart.

3. If someone attempts to belittle you or your work in your presence, don't let their treachery go unchallenged. Respond immediately—but keep your cool! You can say something along the lines of, "You misunderstood what happened. What I did was…" If the person continues to challenge you, don't get into a debate. Instead, reply with a comment like, "I understand you have your opinion, [slimy co-worker,] but everyone else seems to have a different impression of the situation." You can also try to respond with humor. This reveals your slimy co-worker as the jerk he or she clearly is.

4. If at all possible, put some distance between yourself and the kneecapper.

5. Position yourself for advancement by being in the loop and doing great work.

6. If all else fails, consider a transfer to a new department if you continually find your self-esteem undermined.

> **Watch Your Back!**
> When you're trying to deflect a backstabber, don't start the Great Memo Wars. A flurry of memos or e-mail might make you look weak and childish. It also leaves a lasting record of problems that people might otherwise forget. In effect, you're rocking the political boat. Instead, create your own file that you can use to refresh your memory if the matter isn't resolved quickly.

> **Protect Your Assets**
> When you're holding a meeting with an obnoxious colleague, give yourself the edge by setting a time when you and your listener will be most receptive; the middle of the morning or afternoon are usually good times. Try to avoid right before lunch, when people are hungry and often grouchy.

Quitting a job should be your last-ditch resort. Don't let a backstabber drive you away from a good job. Realize that some on-the-job friction is a fact of life, like middle-age spread.

I'm Your Puppet; Pull My Strings

The manipulative backstabber blackmails you to meet his or her selfish needs. Sometimes, they exploit your emotional vulnerability by clinging more tightly than high-priced plastic wrap. "I don't know what I'll do if you don't back me on this" is a common refrain, along with the ever-popular "If you were *really* my friend, you'd..." Even though this is strictly junior high stuff, it still works. Why? Because it taps our need to be needed.

Backstabbers who practice emotional blackmail are among the most ruthless "colleagues" you'll encounter—and we hope you never do. To gain power and advantage, they might even threaten to disclose something you have done that will make you look bad or could even ruin your career if it were revealed.

You might have made an error dealing with a vendor or client, for example, but managed to clean it up without the world knowing. Emotional blackmail can also concern doing the horizontal two-step with a client during a trip, getting drunk during conventions, and slipping office secrets. Whatever the dirty little secret, it's sure to accomplish its purpose and smear you good.

Fly on the Wall

It has been estimated that as many as 20 percent of the people you encounter daily are mentally disturbed. Even a psychiatrist might have difficulty dealing with these people, so don't despair if you have problems with them. Trust your instincts. If a colleague seems one sandwich short of a picnic, they probably are.

Here are some questions to ask yourself if you're wondering if you're dealing with an emotionally unstable colleague:

1. Does the person have any friends within the company?
2. What do others say about this person?
3. Why is this person blackmailing me?
4. Have I offended this person in some way?
5. How did the person achieve his or her rank?

What can you do?

1. Resist the emotional blackmail. You're not mommy or daddy. In the workaday world, it's sink or swim, sugar, and some people have to go down with the ship. Amazingly, you'll find that the whiners tend to float. If you let the clinger wrap around your neck, you'll be the one swimming with the fishes.

2. Try to jettison the leech. See if you can get assigned to another project or another partner.

3. If you *do* have to work closely with the emotion-ally needy, try to rope a healthy third party into the dynamic to balance out the situation and keep things productive.

4. It's not easy to deal with extortion. Other than trying to stay clean, the best advice we can give you is to take a page from the politician's unwrit-ten handbook: Admit anything that could harm your career. The threat ceases to have any power once it's out in the open.

To Catch a Thief

People who are insecure and cannot easily work in teams may take credit for an accomplishment that's not theirs. To do so, they listen for ideas that they know will receive accolades. They then appropriate these ideas and pass them off as their own.

For example, say you come up with an idea to save your department a great deal of money. You share your idea with a co-worker, who promptly turns the idea in as his or her own.

What can you do to combat this type of backstabbing?

1. Don't broadcast your great ideas to co-workers, no matter how trustworthy you think they are.

2. If your idea is stolen in a group meeting, let everyone know that it was your concept. Be tactful and firm.

Watch Your Back!
Sometimes your back will be against the wall; you must disengage from a difficult co-worker to protect yourself from anxiety or abuse. It's okay to throw in the towel because more damage than good will result from the relationship. Whatever your reason for backing off, however, don't be too timid to ask others for help if you think the person and the situation warrants it.

Protect Your Assets
People only succeed in taking credit for other people's work when the person doing the work doesn't take credit them-selves.

3. When you come up with a good idea, put the basic concept in writing and distrib-ute it with a note that the complete proposal will be ready by a specific date.

4. Always keep very careful records. Lay a paper trail.

A final piece of advice from two pros: Stand up to backstabbing even if you're not the victim. If you don't stop it, you're part of the problem. So the next time someone tells you that Fred blew a sales presentation, say firmly that it's balderdash. Even if Fred is a total fool, reserve your judgment. After all, there might be a time when you'll want someone to do the same thing for you.

The Least You Need to Know

➤ *Backstabbers* are colleagues who ruin another colleague's reputation.

➤ To protect yourself, make a favorable impression and establish allies from your first day on the job.

➤ Confront devious colleagues and assert your authority.

➤ Practice self-promotion and resist emotional blackmail.

➤ Don't broadcast your great ideas to co-workers, no matter how trustworthy you think they are.

➤ Stand up to backstabbing even if you're not the victim.

Invasion of the Body Snatchers

In This Chapter

➤ Sycophants and toadies manipulate colleagues and bosses

➤ Successful ingratiation techniques

➤ Why flatter, agree with the other person's opinion, and render favors

➤ Ingratiating upward, downward, and across the board

Assmosis: The process by which some people seem to absorb success and advancement by kissing up to the boss rather than working hard.

No matter how high someone rises in a company, they are always sucking up to someone, be it the chairman of the board, the shareholders, or their supervisors. Back in school, we used to call these people *grade-grubbers* or *brown-nosers*. They're the ones who always flatter the powers-that-be to get what they want. In this chapter, we'll show you how to deal with sycophants. You'll also learn that sloppy efforts to ingratiate oneself in to business associates usually backfire—but subtle techniques are often very successful.

Watch Your Back!
Don't confuse *assmosis* with a *seagull manager*. The former is a colleague who tries to get in good with the higher-ups. The latter is a manager who flies in, makes a lot of noise, dumps over everything, and then leaves.

Anything You Say, Buddy

If it walks like a duck and quacks like a duck, it must be a duck, right? Sometimes it can be hard to tell real ducks from duck-wannabees. The same is true for flatterers, the colleagues who will flatter the boss to get ahead. They might just be general nincompoops rather than genuine suck-ups.

Are you working with a sycophant? Take our easy quiz to find out. For each situation, circle the answer that best describes how your co-worker the sycophant would respond.

Sycophant Quiz

1. We needed to put a desk into a new area and realized none of us had a tape measure. The boss said, "You don't need a tape measure!" He went to the desk and "measured" it with his arms out wide. He then walked to the doorway, but when he couldn't get through with his arms out wide, he turned his imaginary desk sideways, went through, and set the imaginary desk in the corner of the new room.

   He turned to us and said, "See, it'll fit."

   Your co-worker the sycophant would say:

   a. "Boss, let's double check with the tape measure just to make sure."

   b. "Wow, boss, you just saved us all those unnecessary steps we would've had to take with that tape measure! They're overrated anyway."

2. My boss was bragging about her ability to write with either hand. She said, "It's great to be amphibious."

   Your co-worker the sycophant would say:

   a. "Boss, do you mean ambidextrous? I confuse those two words all of the time."

   b. "Wow, boss, you're extremely talented. I sure wish I could do that."

3. In a technology meeting with a new client, a very non-technical senior manager was intent on being impressive. To summarize our technical capabilities, the senior manager supplied the following information on the white board: "We use state-of-the-art equipment such as PCs and eunuchs workstations."

   After the meeting, your co-worker the sycophant would say:

   a. "Senior manager, let's have Jane in tech support draw up a summary of our technical capabilities. I think Client XYZ would be impressed if we follow up."

   b. "Wow, senior manager, you really impressed that new client. You know *everything*."

168

4. The boss had software on 5.25-inch diskettes but had only a 3.5-inch disk drive on her computer. Tech support said she had two options: Get a second disk drive or use 3.5-inch diskettes. She called back later, now complaining that her disk drive was making a terrible noise, even though she was using a 3.5-inch diskette, she said. Why? The boss had used scissors to trim the 5.25-inch diskettes to fit the 3.5-inch drive.

   Your co-worker the sycophant would say:

   a. "Boss, if you have any general computer questions, I'm fairly knowledgeable and might be able to help you. "

   b. "Wow, boss, you should be in charge of tech support 'cause you're so creative."

Protect Your Assets
Bosses can also discourage bootlicking at meetings by appointing a devil's advocate. This person can help encourage dissenting views.

5. When informed that we had three injuries in one week on the production line, the vice-president of manufacturing asked, "Do you think this is a union plot?"

   Your co-worker the sycophant would say:

   a. "Well, vice-president, before we jump to any conclusions let's check out the equipment.

   b. "Wow, VP, I never would have thought of that. You really have your finger on the pulse of this operation."

Watch Your Back!
Office sycophants will suck up to anyone, not just the boss. Don't be misled into thinking that a toady is out to be your friend. They're using you like an old rag, sweetums.

Score Your Co-Worker

Mainly a's   Your co-worker isn't a kiss-up; he or she is a champ when it comes to finesse. Take notes!

Mainly b's   Hear that sucking noise? It's the mating call of the sycophant. This person will say *anything* to get ahead. Bootlicking office toadies are the ones who

1. Praise the boss—and colleagues—frequently and effusively.

2. Will rarely deliver bad news to anyone.

3. Won't offer dissent at meetings.

4. Don't rock the boat.

5. Laugh at someone's jokes, even if they're not funny— *especially* if they're not funny.

Protect Your Assets

If you're the boss, one way to discourage flatterers is by rewarding people who disagree with you—in a constructive way, of course. Encourage your staff to express ideas, even if they are dissenting. This will show that you value brain power, not ego-stroking ability. Bootlickers are annoying, even if you're the one wearing the boot.

6. Never offer an opinion without first asking for yours—and then agree with you.

7. Never find anything wrong with anyone's ideas.

8. Play "Bet You Can't Top This" when it comes to doing favors for people.

9. Use praise to manipulate you into doing their work for them, giving them credit where it's not due, or covering for their screw-ups.

10. Often try to look good by making colleagues look bad.

Don't Go There

When dealing with the office flatterer, don't delude yourself into believing that you're the world's best colleague. You only walk on water when the basement floods. It's also a waste of time to respond to a flatterer in kind. He or she doesn't care whether or not you suck up. The office flatterer is completely self-centered.

Also, don't

➤ Reinforce the sycophant's delusions by showing a weakness for flattery. You want a pet? Get a pooch.

➤ Pass up the genuine praise. A skilled yes-person will mix genuine praise with blatant flattery. Enjoy the real praise; odds are, you earned it by your good performance (or by virtue of putting up with such a suck-up).

Go Here

How can you deal with the office toadster without losing your patience—and your wits? Try these suggestions:

➤ First, determine if you are doing anything to encourage sycophants to assume that flattery works with you. If you don't want co-workers to flatter you, don't fish for compliments and don't reward their behavior.

➤ Tell suck-ups that you don't like their behavior. Try these words on for size and then tailor them to fit your personal style: "I'm not sure how you got the idea that you have to flatter me, but please don't do it anymore."

You're Looking Particularly Lovely Today, Mrs. Cleaver

Why not take a page out of the sycophant's book? (Notice we're talking a page here, not a chapter.) Sycophants mistakenly believe they can get ahead by blatant flattery. Close, but no cigar. Flattery will get you everywhere—*if* it's used properly.

There are ways to get in a boss's good graces or to enlist a co-worker's enthusiastic cooperation without losing your lofty ethical stance and sense of moral superiority. Best of all, using flattery properly helps get the job done and creates a more pleasant office environment for everyone.

There are three main ways you can ingratiate yourself into someone's good graces:

➤ Flattery

➤ Agreeing with the other person's opinion

➤ Rendering favors

Let's look at each one in detail.

Flattery Will Get You Somewhere

Question: Why did the chicken cross the road?

Answers:

➤ Freud: The fact that you thought that the chicken crossed the road reveals your underlying sexual insecurity.

➤ Grandpa: In my day, we didn't ask why the chicken crossed the road. Someone told us that the chicken had crossed the road, and that was good enough for us.

➤ Emily Dickinson: Because it could not stop for death.

➤ Ernest Hemingway: To die. In the rain.

➤ Bill Gates: I have just released the new Chicken 2000, which will both cross roads *and* balance your checkbook.

➤ Saddam Hussein: It is the Mother of all Chickens.

➤ Dr. Seuss: Did the chicken cross the road? Did he cross it with a toad? Yes the chicken crossed the road, but why he crossed it, I've not been told!

➤ Colonel Sanders: I missed one?

Question: Why do workers flatter their bosses and colleagues?

Answer: Because it works.

Of the three techniques for subtly influencing others, flattery is by far the most potent. It's as strong as the known forces of the universe, including gravity, duct tape, and your

Corporate Mumbo-Jumbo

The technical name for *flattery* is "other enhancement." See, and you just thought it was regular old bootlicking.

Watch Your Back!

We strongly advise you to stay away from personal compliments; that is, those based on an aspect of a person's appearance. In today's politically charged corporate climate, personal comments can backfire and be taken as evidence of sexual harassment.

Corporate Mumbo-Jumbo

The technical name for *agreeing with someone* is "opinion conformity."

mother-in-law. It's a quasi-scientific fact: Most cows give more milk when they listen to music—and most people give more favors when they're flattered.

Say you want to win over a new supervisor. You might mention to a colleague how impressed you are with the supervisor's business savvy or leadership style, for example. The colleague might take the compliment on face value and never give it another moment's thought. However, the colleague might pass the comment along to the supervisor. If so, you've hit the jackpot. When other people compliment on your behalf, your ulterior motive is not as obvious. As a result, the compliment appears more genuine and has more power to advance your career.

That said, it's not advisable to make such compliments if you don't actually believe them. False praise has a way of coming back and biting you in the butt.

Going with the Flow: Agreeing with Another Person's Opinion

Danger, Will Robinson: Agreeing with *everything* a boss or co-worker says can be dangerous to your career, because you might be construed as being wishy-washy or a bootlicker! If you simply nod whenever someone voices an opinion, people will assume you don't have any opinion of your own. Further, they might assume you're empty-headed.

Remember what you learned in the beginning of this chapter? Executives rarely want yes-people. They often admire people who share valid suggestions and constructive criticism.

So how can you turn agreement into a successful political tactic? Try these three ideas:

1. Don't agree right away. Allow enough time to pass so that it appears as though you have let yourself be persuaded by the arguments your boss or colleagues present. This makes you appear to be more careful and thoughtful.

2. State your concerns. If you provide some initial resistance, you're also giving co-workers and supervisors the chance to more fully explain their opinion.

3. Find out the other person's point of view ahead of time. Then adapt that position to your own if possible.

Bet you're thinking we're about as deep as a thimble right now. We know our argument to agree with someone else's opinion might sound somewhat superficial, but it's really all about analyzing your audience. All successful managers, supervisors, and bosses know they must spend time understanding and addressing the concerns of their own supervisors—be it profit, shareholder value, or long-range planning.

In the same way, successful directors must understand and address the concerns of the people they supervise—be it duties, responsibilities, salary, benefits, or advancement. Good bosses and colleagues set aside their own agendas to match another's vision.

There's a big difference between caving in and getting things accomplished. It's all a matter of give and take, compromise and concern.

One Hand Washes the Other: Doing Favors

Quick—you're trapped in the following situation:

Your comptroller has made some spiffy black-and-white pie charts, neatly showing each different category of revenue and expense. When they're finished, the Executive Director looks them over approvingly and says, "Great! These are perfect. Now, just one more thing. There's a copy shop across the street that can make color copies. Take these over there and have them copied so this section is red, this one is blue, this one is yellow…"

Do you

    a. Begin to twitch uncontrollably?

    b. Eat a dozen donuts, a bag of fried pork rinds, and a pencil?

    c. Say "We're proactively prioritizing this quality mission objective in an attempt to reach a strategic consensus"?

    d. Take the pie charts across the street and have them colorized, even if it involves a toddler with some crayons?

And the answer is…d! You make your boss look good, even if your boss has the brains of an amoeba.

Any good sycophant knows that the best way to ingratiate yourself with the boss is to do all you can to make him or her look good. This is best accomplished by anticipating the boss's needs and then addressing them. For example, if your boss has a presentation to make, pull it together without being asked. And if you're asked, make it so.

Watch Your Back!
Ever hear the phrase, "To make money, you have to spend money"? It's the same with favors. Think of them as an investment in your future. Focus on the boss's needs and do what you can to meet them. This will often involve granting favors. Remember, the great thing about favors is that someday you can cash them in when you truly need it. Focusing on your own needs will mark you as self-serving and possibly even ruthless.

What Goes Up Must Come Down

Someday, the people who know how to use computers will rule over those who don't, and there will be a special name for them: secretaries.

Protect Your Assets
Ingratiating downward is easier than ingratiating upward because subordinates don't perceive an ulterior motive when the behavior comes from a person with more power and authority.

Good leaders don't assume that they only have to ingratiate upward, to their bosses. They realize that secretaries, receptionists, and others with e-mail name plates hold a lot of power in any organization—especially in today's self-directed, team-driven companies.

Working to gain the respect of lower-level employees might be the most important form of ingratiation of all. When decisions are made, involve *everyone* who will be affected It's not flattery, just good business sense. You'll get much further in a company because you'll be building invaluable good will and influence.

Ingratiation techniques don't work the same way with subordinates. Try these methods to win the hearts and minds of your colleagues and subordinates:

1. Work to gain greater understanding of the needs of the people you want to influence.

2. Target your behavior toward people with high self-esteem. You'll be more effective.

3. Be willing to participate in teams.

4. Take risks with employees.

5. Work across the organization to understand the needs of others.

6. Be accessible to subordinates—no matter how far down they are in an organization.

7. Demonstrate your honesty, integrity, and basic sense of humanity, rather than just talking about it.

8. Use one technique at a time rather than coming on like gangbusters.

9. Be democratic. Spread the ingratiation around rather than targeting one person or group.

10. Most of all, be subtle.

What's the bottom line? Can a skillful and subtle use of flattery, doing favors, and agreeing with someone's point of view help you get a raise and promotion? Can it help you get a bigger budget for your department or lead employees where you want them to go? Yes, yes, yes. Kissing up on its own will hurt your career. Using shrewd and sophisticated ingratiation combined with solid performance will help your career.

The Least You Need to Know

➤ Bootlicking office toadies suck up to manipulate colleagues and bosses.

➤ Discourage their behavior but adopt their techniques that work for you.

➤ Ingratiate yourself upward, downward, and across the board.

➤ Working to gain the respect of low-level employees might be the most important form of ingratiation of all.

➤ Using shrewd and sophisticated ingratiation combined with solid performance will help your career.

Chapter 16

Tomorrow, Tomorrow, Tomorrow: Procrastinators and Buck-Passers

In This Chapter

➤ How procrastinators drive you 'round the bend

➤ Why people procrastinate

➤ Methods for dealing with procrastinators

➤ How "buck-passers" subvert you

➤ Ways to deal with shirkers

A buck-passer, a shirker, and a procrastinator find themselves together in a lifeboat after surviving the sinking of a luxury liner.

After days of floating in an empty sea, they spot a rescue ship on the horizon. Realizing that they must somehow signal it, the buck-passer says, "Quick, start waving your shirt at them."

The shirker shakes his head and say, "Me? That's not my job!" He points at the procrastinator. "Tell *him* to do it."

"No problem," says the procrastinator. "Do you think I should wave my shirt? Or maybe my hat? Or maybe just my arms?"

Some people just get things done. You know who they are: the colleagues you can depend on to pull their own weight. Others, unfortunately, just can't get out of their own way.

And if they can, they don't want to because they're just too darn lazy.

In this chapter, you'll learn effective ways to deal with procrastinators, buck-passers, and similar scourges of your work existence. And on the very, very, *very* odd chance that you like to put off until tomorrow things you should have done yesterday, you can pick up some effective techniques for getting your work done and becoming a more effective—and promotable—employee.

What Is It, Girl? Did Timmy Fall Down the Old Mine Shaft?

Our friend and long-time colleague S.J. told us a wonderful story about a freelance writer who worked for him. Let's call her "Louise." Here's the story:

> On a Friday, I assigned Louise a writing assignment and told her that it was a rush job; I needed it the following Friday. That was my first mistake. Even though she's a great writer, I knew that she tends to promise more than she can deliver. Sometimes it's almost impossible to get her to hand over a job. To keep her nose on the grindstone, I called her every morning to make sure that she was on track. Over and over, she assured me that everything was hunky-dory.

> Friday came and no job. I called, but no answer. I called Saturday, Sunday: ditto. Monday, Tuesday, Wednesday: still no answer. By then, I figured she had been kidnapped by Martians or checked into the Hotel California.

> On Wednesday, she called to tell me that she had indeed finished the job on Friday, but she had tripped, fallen down, and knocked herself unconscious. As my jaw dropped faster than the Dow on Black Friday, she said, "I lay unconscious on my apartment floor the whole weekend! I didn't come around until Tuesday, and then I couldn't get off the floor until Wednesday."

Corporate Mumbo-Jumbo
The root of *procrastination* is the Latin word meaning "belonging to the morrow." To procrastinate is to "put off doing (something unpleasant or burdensome) until a future time; especially to postpone (such actions) habitually."

"Louise" is a procrastinator. Like her fellow procrastinators, she'll promise you the sun, moon, and stars, but when the deadline comes, all you get is air.

Three on a Match

There are three main types of procrastinators: *perfectionists*, *slackers*, and *evaders*. Let's look at each one more closely.

1. The Pursuit of Useless Perfection

   Let's give this the best spin we can. Procrastinators may be perfectionists who want everything faultless before they act. You know those anal retentive types: It's never *quite* good enough to satisfy their exacting standards.

2. Couch Potatoes

   These lazy sots would much rather watch 20-year-old reruns of *Saturday Night Live* than finish the report they took home and promised to complete. "You'll have it Monday, no problem," they swear. In your dreams, baby. You're only young once, but you can be immature forever.

3. No News Is Good News

   A friend sent us this example of a procrastinating boss: "I know your performance review is due today, but let's wait until tomorrow. I'm not in the mood for all that negativity right now."

   Sometimes "do-nothing" co-workers can accomplish tasks that are fun but simply cannot face unpleasant tasks such as writing performance reviews or terminating employees. As a result, they keep postponing the things they don't want to do. (This is a hint to call your mother, clean the closets out, and maybe even file your 1980 income taxes.)

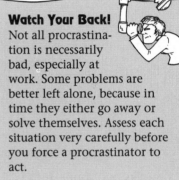

Watch Your Back!
Not all procrastination is necessarily bad, especially at work. Some problems are better left alone, because in time they either go away or solve themselves. Assess each situation very carefully before you force a procrastinator to act.

Whatever their motivation, procrastinators can drive you crazy faster than a room full of cranky toddlers.

Down for the Count

The following chart shows how busy people can be at work. Is it any wonder they don't get to your task, the task at hand, or any important task at all?

Corporate Exercise Calorie Chart

Exercise	Calories Used
Beating Around the Bush	75
Jogging Your Memory	125
Jumping to Conclusions	100
Climbing the Walls	150
Swallowing Your Pride	50
Passing the Buck	25
Grasping at Straws	75
Beating Your Own Drum	100
Dragging Your Heels	100
Pushing Your Luck	250
Spinning Your Wheels	175

continues

continued

Exercise	Calories Used
Flying Off the Handle	225
Hitting the Nail on the Head	50
Turning the Other Cheek	75
Wading through Paperwork	300
Bending Over Backwards	75
Jumping on the Bandwagon	200
Eating Crow	225
Fishing for Compliments	50
Tooting Your Own Horn	25
Adding Fuel to the Fire	150
Pouring Salt on the Wound	50
Wrapping It Up at Day's End	12

How can you tell if you're dealing with a procrastinator? First of all, the condition strikes co-workers and supervisors alike, so rank alone won't help you.

Try our simple quiz. Just check off each excuse you've gotten from your colleagues or bosses.

Excuses Quiz

❑ 1. "I'll wait until I'm in the mood to do it."

❑ 2. "It's okay to celebrate now. I'll get to the project tomorrow."

❑ 3. "Calm down. We have plenty of time to get it done before the deadline."

❑ 4. "Why does the boss give us so much to do? It's not fair."

❑ 5. "It's too hard to talk about it. You're really getting on my nerves."

❑ 6. "I don't know where to begin."

❑ 7. "I work better under pressure, so I don't need to do it right now."

❑ 8. "I've got too many other things to do first."

❑ 9. "It's all done. I'm just checking some numbers. It will be on your desk first thing in the morning. I promise."

❑ 10. "I'm waiting for marketing to give me their input."

❑ 11. "There's tons of air in the schedule."

❑ 12. "Nobody else has finished theirs yet" (said in a whiny voice).

❑ 13. "I learned the project is going to be back-burnered anyway."

❑ 14. "Stop pressuring me. You're stressing me out."

❑ 15. "How can I do the project and learn Esperanto at the same time? You know I have my priorities."

Head Games

Some people procrastinate because they are afraid. They believe that by acting, they will get into trouble. Procrastination protects people from these basic fears:

➤ Fear of Failure: If I delay, my failures won't reflect my ability.

➤ Fear of Success: If I delay, people won't expect too much from me.

➤ Fear of Losing Control: If I delay, I remain independent because I control my activities.

➤ Fear of Separation: If I delay, I won't be left alone.

➤ Fear of Attachment: If I delay, I won't get too close to others.

Now that you know what motivates a procrastinator, how can you use your political skills to make sure they do their work so you're not left holding the (empty) bag?

Protect Your Assets
According to some sources, learning problems such as Attention Deficit Disorder (ADD) can make it difficult for people to stay on task. Many people get relief from these conditions with medication. Unfortunately, it is not your place to suggest such treatments to a colleague, although you might benefit from the information for yourself or family members.

Deal with It

How can you cope with these especially annoying co-workers?

First, recognize that it's a mistake to leave it up to the procrastinators to act. They won't. It's also a waste of time to accept the procrastinator's unrealistic commitments. Their promises are usually more full of hot air than a bag of microwaved popcorn. Who has the time to figure out if this time they'll finally come through? Who will be the one left making shadow puppets during a presentation? All too often, it will be *you*.

You can help the procrastinator stay on task by defining the problem and structuring its solution in terms of specific goals and deadlines. Here are some other methods we've used with success:

1. Set priorities.
2. Break the task into little pieces and set small, specific goals and deadlines—and stick with them.
3. Create visual means to track progress. Schedules, timetables, calendars, and timelines are often helpful. Post these where they are clearly visible.

Watch Your Back!
Many procrastinators have an unrealistic view of time. For example, they might honestly believe that sorting through a stack of papers as high as the Hoover Dam will be a snap. It's not.

4. Optimize a procrastinator's chances for success by having them choose whatever conditions are optimal for them to get their work done. This might not always be possible, of course.

5. Maintain as much control as you can over the situation. Don't delegate responsibility when you're dealing with a procrastinator, unless you want to sabotage a colleague by making him or her deal with the mess. This is not good office politics.

6. Have the procrastinator sign off on deadline schedules to help track responsibilities and keep the person on task.

7. If possible, set sanctions for missed deadlines. "Louise," the writer described in the opening story, was penalized monetarily for each day she missed.

8. Cover yourself. Issue frequent memos to track progress and assure the higher-ups that you're on top of the situation. Always keep copies of the memos in case the procrastinator later denies being told of specific deadlines.

9. Force yourself into the process at key points to keep it moving. For example, you can say, "We need an update at 2:00 this afternoon. Bring what you've got to me at that time."

Protect Your Assets
Help empower people to change their difficult behavior. For best results, focus on the person's behavior—not your ego.

10. Raise their level of discomfort by rejecting promises you don't believe they'll keep. Try this line: "If you commit to that, you'll be hanging the rest of us out to dry if you don't deliver."

11. Confront procrastination and bring any related issues into the discussion.

12. Offer praise for decisive, correct action.

And one last suggestion: Build a safety net for yourself. Never let a procrastinator take a project off-schedule so far that you can't save it if you have to.

Pass the Buck

The answers listed below won't make you rich. Nor will they assist you in your pursuit of fame, fortune, or happiness. They won't help you get hot dates, show you how to make a million from real estate you don't own, or tell you how to give your 73-year-old skin a youthful glow.

They will, however, help you identify dishonest, lazy co-workers who shirk work and pass the buck. You know the types: like a blister, they come out when the work is done.

The excuses or answers they'll give you include

1. I'm just not ready to make a commitment to do that assignment.
2. If I *had* the time, I would gladly help you. Unfortunately, I just don't have the time.
3. I wasn't in the office for that meeting.
4. When hell freezes over.
5. Because the world would be a lot better off if things were done my way all the time.
6. You'll break your mother's heart.
7. I could tell you, but then I'd have to kill you.
8. It's not my job.
9. It's not in my job description.
10. They don't pay me enough.
11. They don't pay me to do that.
12. No.
13. No.
14. *No!*

Shirkers are different from procrastinators. The latter *want* to do the work but just never seem to get around to it. The former, in contrast, simply don't want to pull their weight—or anyone else's, for that matter.

It's Not My Responsibility!

This story came from a friend:

> While doing some after-hours work at a state agency, my boss came by to let me know that he was going to hire a new assistant division head—a second in command. He said he needed someone to serve as a buffer, someone who would be accountable for any problems or difficulty.
>
> When I pointed out that *he* was the division head and ultimately accountable, he paused and replied, "Yeah, but an assistant would be my first line of defense. Therefore, the assistant would get fired first."

How can you tell a buck-passer?

➤ They always seem to try to take credit but never shoulder the blame.

➤ They try to ride on the coattails of others.

➤ They don't carry their share of the work and when called on the carpet, they'll claim the job was someone else's responsibility.

➤ They have mastered sign language: They're great at pointing the finger, usually after the work has all been completed, and especially if something has gone wrong.

➤ They try to pin the blame on someone else who isn't present at the time. This helps them avoid a face-to-face confrontation.

➤ If they're really good, they seem to be made of Teflon. Stuff gets thrown in their direction, but nothing seems to ever stick. They're never the ones in the firing line.

➤ When confronted with their own failure, they divert attention to someone else's mistake.

In general, buck-passers are at their best when they are working on a joint task with others. This makes it much easier for them to slough off their responsibilities on their co-workers.

The Buck Stops Here

A computer is an invention that will never be the equal of a worker until it can put the blame for its mistakes on some other computer.

Shirkers have mastered the fine art of looking much busier than they could ever be without collapsing from complete exhaustion. The good news? These co-workers are usually too busy to stir up any real trouble. The better news? They eventually get caught. How can you help speed up this process? Try these political moves:

➤ Try to avoid working with them in the first place.

➤ Because everyone knows who the buck-passers are and they seem to reproduce like rabbits, odds are you're going to get stuck with them. In this case, make it really clear to all, including higher-ups, who is responsible for which part of the work.

➤ Keep a paper trail. Try to get as many of the shirker's empty promises in writing (this is when e-mail really comes in handy).

➤ Let your supervisor know how the duties have been divided. This short-circuits the buck-passer's attempts to stick you with the blame.

➤ Speak to the boss first. That way, when the jerk starts pointing the finger in your direction, it will likely be seen for what it is: a tacky excuse to avoid blame.

➤ Ask your boss how he or she would handle a colleague whose laziness and poor morale meant extra work for the rest of the team—but don't name names!

The Least You Need to Know

➤ Whether they are *perfectionists*, *slackers*, or *evaders*, procrastinators don't get their work done. This leaves you in a lurch.

➤ Help procrastinators by defining the problem and structuring its solution in terms of specific goals and deadlines.

➤ Maintain control and cover yourself.

➤ Shirkers try to avoid doing their fair share of the work.

➤ Short-circuit the buck-passer's attempts to stick you with the blame.

Chapter 17

Hey, Look Me Over

Feldman, the sales manager, stood before a group of key clients who had been gathered to observe a demonstration of his company's brand-new, state-of-the-art computer.

The rep's screen blurred and rolled. His attempt at a telecommunication link failed. Feldman phoned his company for help, but his liaison was gone for the day. He took a deep breath, faced the group, and said, "This concludes my demonstration of our competitor's product. Next week I'll come back and show you ours."

How do some people manage to snatch victory from the jaws of defeat—while you're always snatching defeat from the jaws of victory? How do these co-workers manage to snare all the goodies—while you're left with the crumbs? Why are they the apple of the boss's eye—while you feel like the pits?

It's more than simply having the smarts. These co-workers know how to impress the bigwigs. They have figured out how to position themselves for success. They're the office superstars, the show-offs, the celebrities. And they can make your life miserable by outshining your efforts.

In this chapter, we'll show you how to deal with the office darling who always comes out smelling like a bonus. Then we'll teach you how using office politics can help you become A-#1, top of the heap, king of the hill—even against genuine superstars.

The Power and the Glory

R.J. and his colleagues at the Big Fancy Financial Company always seemed to be at loggerheads. Their jobs, selling the company's financial services, required them to collaborate on marketing strategies, but one member of the team consistently (and skillfully) claimed credit for every good idea. There wasn't even a mention of the team's effort when a trade journal did an article on one of their joint efforts. The group sparred for more than two years, accomplishing their professional mission but acting like siblings squabbling for parental attention. Tired of their battles, R.J. finally asked the boss to intervene. The boss's response? "Work it out yourselves."

Protect Your Assets
Battles with office superstars and other co-workers strain relationships and make it hard to get the job done, but disagreements don't have to be destructive in the long term. At best, interpersonal conflicts energize people and lead to creative strategies that benefit a company and its employees. (At worst, you push the pain-in-your-neck down an elevator shaft, but let's not go there.)

Sound familiar? R.J. is battling with the *office superstar*.

Remember teacher's pet, the apple of the teacher's eye? Well, the class winner has grown up and is working in the next cubicle. Doesn't it seem like these colleagues spend most of their time hatching nefarious schemes to get praise and promotions? That's because many of them do. We discussed these colleagues in Chapter 13 from the vantage point of the boss. Now let's look at them from the other side of the desk.

The office superstar is a master of aggrandizement and showing off. The office superstar's skill at taking center stage can heighten your competitive impulses, intimidate you, or just plain tick you off.

Blind Ambition

There's nothing wrong with a little ardor and a few aspirations. Ambition is a good thing. But there *is* a difference between healthy ambition and glory seeking. We've laid it all out for you in this nifty chart:

Healthy Ambition	Glory Seeking
Master new skills	Learn just enough to fake it
Have solid friendships	Pretend to like everyone
Take initiative	Seize the limelight
Offer solutions	Create problems
Is a team player	Be the big cheese
Take risks	Only work on a sure thing

Fit to Be Tied

A friend shared this tale of frustration:

> Several years ago, the company I worked for went through an exasperating time of reorganization and expansion. Employees and customers were both extremely frustrated, and we lost a number of each. Morale dropped to new lows. Senior management decided to stage a party to lift the spirits of the employees.

> The president chose to make a few remarks of appreciation: "We could not have done this without the patience, perseverance, and understanding of Rex, the Wonder Worker. He did a great job handling all the problems. Even you 'lower people' contributed something."

Been there, done that, got the T-shirt to prove it? Well, you're not alone.

Try on this scenario for size:

You've been assigned the job of making all the arrangements for the annual convention. Even though you think it was probably easier to set up the D-Day invasion, you rise to the convention challenge and virtually single-handedly pull it together. Everything runs so smoothly that at the banquet your boss is moved to praise the accomplishment. Unfortunately, your boss heaps the praise on your colleague, the Office Darling, who had almost nothing to do with the conference planning but jumped in at opportune moments during the convention to give the impression that he or she had been involved all along. You smolder in the shadows.

You *can* out-maneuver the office star while maintaining your integrity (and without going ballistic). "But I'm the Alpha Geek," you protest. Okay, we'll bite: Let's say you *are* the most knowledgeable, technically proficient person in an office or work group. So why is the Office Favorite (a real cement head) getting all the glory—and the money?

> **Watch Your Back!**
> Never lose track of where you want to be in your career. If you set aside your goals and desires just for the sake of advancement, you could end up in a position you neither like nor do well in.

Read on to find how *you* could be sitting in the catbird seat. The following political solutions can help you create a win-win situation for all.

I Coulda Been a Contender

True story:

> After years of increasing sales to record levels in my store, I was passed over for an outside sales position. When I asked my boss why, he said, "I forgot about you!"

Never forget that good work alone is *not* enough to get you the recognition you deserve. We can't emphasize this fact of office life enough: No matter how good you are, it doesn't matter for squat if no one knows that you're the greatest thing since Velcro.

"Nature has a way of compensating for weaknesses, which is why stupid people have big mouths," you chime. Nonsense. Your silence makes it easier for someone else to steal all your thunder—and shine while you storm.

First, take preventative measures. One way to make sure you get the credit you deserve— and maybe even become the office star yourself—is to let others know of your efforts while you're doing the work, not just after the job is done. As you're working on a project, let everyone know what you're doing. Make sure word of your success gets to your boss, your boss's boss, and all the key players in the corporation.

You don't have to take out a full-page newspaper ad, shout it from a rooftop, or schedule a press conference. Subtle buzz about your myriad of shining accomplishments works *if* the word of your efforts does indeed get around. Being subtle prevents you from sounding immodest or overly aggressive. Rather than bragging, you're just keeping everyone on the same page (and advancing your career).

Twinkle, Twinkle, Little Star

Protect Your Assets
Try to find some common ground with the office show-off. Once you stop telling people why the show-off is making you crazy, you can focus instead on the goals you share.

Next, take a lesson from the Office Star's self-help manual and fine-tune your professional image. What are your special strengths? How can you capitalize on them to get the recognition you deserve? Do an honest self-assessment.

Assuming you are producing great work, look a little deeper. Why are you being outshone? Here are some possibilities to consider:

➤ Your hair, clothes, or grooming don't match the company's image. The star shines; you're dull, disheveled, or even dirty. If you want to get respect and be seen as a player, strive to look professional and act professionally in all circumstances.

➤ Your speech is riddled with regional expressions, errors, or even profanity. The company can't dress you up or take you out.

➤ You're not out to win friends and influence people. As a result, you haven't built up a network of allies. No one will throw your name in the hat (or even pass you the hat), making it easier for the office superstar to seize all the credit from you.

➤ You think you're too good for all this political stuff. If you won't play the game, why should anyone consider you a contender?

Method Acting

"There's no way I can outmaneuver the office shining star," you moan. Stop moaning, buckaroo. Instead, imagine that you're an actor preparing for a big scene. You need motivation to appear sincere. Here's your motivation: It's easier to become the office star if you present a valid reason for seeking recognition. Further, by justifying your ambition, you won't seem unduly pushy with the boss.

For example, you might tell your supervisor, "I am trying to succeed in this company. It would help me if you could document my performance. Because I did the majority of the work on the new automated shipping system, would it be possible for my name to appear on the top of the report?"

Can't Beat 'Em? Join 'Em!

Who says you necessarily have to beat the office superstar? Why not join 'em? After all, nothing breeds success like success.

The rising star

➤ Exudes an aura of glamour

➤ Is adept at spinning the truth to create an exciting image

➤ Is in the right place at the right time

➤ Rides the crest of accomplishments

Watch Your Back!
Want to ride on the coattails of the office superstar? Not a bad idea, but beware! Hitching a ride in someone else's wake is not without risk. If you're along for the ride, the day will come when you'll have to take sides. It might not manifest itself as a need to declare your position outright, but when push comes to shove, you'll be wiped out if you won't stand up and be counted.

Whatever the reason for the star's success, the star's name seems to move mountains. Mention it, and you get three extra keys to the executive washroom.

Logic tells us that when superstars ascend to their corner offices, those riding on their coattails will come along for a great ride. Should you climb aboard? As you weigh your options, be sure to learn as much as you can about the star of the moment. You can use the following handy-dandy worksheet to focus your thinking.

Superstar Assessment Worksheet

1. What makes this person so successful? Is it knowledge, technical competence, brilliance, efficiency, hard work, political skill, or charm?

   _____

   _____

   _____

2. What is this person's track record? Why did he or she leave their last job?

   _____

   _____

   _____

3. Is this star protected by an even bigger star? Is this a smoke-and-mirrors deal, or does the person have some solid backing that can help protect me in the future?

   _____

   _____

   _____

4. What's the office scuttlebutt on this person? Do people think he or she can be trusted in the clutch?

   _____

   _____

   _____

5. What's my gut reaction? Do I feel confident or uneasy?

   _____

   _____

   _____

If the star is no more than a brief flash in the pan, steer clear. When the person goes nova, you'll be safe. If you're in a position that matters, he or she might try to ostracize you, but take heart: You'll be vindicated in the end. If, on the other hand, the lab tests prove the star shines true, climb aboard.

Star Wars

So far, we've been helping you deal with your normal, garden variety office superstars, the utterly frustrating everyday colleagues who manage to claw their way to the top by your average backbiting, manipulation, and shrewdness. But what happens if a colleague has actually trained to seize the spotlight? What happens if your colleague is a genuine honest-to-goodness 14K superstar?

The computer isn't the only new presence in corporate America. Increasingly, stars shine brightly in every business. More and more, powerful media personalities are the norm in business. You've been told that their primary purpose is increasing the bottom line, but they really seem to exist to make life more interesting for chief executives. Everyone's star struck—and your boss is no exception.

This practice has existed quietly for a long time, but it really got rolling in the 1970s, when Revlon hired Michael Bergerac from ITT and gave him an employment package that included a seven-figure bonus for signing—a practice until then confined to sports stars. Upon leaving Revlon, Mr. Bergerac had an eight-figure platinum parachute. Nice work if you can get it. He's not alone.

➤ After serving as president of the City Council in New York, Carol Bellamy sallied down to Wall Street and became a vice president of Morgan Guaranty.

➤ Lee Iacocca parlayed his business stardom by attaching his name to patriotic projects beginning with the Statue of Liberty restoration.

➤ Peter Dawkins went from a general in the Army to a tycoon on Wall Street.

➤ Peter Ueberroth, the businessman who gave us a boffo Olympics, then took a plum job as commissioner of baseball.

➤ Opera star Beverly Sills serves on the board of Time Warner.

While you might not have superstars like this in your business life, chances are increasing that somewhere along the line a star will come into it. It might be a corporate star, someone who is red-hot in another company, or a media star who has switched careers. What do you do if a star enters your galaxy? How can you, a mere mortal, compete with this strange visitor from another planet?

Watch Your Back!
Sometimes the arrival of a star causes a ripple effect, as people are outsourced to make room for the new world order. Management decides to downsize your boss and his or her staff to clear the way. Be alert to shifting loyalties. Jettison your boss when the handwriting is on the wall that he or she is on the way out. Then get on the new person's dance card as fast as you can.

Hitch Your Wagon to the Star

Let's be real: There's no way you can eclipse a star of this magnitude. Your best bet is getting on board, and fast. When a new star enters your company, dollars to donuts there's a lot invested in his or her success. Someone in the corporate stratosphere is committed to that person's success. Here's how to hitch a ride.

Approach your boss and say, "With Superstar coming on board, I think I can be very helpful. I want to be sure, of course, that you agree. Here's what I can do..."

Keep Your Head When Everyone Else Is Losing Theirs

Bob says:

> As a director of a division of the entertainment giant Time Warner, I've met Big Stars with astonishing frequency. I've run into such notables as Gene Shallit, Barbara Walters, Dave Winfield, and Robert Redford in the elevator. I dealt with Christopher Reeve years ago when he chose the winners of a *Superman* movie contest. I even smuggled him out of the building as his fans crushed the lobby. Mel Torme, the "Velvet Fog," once visited our offices; Gilbert Gottfried, the crazy-talking movie host, stopped by. Burt Ward, who played Robin on the *Batman* TV show, came to visit, too. Novelist Mario Puzo came for story conferences before scripting the first *Superman* movie. Beverly Sills' daughter worked for me for nearly a decade. The important thing is to be yourself. These are famous and important people, but they're still people. After all, even superstars still put their pants on one leg at a time—and I found out that Mario Puzo doesn't like to wear socks.

"Easy for Bob to say," Laurie responds. "If Robert Redford shook my hand, I wouldn't wash it for a week."

Protect Your Assets
Remember the techniques you've already used to disarm toxic colleagues: building alliances, enlisting the support of co-workers, showing appreciation, recognizing other people's priorities, being accommodating, and covering for co-workers.

That's why we're listening to Bob now. Here's how to deal with Big Stars, Little Stars, and Stars-in-the-Making:

➤ Stay cool. Don't fawn and act overly impressed.

➤ Don't pretend you don't know who they are. Unless you've been living in a cave for the last decade or you've lost the TV remote control, you'll know who the stars are.

➤ Treat the star with all the manners and respect due to any rich and powerful person who has the ability to affect your life.

➤ Don't be blinded by star power. Be alert to the person's motives and ways that you are being used. In certain circumstances, even people on the bottom rung of the corporate pecking order can be useful to Big Stars.

The Least You Need to Know

➤ Office superstars have positioned themselves for success. So can you—and maintain your integrity.

➤ Good work alone is *not* enough to get you the recognition you deserve. You must let others know of your success during and after every project.

➤ Polish your professional image until it shines like your work.

➤ Give the boss valid reasons for making you the Favorite.

➤ Consider riding on the Great One's coattails to the top.

➤ Don't be intimidated by office superstars, even ones drawn from media and politics.

Part 5
Socializing

The Worker's Plea

*Grant me the serenity
to accept the things I
cannot change.
The courage to change the
things I cannot accept,
and the wisdom to hide
the bodies of those people
I had to kill today
because
they acted like nitwits
and also,
help me to be careful of
the toes I step on today,
as they may be connected
to the butt that I may
have to kiss
tomorrow.*

In this section, we'll show you why it's so important to socialize with your colleagues and supervisors. We'll even teach you how to do it without going postal.

Chapter 18

Culture Club

In This Chapter

➤ The open culture and hidden subcultures within a company

➤ Hints for analyzing a company's traditions, values, and style create its culture

➤ Ways to figure out your company's culture

➤ How to package yourself

Abused as the idea of "corporate culture" has become, it is a fact of life. Every company has an open culture, as well as layers of hidden subcultures, social networks, and alliances. In this chapter, you learn how to recognize them and find out why they're so important to your career. You also learn how to fit in without selling out.

One Big Happy Family

The people you work with are like family—and we don't mean this in a nice way. Let's face it: Offices and families are similar in more ways that not. (The phrase *dysfunctional family* is, of course, redundant. Show us a functional family, and we'll show you how to change the channel on the TV set you're watching.)

How are your co-workers like family? Consider these eerie parallels:

➤ You spend a tremendous amount of time with them. Odds are that you're with your co-workers more than you're with your family members.

Protect Your Assets
Understanding the style of the place where you work and the ways it filters through the company is often the key to a successful relationship with that company.

Corporate Mumbo-Jumbo
A company's *culture* comprises the company's history, traditions, values (spoken as well as unspoken), management style, and market position.

➤ When you're not with them, you're thinking about them, obsessing about them, worrying about them.

➤ At home and at the office, you struggle for dominance.

➤ You're stuck with them, which is the most important commonality between the people clustered around the dinner table and conference table.

This isn't to say there aren't some big differences between your genetic clan and your office clan. The main difference? The people in your office know more about you than your relatives would ever dream of noticing. Your colleagues have observed you in minute detail. They know your height, weight, and whether you prefer cola or the uncola. They've been making a list and checking it twice. Family members, in contrast, only want to know if you'll drive Aunt Edna home from the podiatrist on Saturday.

And whether you're at the dinner table or the conference table, you have to fit in. Otherwise, you'll be labeled the oddball, eccentric, weirdo, or kook. You know, like Uncle Elmer, who wears kimonos and speaks only Esperanto, or Jocko in shipping (the one who does strange things with lawn clippings, light bulbs, and hair nets).

Of course, you can distance yourself from your co-workers. (You're pretty much stuck with your family.) But if you refuse to play, you'll pay. That's how the corporate culture works. You can use office politics to uncover the culture in your office and set about becoming comfortable with it.

Square Peg, Round Hole?

First of all, are you normal? Take this quiz to see. Check each answer that applies to you.

Normalcy Quiz

❑ 1. You store your paper money in rigid order from singles to hundreds.
❑ 2. You drink orange juice every day.
❑ 3. You depend on alarm clocks to wake you up.
❑ 4. You would tell an acquaintance to zip his pants.
❑ 5. You speed up at a yellow light.
❑ 6. You regularly sneak food into movie theaters to avoid the high prices of snack foods.

❏ 7. You eavesdrop.

❏ 8. You have suffered from hemorrhoids.

❏ 9. When nobody else is around, you drink straight from the carton.

❏ 10. You reuse aluminum foil.

❏ 11. You peek in your host's bathroom cabinet—and occasionally, you've been caught.

❏ 12. You've called in sick to work when you weren't feeling sick.

Score Yourself

1. Seventy-five percent of all Americans store their paper money in rigid order from singles to hundreds.

2. Seventy percent of us drink orange juice daily.

3. Ninety percent of us depend on alarm clocks to wake us.

4. Eight-one percent of us would tell an acquaintance to zip his pants.

5. Sixty-six percent of us speed up at a yellow light.

6. Fifty percent of us admit we regularly sneak food into movie theaters to avoid the high prices of snack foods.

7. Seventy-one percent of us eavesdrop.

8. Eighty percent of us have suffered from hemorrhoids.

9. When nobody else is around, 47 percent of us drink straight from the carton.

10. Forty-four percent of us reuse aluminum foil.

11. Thirty-nine percent of us peek in our host's bathroom cabinet. Some of us—17 percent—have been caught.

12. Sixty percent of us have called in sick when we weren't under the weather.

Okay, so now that you're normal (or as close as you can be after dealing with *your* boss), you can begin to learn how to walk the walk and talk the talk on the job.

Imagine that you're planning a trip to Tanzania. The first thing you'd do is read the travel brochures and guidebooks. Maybe you'd study a map of the region and take a crash course in the language. Why? Because you're one smart cookie. You know that the success of any trip depends in large part on your advance knowledge of the geography, customs, history, and language of the place. And if you planned to live there, even briefly, you'd find out how to dress, eat, act, and talk like the natives. The name of the game? Blend, blend, blend.

Corporate America is a foreign land, probably more alien than any place you can find on a world map. Fitting into the corporate culture requires keen analysis of its *culture—*

how it does business internally and externally. Each organization has its own style, which is a combination of management's behavior and fantasies, middle management's interpretations, and the average worker's understanding of what's really valued. Here's how the process looks visually:

Corporate Culture

⇓

Management's actions and daydreams

⇓

Middle management's reading of reality

⇓

Average worker's interpretation

These groups don't always agree, which can make it even more difficult to figure out the company's culture. Think of figuring out the company's culture as an especially diabolical game of "telephone," in which the message gets more and more garbled as it is transmitted further down the line.

Culture Vulture

Your task? Study the clues to figure out the organization's culture. Are you working for laid-back, hippie-style, Birkenstock-and-latte-types? Or are you caught in Dilbert hell where the unspoken motto is "Eagles may soar, but weasels don't get sucked into jet engines"?

Watch Your Back!
A company's culture is usually formed from top to bottom, but even you, a lowly serf on the bottom of the food chain, can't have a significant influence on the company's culture. Once you're firmly entrenched in a company, you can help shape its culture—but always work slowly and carefully!

A company's culture is conveyed both directly and indirectly. Here are some ways it gets transmitted:

1. Who gets hired—who gets fired?

   Studying who makes the cut and who doesn't can help you figure out what values the company rewards and which ones it punishes.

2. What is said at employee orientation sessions?

   Also "read" the subtext: What is implied?

3. What rules and guidelines does the employee handbook outline?

   How stringently are the rules enforced? How?

4. What does the company teach in its training programs?

Also be alert to the emphasis the company places on training. If training is a priority, the company is probably a high-powered organization, focused on grabbing market share.

5. What is the company's avowed mission?

   All things being equal, for-profit companies have a very different culture from nonprofit groups.

6. What is the company's marketing position?

7. What types of advertisements does the company use?

8. Observe other people. Do they come early and stay late?

Protect Your Assets
You can also pick up ideas about the company's culture by reading its literature—annual reports, brochures, and manuals. See how they describe the company. What personality profile can you draw from them?

This answer tells you whether the culture rewards nine-to-five folks or nine-to-nine lunatics. Who's playing with whom?

9. Tune in to the office grapevine. (Like you'd ever be silly enough to tune out your informal lifeline.)

   For example, does the gossip focus more on people who succeed or those who fail. If the rumor mill hums with the news that someone was passed over for promotion, you'll know this company places tremendous importance on independent achievement rather than consensus-style management.

10. Talk to people to learn the unwritten rules.

11. Listen to stories. Who are the company heroes? What did they do that helped them win admiration? Who are the company villains? What did they do to incur corporate wrath?

12. How formal or informal is the language used in the office?

    What's the position on an occasional barnyard epithet, for example?

13. Note how people dress. More on this later.

14. Where do colleagues and bosses eat lunch—and what do they eat?

    Do they go out to lunch often with coworkers or clients? Do they eat at their desks with the door open and work through lunch? Or do they look for some downtime during lunch and close the door or go out on their own? The crowd that eats a lettuce leaf and then power walks for 45 minutes is very different from the crowd that chows down on a 22-ounce porterhouse and then smokes a stogie.

15. Note the types of parties, gatherings, and social events the company holds and endorses.

    See "Party Hearty," in Chapter 19 for details on corporate socializing.

Corporate Mumbo-Jumbo
Face time is the trendy term for meeting someone in person, as in "I got 10-minutes of face time with the boss on Thursday."

Protect Your Assets
In very conservative organizations, specific aspects of the culture, such as promptness and productivity, may be defined in writing. In contrast, smaller organizations may pay lip service to these ideas, but not do anything specific to enforce the "rules" or to punish transgressors.

16. Pay attention to the method of communication used in the company.

   Do people interface through technology—e-mail and phone—or do they prefer real face time?

17. Check the tone of company newsletters.

   Are they cheery little missives about Lou's son Nick playing shortstop on his Pee Wee baseball team or terse reports on Lou's ability as a visionary planner to decentralize empowered team dynamics? The former indicates a more relaxed, even folksy atmosphere; the latter, duck-and-cover country.

18. Ask your boss to critique your memos—and pay attention to the comments. If the boss circles typos and revises your sentences, that's a clue to what's valued in the company. The folks there are clearly into getting it *all* right, down to the last itty-bitty detail.

19. How do people get ahead? Are the organization's rewards based on seniority, education, being well-liked, making technical discoveries, or serving customers? Are rewards available to only a few top people, or is everyone expected to succeed?

20. Does the organization value diversity or homogeneity? Does it value independence and creativity or being a team player and following orders?

Many companies still maintain a clear corporate culture based on dusty, traditional models; some have adapted their internal company culture to keep up with the trends and multicultural makeup of the real world. Never assume that everyone is as enlightened about cultural change as you are. That's why it's so important to do a complete analysis of your company's culture.

Give it a shot now. Read the following scenarios and then briefly describe the culture in each company.

Company Culture Worksheet

My company recently got a new boss—one trained in the ways of the New Age I-feel-your-pain sensitivity school. On his first day, he told us that work should be fun and the office should be an enjoyable place to work.

Today I got a written reprimand for "not having a fun attitude."

1. The company's culture can be described as

_____

_____

_____

I work in the library of a major college. The director instituted a computerized card catalog and checkout system that required the staff to apply bar codes to all 100,000 books. The director wanted the job to get done quickly and announced that everyone would be working a full day on Saturday. We all showed up and worked 9 hours.

On Monday we learned there would be no overtime pay for Saturday. When approached, the director said, "Oh, Saturday, that was volunteer work."

2. The company's culture can be described as

_____

_____

_____

My supervisor recently downsized the corporation. A number of individuals from different departments were selected for layoff, including one young man who was planning to get married the day after the layoff.

When questioned about the compassion and timing of this layoff, my supervisor replied that it was actually kinder to do it this way. He said, "The young man is preparing for a new life and now he has several dimensions to his new beginning."

3. The company's culture can be described as

_____

_____

_____

My manager reprimanded our team for not adhering to the company "process." The process she was referring to was explained in the brand-new company rule book that had not yet been distributed to the staff.

I asked for a copy of the process so that I could follow it more effectively.

After a short pause she said, "I don't think that's a good idea."

4. The company's culture can be described as

_____

_____

_____

Score Yourself

1. They're a bunch of hypocritical weasels and tyrants. The company's culture endorses hedging and shading the truth, which is just a nice way of saying they're a bunch of liars. To get the full picture, you have to fill in the blanks, as the following examples show:

Truth	Unstated Part
I'm concerned...	when it comes to my future.
You're next...	on my list of people to ax.
I'll call you soon...	as hell freezes over.
We value your work...	as much as we value road kill.
You're important...	in your dreams.

2. They're petty and cruel, ready to squeeze you dry and throw you down the airshaft. Expect these tightwads to focus on self-serving strategies, like taking credit for the work of others.

3. They're absolutely, positively clueless—about as smart as bait and proof that evolution can go in reverse. This type of corporate culture would not value someone who went around pointing out the humane and intelligent way to behave.

4. This company values form over substance. A lot of papers get shuffled, but nothing ever seems to get done because everyone is too afraid to reveal the "secret." People are likely to be very good at looking busy and exaggerating their talents. Here are some scams to watch for (or try yourself):

Actual Work	Claims
Attended a meeting, drank some coffee	Designed a new paradigm; positioned the company for the 21st century
Got stuck organizing the company's blood drive	Stabilized the health care system of the most powerful nation on earth
Worked on a project that got canceled before completion	Redesigned the company's international strategic visibility strategy

It's All in the Packaging

What can happen if you package yourself incorrectly? Well, let's take a look at what happens when advertising goes awry. Here are some products that didn't get the packaging quite right for foreign markets:

➤ Frank Perdue's chicken slogan, "It takes a strong man to make a tender chicken," was translated into Spanish as "It takes an aroused man to make a chicken affectionate."

➤ Scandinavian vacuum manufacturer Electrolux used the following in an American campaign: "Nothing sucks like an Electrolux."

➤ Pepsi's "Come alive with the Pepsi Generation" translated into "Pepsi brings your ancestors back from the grave" in Chinese.

➤ In Italy, a campaign for Schweppes Tonic Water translated the name into "Schweppes Toilet Water."

➤ Coors translated its slogan, "Turn it loose," into Spanish, where it became "Suffer from diarrhea."

➤ When Parker Pen marketed a ballpoint pen in Mexico, its ads were supposed to have said, "It won't leak in your pocket and embarrass you." Unfortunately, the company thought that the word *embarazar* (to impregnate) meant "to embarrass," so the ad stated: "It won't leak in your pocket and make you pregnant."

Watch Your Back!
What happens if the company's culture is totally opposite to your own style? Get out—then find a place that better suits your values. Otherwise, you're likely to be labeled "inflexible" and "resistant to change" on your performance review, which could make it very hard for you to get another job when you are finally fed up to *there*.

Corporate Mumbo-Jumbo
MO stands for "modus operandi," which is Latin for "method of operation"—your company's way of getting things done.

To make sure that *your* message doesn't get lost in the translation, you must be aware of who your audience is and what it wants. That means you must figure out your company's style. Being aware of your company's style is crucial because it tells you what your co-workers and managers value. You should study your company's MO and, during working hours, adopt it as a way to package your ideas and accomplishments successfully.

Packaging yourself doesn't mean surrendering the last vestiges of your individuality and marching in corporate lock-step. Rather, it means putting your ideas into a format that makes them acceptable to the people with whom you work. It's the most effective way to sell everyone on your ideas and you. After all, what good are all your good ideas if no one takes them seriously?

But Darling, It's You!

A traveler became lost in the desert region of Algeria. Realizing that his only chance for survival was to find civilization, he began walking. Time passed, and he became thirsty. More time passed, and he began feeling faint. Reduced to crawling, he was on the verge of passing out when he spied a tent about 500 meters in front of him. Barely conscious, he reached the tent and called out, "Water...."

A Bedouin appeared in the tent door and replied sympathetically, "I am sorry, sir, but I have no water. However, would you like to buy a tie?" With this, he brandished a collection of exquisite silken neckwear.

Protect Your Assets
The boom in "business casual" in part reflects larger changes in how Americans work. With laptops and faxes, more people work at home or on flexible hours, blurring the lines between work and home.

"You fool," gasped the man. "I'm dying! I need water!"

"Well, sir," replied the Bedouin, "If you really need water, there is a tent about 2 kilometers south of here where you can get some."

Amazingly, the man summoned sufficient strength to drag his parched body the distance to the second tent. With his last ounce of strength he tugged at the door of the tent and collapsed.

Another Bedouin, dressed in a costly tuxedo, appeared at the door and inquired, "May I help you sir?"

"Water..." was the feeble reply.

"Oh, sir," replied the Bedouin, "I'm sorry, but you can't come in here without a tie!"

Protect Your Assets
Not sure what to wear when you meet with a client? Call ahead and speak to a secretary or administrative assistant. Ask about the dress code straight out; forewarned is forearmed. If the two cultures clash, follow your client's clothing style. Your aim is to put your client at ease. That's good manners—and good office politics.

In addition to getting a handle on the company's culture line, you've also got to check out its clothes line. Packaging includes all elements of your appearance. Clothes make the man and the woman. Look around your office and take note of who's getting the promotions; bet they don't just sound good—they look good, too.

Unfortunately, dress codes have become a bit confusing in the late twentieth century. Getting dressed for work used to be a snap—until companies started going casual. In the old days (as far back at 1980), workers on the move up wore well-tailored suits, expensive shoes, and elegant watches. Of course, men were never seen without a tie. But that was then; this is now.

High-tech engineers and creative sorts have long been casting aside suits, and much of corporate America has followed their example by implementing dress-down Fridays. But in the last two years, more buttoned-down corporations—including Proctor & Gamble, Boeing, Burlington, and Northern Santa Fe Railroad—have given their work forces a jolt by giving khakis full rein every day.

According to a recent poll, more than half of all white-collar workers can now dress more casually every day, compared to one-third who could do so a few years ago. Double-breasted suits are out; cardigans are in. That hasn't stopped some employees from trying to announce their power by trading sweaters for sports coats or carrying fancy briefcases, however. That's because some people feel they lose authority when they're dressed casually—and they have a point.

Style for the Flair Impaired

David Neuman, 37, decided he needed a makeover when he became president of Touch-stone Television. Accustomed to wearing sleek Armani suits for his former position as an executive at Whittle Communications, Neuman was flummoxed when he crash-landed at Disney's J. Crew-and-jeans work environment. "Every company has its own corporate culture," Mr. Neuman said. "Disney turned out to be casual. But there's casual, hanging-out-with-your-friends-on-the-weekend casual, and then there's corporate casual."

Neuman hired a stylist to help him select the correct wardrobe. She cleaned the outdated, unsuitable clothes from his closets and added shoes, plaid shirts, and suede blazers to create that "casual chic" look. The stylist's fee? $1,500 to $5,000 per day—not including the price of the clothes.

Image consultants and personal shoppers have been around for years. Lately, however, serious movers and shakers have been getting makeovers to help give them that extra edge when it comes to blending with the prevailing corporate culture—especially when they change jobs or industries. You can probably dress for success by studying what the people on your level wear—and then just kicking it up a subtle notch. They're going for khakis and striped shirts? Get a slightly better grade of clothing, perhaps a really good belt and shoes, and then add a well-cut blazer for client days.

Besides, doesn't personal dressing conjure the image of a thumb-sucking child standing in front of a bulging closet and howling, "Mommy, I don't have a thing to wear!" Okay, so it is a little extreme, but if you're flair impaired and a shopping phobic, a stylist is a viable (if costly) option.

Watch Your Back!
Warning: Traditional corporate clothes are still de rigueur for any jobs involving money—investments, banking, and so on. Men, that means long-sleeved white shirts, dark suits, and ties. Women, we're taking suits, one-inch heels on shoes, and conservative makeup and jewelry. Remember: Dark gray or navy suits just scream authority. Nix on the nose rings for either sex.

Don't have the bucks? Not to worry. Virtually all department stores offer this service for free, as long as you buy their clothes! A personal shopper will walk around with you and help you pick the outfits that work for your style and job.

The Least You Need to Know

➤ Every company has an open culture as well as layers of hidden subcultures, social networks, and alliances.

➤ A company's culture encompasses the company's history, traditions, values, and style.

➤ Study the clues to figure out an organization's culture.

➤ Package yourself carefully; dressing well and appropriately for your job adds clout to your ideas and accomplishments.

➤ Dress for success by wearing clothing that suits your company's culture.

Company Manners

In This Chapter

➤ The importance of socializing in the office

➤ Breakfast meetings

➤ Power lunches

➤ Dinners with co-workers and clients

➤ Parties, the business of socializing

➤ Office functions, such as showers and weddings

President Calvin Coolidge once invited friends from his hometown to dine at the White House. The guests, worried about their table manners, decided to do everything that Coolidge did. This strategy succeeded—until coffee was served. The president poured his coffee into the saucer. The guests did the same. Coolidge added sugar and cream. His guests did, too. Then Coolidge bent over and put his saucer on the floor for the cat.

The moral of the story? Pick one:

a. Never have a business lunch with Calvin Coolidge. (No problem—he's dead.)

b. Before you eat at the White House, always check the plate for cat hairs.

c. Order tea, not coffee.

d. Know your table manners.

The envelope, please. The answer is...*d*! You got that one, you party animal.

Much of business is a matter of seduction—and there's no better place to conduct the affairs of business than at a business breakfast, lunch, dinner, or party. Being a copycat will take you just so far in the business social whirl. So, you better know a fork from a spoon—and a whole lot more.

In this chapter, you learn the "whole lot more." First you learn the importance of making the scene with your co-workers and clients. Then you master proven techniques for doing business at breakfast, lunch, and dinner. Finally, you go on a whirlwind tour of business parties across the country. With our help, you'll be ready to work the room like a pro.

You're Known by the Company You Keep

You may wonder why something as seemingly harmless as whom you socialize with at the office can have an impact on your career. This is especially true if you don't socialize enough. Here's the splash of cold water: The people you socialize with at the office can have a profound influence on the success of your career.

While making the *wrong* friends at work is rarely fatal to your chances for advancement, making the *right* social contacts can propel you up the ladder much faster than you might imagine. Even though you're probably inclined to view your friendships at work as your own business, in certain instances you may have to decide how important particular friendships are when balanced against career considerations. Of course, the choice is yours—but so are the rewards and risks.

One of the most important ways to connect with colleagues and clients is at meals. The business of eating is not just a business—it's an art. And the first thing to know is which meal to choose for your goals. Breakfast? Lunch? Dinner? The next sections serve the right information.

Breakfast of Champions

Watch Your Back!
No power breakfasts for artsy types and freelancers, however. They rarely like to get up and out that early. About 10:00 a.m. is the earliest you can get creative folks to confront food and work together.

Breakfast is an excellent time to make contacts, trade news and views, arrange deals, and win allegiance since it adds profitably to a person's work day. A business lunch is a more relaxed meal; a business breakfast, in contrast, conveys a certain power and panache. There's an unstated urgency to a breakfast meeting: a we-are-really-important-people-aren't-we tone. In addition, it can be much easier to book important colleagues and clients for a breakfast than a lunch or dinner.

And thanks to the Puritan work ethic, we all feel good about this type of multitasking. Over grits and gossip, we can crow, "Hey, look at me; I'm starting my day with a deal and a meal!"

Let's Do Lunch

An older couple met their demise and were transported to Heaven. As they were waiting to be processed, they began to look all around at their setting for eternity.

The wife was amazed at the beauty, the peace, and the contentment she felt and commented over and over about what a nice place Heaven was and how fortunate she felt to be there.

The husband sneered, "If it weren't for you and your damned oat-bran muffins and health food crap, we'd have been here 15 years ago."

Lunch meetings are a standard time to do serious business with co-workers as well as with clients. Taking a break in the middle of the day allows you to recharge your batteries while pumping associates for news, forging bonds, mending fences, and hashing out details of key deals. A lunch meeting also lets you connect with clients and build a valuable network of business alliances. The meal can take place in a fancy restaurant, a low-key coffee bar, or the company cafeteria. Might as well start with the top of the line bistros, where the elite meet to eat.

If you're doing the inviting, always give your guest the choice of at least two restaurants; hey, not everybody's into nuts and berries. This gesture prevents problems with specific dietary preferences and restrictions.

Here are some additional tips for making a business lunch go smoothly:

➤ The day before an important business lunch, visit the restaurant if it's new to you. Meet the maitre d' and pick a table. Avoid tables facing mirrors, tables next to rest rooms, and tables near the kitchen.

➤ Get the reservation carved in granite; you can kill the meeting by having to wait for a table. It makes you look weak and careless.

➤ The early bird catches the business. Never keep a guest waiting. If you're meeting at the restaurant, arrive early.

➤ If you can't pronounce it, don't order it.

➤ Try to eat like a native. Don't order sushi in a steak house or bagels and lox in a Tex Mex grill.

➤ Candy is dandy but liquor is quicker...to destroy the lunch. Liquor makes people sloppy and stupid. Order a drink if your guest does but nurse it—don't pound drink after drink.

➤ Get to the point before you get to dessert.

➤ Handle the check privately by having your credit card receipt signed and stamped in advance. You can arrange this ahead of time easily.

Protect Your Assets
When it comes to business entertaining, we patronize a select handful of restaurants and suggest you do the same. Since we go to these places often and tip well, we know what to expect and we get treated like royalty.

213

Wine and Dine

Dinner is the trickiest of the three meals at which to do business. Everyone is tired at the end of the day, so there's always the chance of eating too much, drinking too much, and saying too much. The result? Too little business gets done.

Watch Your Back!
Never assume that your guest's dinner hour is the same as yours. Midwesterners generally chow down around 6 p.m.; New Yorkers rarely lift their forks until 8 p.m. And we haven't even gotten to the issue of Europeans. By the time *they* have dinner, Laurie's ready for breakfast.

That said, figure on participating in business dinners a fair amount of the time, depending on your line of work. Business dinners are the gold standard for wining and dining important clients from other areas. These out-of-towners often expect the four-star treatment—dinner—not a mere breakfast or lunch. You may also be expected to take a client to some after-dinner entertainment, such as a show, nightclub, or local attraction.

As a key player in the production and manufacturing of comic books, Bob is often feted this way. He's been to exotic, expensive, and eccentric restaurants from sea to shining sea. He's learned to eat light after 10 p.m., avoid booze, and catnap when he can. And so can you.

Party Hearty

Work today is a 24-hour-a-day event. More and more, the lines between social life and business life are blurring, and hosting is becoming a new business art.

In general, business parties reflect the corporate culture. As a result, the style of the party changes with the location. As you travel around the country or change companies, it's important to remember that what works at business parties in one city will not necessarily work in another.

Protect Your Assets
Laurie says, "Bob always makes fun of me for doing this, but I *always* eat a real dinner before I go to a business cocktail party. First off, with my belly full and happy, I can concentrate on doing business. Second, I'm a really picky eater; I won't eat anything I can't recognize and avoid most of what I can." Also, you won't get tipsy as easily!

There are as many different types of entertaining as there are companies, but odds are good that you can count on being invited to a slew of cocktail parties. That's because a cocktail party is a business way of getting a lot of people into a small space without spending too much time, money, or preparation effort. A cocktail party is perfect for the following events:

➤ Introducing products

➤ Announcing events

➤ Saluting associates

➤ Making important business contacts

Remember what you learned about building alliances, networking, and business socializing in previous chapters.

The rule is, Be There or Be Square—even if you're not a party animal. Business parties are the same as business. Think of them as business meetings that start with mystery meat on a cracker, follow with a rubber chicken, and end with something that was probably ice cream in its first life. But even if the food is great, you're not there to eat; you're there to see and be seen.

The Name Game

When you go to these corporate mingling events, chances are you'll be meeting new people. They could be clients or co-workers from a different department within your company, but they all have one thing in common: a new name you have to remember. If remembering names or matching names to faces is a problem for you, never fear. Everyone blanks out now and again. Try these ideas if you're stumped:

➤ Before going to a party or convention, get the guest list. Study up.

➤ Ask for business cards.

➤ Life is short. Be blunt. Say, "Please tell me your name again," or "Could you repeat your name, please?"

➤ Don't be a hero. Ask people in a group to introduce themselves.

➤ When you're the host, give everyone a break—use name stickers and place cards.

Watch Your Back!
Europeans find it incredibly rude to define people in introductions. Americans, in contrast, think it's better to give guests a clue about where to start the conversation. What to do? Follow the custom of the country where the party is being held.

The New York Cocktail Party

If you're invited to a company cocktail party in the Big Apple, everyone assumes that you'll go to the party directly from your office. Therefore, you'll be wearing business clothes and carrying your briefcase. (There will be a place to check your briefcase—just remember to pick it up after the festivities.)

Cocktail parties generally run from 5 to 8 p.m. If the New York party is scheduled to start at 5 p.m., you're not expected to show up before 5:30 unless you're hosting the party. Stay past closing time only if you are having a very profitable time.

Cocktail parties are held in discos, restaurants, clubs, and private apartments. The typical conversations will cover the following topics:

➤ The price of apartments in New York City

➤ The availability and price of summer rentals on the East End of Long Island (the Hamptons, Mattituck, Greenport, Shelter Island, and so on.)

Protect Your Assets
New Yorkers pride themselves on their food. Be prepared for sushi (raw fish with an attitude), clam and oyster bars, and other finger foods that cost more a piece than you make in a week. Currently, tapas (a Spanish word meaning appetizers or snacks) are big in the Apple.

➤ Sizzlin' new restaurants

➤ Trendy new people and their adventures

➤ The latest plays (on and off Broadway)

➤ The latest movies (those with subtitles are always in)

➤ Shopping bargains of the decade

➤ New York teams (How about those Mets?)

➤ New York gossip

➤ Oh, yes, and some business deals—a lot of business deals

How can you prepare yourself to do business at a New York City cocktail party?

➤ Read this week's issue of the *New Yorker,* today's *New York Times,* and this morning's *Wall Street Journal.*

➤ If you can't get to the plays and movies, read the reviews. The Friday Arts and Leisure section in the *Times* makes a great crib sheet. Also, the *New Yorker* has quick reviews in the front of the magazine and more detailed articles on books, plays, and films in the back.

➤ Read all the latest books. No time? No surprise! Cram with the Sunday *Times* Book Review.

➤ Catch up on the latest New York trends. *Time Out* will fill you in on what's hot on the social scene in New York. The "Styles" magazine section from the Sunday *Times* also has it all.

➤ Dress right. Women, get a good black dress and elegant pumps. Men, procure a good blue suit (not black) and understated dress shoes (no rubber soles).

The Washington Cocktail Party

Washington business cocktail parties aren't about the cocktails and they aren't about the party. They are strictly about the guest list. The value of the party is judged by the number of important movers and shakers in attendance.

Washington, DC, is a company town; nearly everyone works for the government in some capacity, so everyone knows why he or she was invited. Be prepared to hear bills lobbied and law cases argued.

In Washington, parties always begin and end on time. The Washington crowd is a punctual bunch, if not well fed. That's because there is always a bar, but don't count on food.

How can you prepare yourself to do business at a Washington cocktail party?

➤ Read today's *Washington Post*, the *New York Times,* and a third newspaper. We recommend the *London Times* or the *Los Angeles Times*.

➤ If at all possible, get a copy of the guest list or at least try to find out ahead of time who will be there. You're expected to know everyone without necessarily being introduced.

➤ Practice not gawking. And never, never, never ask for autographs.

➤ Ditto on the black dress and good business suit.

Watch Your Back!
Never ask personal questions at a Washington "business" party. It is assumed that if you are important enough to be at the party, you must be influential in government. Asking a personal question reveals your lack of clout.

Fly on the Wall

What if you're the host? Take a tip from Sally Quinn, a former political reporter for the *Washington Post* and Washington's social maven. Quinn notes that "Parties are essential elements of the scene in Washington, DC. They help form the relationships that make things happen." Quinn credits advance planning—food preparation, memorizing the names of every guest, testing music and lighting—for much of her success. She also says that when you introduce people, add a biographical tidbit or something they have in common. And if you forget someone's name? Just say, "But of course you two know each other" and then flee. [*Bottom Line*, March 15, 1998]

The California Cocktail Party

In terms of business, California means Los Angeles. With these parties, *time* is a relative term, like "rich" and "family." Since California is already three hours behind New York and Washington, DC, what's the use of hurrying?

Parties in Los Angeles center around the entertainment industry. At each party, be prepared for jockeying among the power players for the bankable directors, stars, and (the bottom of the heap) writers. The food will be very California: Tex-Mex, sushi, and weird fruits and veggies. Things will look too good to eat and glow as though radioactive.

Typical conversations at a business party in La-La Land dwell on the following topics:

➤ How much money a movie made (called the "gross")

➤ What's hot and what's not

➤ Tummy tucks, face lifts, and other body sculpting

➤ Hairdressers

➤ Exercise coaches who make house calls

➤ The "next" restaurant or spa

➤ The "next" star

➤ Decorators

➤ Gardeners

➤ Real-estate prices

➤ Who's moving out to California and who's moving back to New York

➤ Kids and nannies

How can you prepare yourself to do business at a California cocktail party?

➤ Realize that the guests will be too cool for words. Men, ditch the jacket and tie. Ties are illegal in Los Angeles. Women, wear something short and tight. Better be buff and tan.

➤ Read the daily *Variety, Hollywood Reporter,* and possibly *Billboard.*

➤ Check out the cover story in *People* magazine.

The Midwest Cocktail Party

In the Midwest, unlike the rest of America's business centers, business associates tend to be friends. Their business parties are social events as much as business events, which is rarely true elsewhere in the country.

Business friends often entertain in suburban settings and downtown hotels. Since everyone works downtown in the business center, people often gather around 6 p.m. and get out at a reasonable time to have a real home life.

Typical conversations at business parties in America's breadbasket cover these popular topics:

➤ Golf games

➤ Vacations

➤ Children and their admission to select colleges and universities

➤ Hobbies

➤ Mutual acquaintances

How can you prepare yourself to do business at a heartland cocktail party?

➤ Read the *Wall Street Journal* and the local daily newspaper.

➤ Read any business magazine that has featured a story about the host company within the recent past (say six months to a year).

➤ Don't count on eating endangered species or almost-but-not-quite poisonous blow fish. A party in the Midwest is more a Miracle Whip/deviled egg affair.

➤ Don't expect dowdy (many Midwesterners have real style) but don't do the LA tart thing or the New York vamp. Go classy.

Protect Your Assets
Midwest business cocktail parties still tend to be primarily male. No one drinks very much, and everyone's gone within 15 minutes of the end of the party.

Working the Room

North, South, East, West. No matter where the business party is held, here are six actions you can take to make the most of your time:

1. Approach strangers, introduce yourself, and learn why you both are there.

2. Do business. That's why you're there. Remember: This event is a business party, although it may appear to be a social gathering.

3. Trade business cards. It's much easier to exchange business cards than to scribble down names and addresses on soggy cocktail napkins.

4. Eat and drink lightly. You're there to do meet and greet, not to win the all-you-can-eat contest or a beer-guzzling competition.

5. Thank your host before you leave.

6. Send a formal thank-you note to your host the following day.

The Art of Spousemanship

Back in the middle ages of corporate life (a generation or so ago), it was de rigueur for management to look at wives as well as their hubbies (a.k.a. "the employees") when selecting the next president of Widgets, Inc. Would she adjust to life in Upper Armpit or Lower Slobovia? Would she get into the right clubs and service organizations? Could she make a cunning salad from lime gelatin and miniature marshmallows?

Watch Your Back!
Never make a spouse look bad. That includes your own, your client's, or anyone else in the spousal role. It's embarrassing and bad for business.

But times have changed. Today the future president of Widgets, Inc., is just as likely to be the Mrs. as the Mr. As a matter of fact, she's more likely to be a *Ms.* According to a recent survey in *USA Today,* 44 percent of all women ages 18 to 44 are child free—and have no intention of ever having children. The most frequent reason these women gave for not having children? They want to be free to get ahead on the job.

Nonetheless, the spouse role still exists, except that now it's just as likely to be a man as a woman playing second fiddle.

In Love and War

If you're not already employed by your spouse's employer, don't look for a job at the same place. We know we sound as out-of-date as the hula hoop, but we're right. How right? Some companies even have rules prohibiting spouses to work in the same department. Most have rules forbidding a spouse to supervise his or her partner. Some companies extend the rules to live-in partners, too.

There's nothing romantic about being in business with your lover. Very few people have the maturity, the time, and the patience to nurture a marriage and identical career. It's hard enough to run a house together without trying to run a business. If you do already work for the same company, make sure that your responsibilities don't overlap.

Strategic Visibility

In addition to company parties and shindigs with clients, you're going to get invited to a lot of parties given by colleagues for colleagues or just for fun. (At least you'd *better* be invited. If not, you haven't been reading very closely.)

If people in the office are holding an event, you have to decide if you'll make the scene. Your decision depends on your relationship to the honoree: colleague to colleague, boss to colleague, colleague to boss. Always consider the balance-of-power relationship as you make your decision. Evaluate the situation by asking yourself these questions:

➤ What message does my attendance (or lack thereof) send?

➤ Will people expect me to show up? Why or why not?

➤ How can my attendance help—or hurt—my career?

➤ If I should attend, but cannot, do I have a strong enough excuse?

Protect Your Assets

Even if you hate the retiree, show up at a retirement party. Especially your own.

If a specific person isn't being honored (as in a birthday party, retirement party, or baby shower), you have to weigh the nature of the event. Some events are clearly off-limits—such as a weekend in a hot tub with your staff—while others are harder to evaluate. The following chart can give you a starting point for weighing your options.

Weighing Your Options

Event	Attendance
Retirement party	Colleagues: always (hey, don't you want people to show for you in 50 years?)
	Boss: always (and you better make a great speech and a toast)
Birthday parties	Colleague: always
	Boss: make an appearance, tell a joke, split fast
Baby shower	Colleague: yes
	Boss: optional (but always send a nice gift)
Bridal shower	See above
Wedding	Colleague: yes
	Boss: yes (show of respect)
Ski weekend	Colleague: sure
	Boss: no way on Earth
Opening of a new nightclub	Colleague: of course
	Boss: no, no, no

The Least You Need to Know

➤ The people you socialize with at the office can have a profound influence on the success of your career.

➤ Network, cement relationship, trade gossip, and make deals at breakfast, lunch, and dinner.

➤ Business parties are the same as business, so make the scene.

➤ Business parties reflect the corporate culture and geography. Study up on the culture and blend in.

➤ In many companies, spouses still matter.

➤ If you're not already employed by your spouse's employer, don't look for a job at the same place.

➤ Consider your relationship with the honoree or host before accepting an invitation to an office party.

Chapter 20

Interoffice Romance: Your Cube or Mine?

In This Chapter

➤ Reasons for office romance

➤ Love and work

➤ Passion among the paper clips

➤ Rules for keeping both your sweetie and your job

It's tough to meet your mate when you're working 60-plus hour weeks. But what happens when the cubicle walls come tumblin' down, and you find yourself in a lip-lock with a sexy co-worker? We've all lusted after an office-mate or two (or three or four), but how many of us have sealed the "real" deal? If you've redefined power lunch protocol and still have come back hungry for seconds—or even pondered the very thought—this chapter is for you.

First, we'll show you who's doing what with whom on company time. Then you'll learn the effects of office romance so you can decide if the potential rewards are worth the sure risk.

Finally, we'll teach you how to use office politics in your favor when love is in bloom so you won't lose your job while you're losing your heart.

The Birds and the Bees—and Office Politics

Interoffice love affairs are as common as summer reruns, overpriced designer coffee, and uncomfortable shoes. Indeed, if studies are to be believed, making whoopee on company time is on the rise. We present the following proof:

➤ More than 40 percent of employees report they have been involved with a co-worker at some time in their careers, according to a survey by the American Management Association.

➤ Bosses aren't left out of the fun. Nearly one-quarter of 500 managers and executives in the same survey said they'd had an office romance.

Increasingly, work is a natural place to find love. For many people, dating a co-worker is a safe and attractive alternative to pursuing romance in riskier venues, such as bars, parties, or health clubs. "I got to know my fiancé pretty well before we even started dating because we worked in the same law firm," said a Washington attorney. "That was important to me, and everything's working out fine."

The Heat Goes On

It's no wonder that so many romances start on the job. In part, that's because love and work have a great deal in common. Don't believe us? Here's an excerpt from Harvard's Kennedy School Career Services Guide comparing successful interviewing to successful dating.

Positive First Impressions

Interview:

➤ Interviewer greets you by name.

➤ Interviewer doesn't make you wait a half-hour.

The first date—Her perspective:

➤ He shows up with flowers.

➤ He opens the car door for her.

The first date—His perspective:

➤ She's wearing a mini skirt.

➤ She reaches over and unlocks his door.

Negative First Impressions

Interview:

➤ Interviewer starts off conversation with: "Considering your ineptitude, I'm surprised that we granted you an interview in the first place."

The first date—Her perspective:

➤ He wears his shirt unbuttoned, revealing multiple gold chains, tattoos, and pierced body parts.

The first date—His perspective:

➤ She says, "I'll be with you in a minute. I'm almost done bleaching my facial hair."

Acceptance

Interview:

➤ Interviewer says, "We'd like you to visit the home office."

The first date—Her perspective:

➤ He says, "I'd love to introduce you to my parents."

The first date—His perspective:

➤ She says, "Should I call you...or nudge you?"

Rejection

Interview:

➤ Interviewer says, "Judging by your diverse experience, I'm sure that you'll find success no matter who you work for."

The first date—Her perspective:

➤ He says, "I should introduce you to my cousin—he comes up for parole next month."

The first date—His perspective:

➤ She says, "I should introduce you to my cousin—she's got a great personality."

Mixing Business and Pleasure

With thousands of employees, the Boeing Company has its share of husband-wife teams and dating couples on staff. Though the aerospace giant doesn't prohibit dating within the workplace, it does require that involved employees maintain peak performance—especially if the romance ends.

A married couple working at Boeing divorced, and the woman had a restraining order placed on the man. To add to the headache, they both worked on the same manufacturing floor. Boeing honored the 100-foot legal restraining order by keeping the man at one end of the floor and the woman at the other. It's situations like these that make companies hate any form of office romance.

Protect Your Assets Accusations of favoritism are common when colleagues pair off, and office morale can suffer as a result. Twenty-eight percent of companies say romances have resulted in charges of favoritism.

Watch Your Back! So you think you're in love with the boss? Think again, we say. Most likely you're just in love with that person's power. And once you get outside the board room, that power fades. It's the same phenomenon that attracts groupies to rock stars, athletes, and politicians. Plus, how do you maintain an equal relationship outside of the office when you're the subordinate in the office? Tricky stuff.

As this story illustrates, work and love don't always go together. Next to mergers and downsizings, office dalliances are the biggest interruptions to workplace productivity. At the very least, rumors of romance lead to gossip galore. Keeping such romances away from the office gossip grapevine is tough. More than 60 percent of managers who had a romance said their co-workers knew about it, according to the American Management Association survey.

At the very most, making time with a colleague can result in icy stares from the unlucky in love, thwarted careers, and even firings for the participants. They can also result in the "my lover's keeper" syndrome, i.e., if it's accepted that you're a couple, suddenly you're both expected to know the whereabouts of your significant other and their reasons for doing things. Sometimes, you can even get bawled out for their mistakes.

Pair Off—and Square Off

We got this story from a friend:

My boss is engaged and plans to marry soon. The other day he called me into his office to confess. He said this was going to be a "mixed" marriage, and he was having some last-minute reservations. He leaned over his desk and whispered, "You know, she's a secretary, and I'm a manager. Do you think it will work?"

Probably the most celebrated office romance case to hit the news involved Bendix Corporation Chairman William Agee and his aide, Mary Cunningham. Cunningham was forced to resign when the two started doing the deed.

More recently, the head of Staples, Inc., Martin Hanaka, resigned after a subordinate accused him of assaulting her during an argument. The pair had apparently been romantically linked at one time. Hanaka was in direct violation of the company's fraternization policy, which prohibits managers from dating subordinates.

Half of all hierarchical love affairs will not work out. They're especially dangerous for a company because they are more likely to result in charges of sexual harassment. In fact, one-quarter of all businesses say that a workplace romance in their company has resulted in an accusation of harassment, according to the Society for Human Resource Management.

A Stud or a Dud?

How can you tell it's over? Here are the top 10 rejection lines given by women (and what they actually mean):

10. I think of you as a brother. (You remind me of that inbred banjo-playing geek in *Deliverance*.)

9. There's a slight difference in our ages. (I don't want to date my dad.)

8. I'm not attracted to you in "that" way. (You are seriously unattractive; in fact, you may be the ugliest nerd in this office.)

7. My life is too complicated right now. (I don't want you spending the whole night, or else you might hear phone calls from all the other guys I'm seeing.)

6. I've got a boyfriend. (I prefer spending the evening with my cat and a half gallon of Ben and Jerry's to you.)

5. I don't date men where I work. (I wouldn't date you if you were in the same solar system, much less the same building.)

4. I'm concentrating on my career. (Even something as boring and unfulfilling as my job is better than dating you.)

3. I'm celibate. (I've only sworn off the men like you.)

2. Let's be friends. (Let's not and say we are.)

1. It's not you, it's me. (It's you.)

Protect Your Assets
The fallout from a break-up can get costly, too. Payouts on out-of-court settlements on sexual harassment cases have ranged, on average, from $25,000 to $50,000, according to David Sterling, chief executive of Sterling & Sterling Insurance Inc., a New York insurer that sells sexual harassment coverage to companies.

God of Eros

Even though many workers play where they get paid, they also have serious reservations about office romances. Here's the result of a nationwide poll:

➤ 38 percent of workers polled viewed romances at work as unprofessional.

➤ 46 percent had concerns about lowered productivity of those involved in the romance.

➤ 60 percent had concerns about the morale of co-workers if a romance ended badly.

➤ 75 percent said there's a great chance of potential for retaliation if the romance ends.

Watch Your Back!
At companies with a workplace romance policy, the consequences applied to workers who violate the policy varied. Punishments included transfer within the organization (42 percent), termination (27 percent), counseling (26 percent), formal reprimand (25 percent), and demotion (7 percent). In addition, 25 percent do not have any consequences.

Kiss and Tell

Despite concerns about the consequences of office romances, a 1988 Society for Human Resource Management Workplace Survey of more than 600 human resource professionals found that while most companies have strict guidelines on employee pilfering, racism, and even sexual harassment, few are sure how to deal with dating. Only 6 percent of the companies polled had written rules on employee dating.

A lot of companies shy away from the issue of romance on the job because they're afraid that employees are going to be upset that the company's intruding into their privacy.

As a result, more and more companies are loosening once-strict rules against romancing co-workers. For example, until the 1970s, Electronic Data Systems fired adulterers. But today, EDS has no written policy on workplace love. "It's not the business of the company," a spokesman offered. "We expect people to behave professionally." AT&T, for instance, treats the issue with "benign neglect" and doesn't have a written policy on love at the office.

Fly on the Wall

"We don't have any written rules specifically against dating," Delta Air Lines spokesman Bill Berry said. "What we request is simply that you maintain professional and businesslike conduct in the office. If the dating leads to marriage, we do not allow a spouse to supervise a spouse. Other than that, if you're in the same department, as long as you maintain proper business conduct, you can work in the same office."

Likewise, Coca Cola Company doesn't have a written policy on office romance. Spokesman Robert Baskin noted, "We're not looking to regulate dating. Managers have to perform their functions professionally. It's certainly not good practice to be dating your subordinate, yet we're all adults who should be able to deal with these things professionally."

The general rule of thumb in dealing with office romances is this: Most companies strongly discourage managers from dating underlings; otherwise, dating among peers is okay, as long as it's discreet and the couple conduct themselves in a professional manner. In some cases, companies will separate couples at work—either by transferring one partner to another department to avoid either person having to report to the other, or at least by having a different supervisor evaluate the subordinate's work.

The Dating Game

➤ 75 percent of all workers think it's okay to date a co-worker;

➤ 40 percent of workplace relationships lead to marriage or a long-term relationship.

(Source: *Time* magazine, February 22, 1998)

Memo to all co-workers who decide to begin a workplace romance: Pursue at your own risk. When something goes wrong, it's usually a big mess. Our motto? Don't start no mess, won't be no mess. If you're just curious about how it would be, stay that way.

That said, we're also realists. Hey, we met each other working together on the college yearbook, so we're not about to go pointing any fingers at that couple making kissy-face in the corner. If two co-workers want to suck face, they will. Try this revised advice: Aim Cupid's arrow with caution.

After all, under certain circumstances, Cupid's presence *can* add life, not just strife, to an office. Romance can bring new enthusiasm, pleasure, and renewed happiness. Additionally, when dating couples can see each other at work, absences decrease.

What I Did for Love

Now, should you take the plunge? Will you be lucky in workplace woo? To see, why not ask yourself the following questions before dating a co-worker. Check *Yes* or *No* for each question.

Co-Working Dating Worksheet

Yes	No	
❑	❑	1. Are we going to date because we both like each other, or is there a political subtext here?
❑	❑	2. Would this person date me only because he or she is afraid to say no?
❑	❑	3. Am I using this relationship—or would the person I date use this relationship—to gain power, influence, or benefits?

If you answered yes to one or both of the last two questions, run, don't walk, from the relationship.

Advice to the Lovelorn

Before you ask out that certain someone in the next cubicle, we recommend that you do the following:

1. Check the company policy on office romances. Some have "no fraternizing" policies, while others are more lenient. Know where you stand before you go somewhere you might not want to be.

2. If you can, avoid getting personal with someone who reports to you or to whom you report.

3. Decide the amount of secrecy you plan to keep about your relationship.

4. Avoid public displays of affection while on the job. We don't just mean within the building. Keeping an office romance outside a general five-block radius of the building isn't a bad idea.

5. Don't exchange romantic or suggestive e-mail or voice-mail.

6. Don't treat business trips like romantic get-aways. They're not.

7. Maintain a professional manner when you and your partner attend after-hours office functions together.

8. If your relationship violates a company dating policy, be the first person to tell your supervisor about it and offer a solution that will bring you and your partner back into compliance.

9. Decide whether you are willing to change jobs or leave the company if a manager decides that your romantic liaison is negatively affecting the workplace or violates company policies—or if the romance goes south faster than a snowbird in the fall.

10. Have an escape hatch ready in case things go awry. Always remember, your options may be few if the relationship collapses or the boss forces you to choose between your job and your partner.

The bottom line? Be very cautious before embarking on a workplace romance, and be certain you're aware of the potential consequences.

The Least You Need to Know

➤ A lot of workers are making whoopee on company time.

➤ Office romances can result in thwarted careers and even firings for the participants.

➤ Most companies strongly discourage managers from dating underlings, but dating among peers is usually okay.

➤ If you do fall for a colleague, check the company policy on office romances. Act like a grown-up.

➤ If appropriate, confide in your supervisor. You'll need an ally if the romance sours.

Chapter 21

Crossing the Line

In This Chapter

➤ Sexism on the job

➤ Some examples of sexual harassment

➤ Nonsexist and bias-free language

➤ Racism, ageism, and lookism

NEWS BULLETIN—Men and women are NOT alike.

Sure, you thought you already knew that. But now we have proof! After countless hours of surveys and studies on the following topics, here's what we've learned:

The Difference Between Men and Women: Haircuts

Women's version:

Woman 1   Oh! You got a haircut! It's so cute!

Woman 2   Do you think so? I wasn't sure when I first looked at it. I mean, you don't think it's too fluffy looking?

Woman 1   No, no, it's perfect. I'd love to get my hair cut like that, but I think my face is too wide.

Woman 2	Are you serious? I think your face is adorable. And you could easily get one of those layer cuts—that would look so cute! I was actually going to do that except that I was afraid it would accent my long neck.
Woman 1	Oh! I would love to have your neck! Anything to take attention away from this two-by-four I have for a shoulder line.
Woman 2	Are you kidding? Everything drapes so well on you. I mean, look at my arms—see how short they are?

Men's version:

Man 1	Haircut?
Man 2	Yeah.

We know that women speak in estrogen and that men listen in testosterone, but that doesn't make it any easier to accept the conflicts that arise in the workplace because of outmoded sexist assumptions and behavior. Men and women *are* different, but gender has nothing to do with a person's ability to get a job done. After all, people of either sex can be jerks on the job. You know the type—they couldn't find their butt if they had a bell on it.

In this chapter, you learn how to recognize sexism in the workplace. Next, you learn how to cope with the unenlightened piggies you're likely to encounter as you make your way up the corporate ladder. Finally, you learn how to use office politics through nonsexist and bias-free language.

Jane, You Ignorant Slut

Ed Duckworth had paid his dues for more than 25 years before being named vice president of a highly successful company. Ed brought a wealth of experience to his new job, which he immediately put to work correcting shortcomings in marketing and spearheading improved quality control. The money rolled in.

Unfortunately, not every aspect of Ed's career was quite as rosy. Three female supervisors, two female managers, and four female administrative assistants had all lodged complaints with human resources about Ed's sexist behavior.

First, there was Ed's language. He referred to women as "girls," "babes," and "pieces." He often shook his finger in a woman's face and screamed, "Now, Missy, I know what's best here. After all, you're just a woman." He ignored the ideas that women proposed. In addition, he consistently promoted less-qualified men over more-qualified women. Finally, he regarded the women in the secretarial pool as his personal harem, placed there to serve his every need.

Since Ed was otherwise an outstanding adminis-
trator, the company tried to correct his sexist
attitudes. Other executives enrolled him in a
sensitivity-training course and had him work
privately with a female management consultant.
They set up meetings with Ed and the women
who had accused him of sexist behavior.

Protect Your Assets
It's not just power and the penis. While the headlines concentrate on men as sexists, women in power can be equally guilty of sexist behavior.

It didn't take. By the end of the year, Ed had been
unable to bring his behavior within acceptable
bounds. "I'm still bringing in the bucks, aren't I?"
he complained. "If the babes can't stand the heat in the office, let them get back
into the kitchen," he said in his defense. "After all, what really matters is the bottom
line. I'm bringing in the bacon."

The women filed a class-action lawsuit against the company and Ed. They
won...and Ed took early retirement.

Unfortunately, a lot of Ed Duckworths are still out there. They haven't been able to adjust
to the realities of the new workplace. Not comfortable with women on the job (especially
women in positions of power), men like this are unable to understand that there's no
room in the boardroom for bias and bigotry. But being clueless doesn't cut it where
sexual harassment is involved.

Sexual harassment in the workplace has been going on since the ozone layer was intact,
but it wasn't until the Anita Hill–Clarence Thomas hearings in 1991 that the taboo
against discussing it was finally broken. Since then, sexual harassment has become the
EEOC's fastest growing complaint.

➤ Between 1990 and 1996, harassment cases filed with federal and local agencies
  skyrocketed 150 percent.

➤ In 1997 alone, 15,342 cases of sexual harassment were filed with the courts, compared to 6,900 in 1991.

➤ A recent survey of human resources managers found that 7 out of 10 handled at
  least one sexual harassment complaint last year (*Time*, March 23, 1998).

Since 1991 juries have returned well over 500 verdicts on sexual harassment—decisions
that often contradict each other and send mixed signals about how we should behave
anytime we meet a co-worker we'd like to see after five o'clock. As a result, this stuff is
still being sorted out.

Too Close for Comfort

A friend told us this story about her experience with sexual harassment on the job:

> After I was promoted to associate editor, I was assigned an author whose books brought in a lot of money. At 6'5" he was physically frightening as well as fiscally intimidating. With his booming voice and towering bulk, he was just plain scary—and he knew it. He loved to flirt with young women. If a woman didn't play his game, he cut her down to size very fast.

Corporate Mumbo-Jumbo
Federal regulations define *sexual harassment* as "unwelcome sexual advances, requests for sexual favors, and other verbal and physical conduct of a sexual nature when submission to such conduct is made either explicitly or implicitly a term or condition of an individual's employment."

Watch Your Back!
Sexual harassment doesn't necessarily exist just because an employee is offended. Instead, the employee must show that "an ordinary, reasonable, prudent person in like or similar circumstances" would have been similarly offended. In other words, the plaintiff can't argue, "Well, I know a reasonable person would have shrugged this off, but I'm not reasonable and I was offended."

We got along okay for a few weeks until he said to me, "You know, you have the sexiest voice in the company. But I bet every man tells you that." Although I was rattled, I decided that humor was the best way to deal with him, so I laughed off his remark.

A few weeks later, he came into my office, closed the door, and came on to me. Again, I was able to deflect his advances, but this time I told my supervisor. I knew that since Mr. Big Shot Writer was such a huge money maker for the company, if the situation escalated, I'd be the one to go, not him. I didn't know if I was technically being "sexually harassed," but I *did* know that Mr. Big Shot Writer was making me feel really uncomfortable.

I spoke to my supervisor. By law, he had to report the incident to human resources. My supervisor then spoke to Mr. Big Shot Writer. It was really embarrassing, but stopping the incident early saved it from becoming really bad later.

Myth   Sexual harassment is the product of radical man-hating feminists.

Fact   Gender discrimination was added to the Civil Rights Act of 1964 by conservative men who thought it would make the bill fail. It didn't.

According to Title VII of the Civil Rights Act, sexual harassment is any "unwelcome sexual advances, requests for sexual favors, and other verbal and physical conduct of a sexual nature when...

➤ submission to such conduct is made either explicitly or implicitly a term or condition of an individual's employment;

➤ submission to or rejection of such conduct by an individual is used as the basis for employment decisions affecting such individual;

➤ such conduct has the purpose or effect of unreasonably interfering with an individual's work performance or creating an intimidating, hostile, or offensive working environment."

It is up to the courts to evaluate each charge of sexual harassment separately and to determine whether you are indeed a victim——or a perpetrator.

Has It Come to This?

It would be easy to determine sexual harassment if your company was as blatant as this fictitious one:

> "Our company does not discriminate on the basis of race, sex, age, or religion...unless the religions are bizarre and unpopular and can be considered cults (and so may be freely discriminated against) or you are a short, fat, bald, ugly guy (and can be picked on without restraint) or are a nerd, smoker, or single person. Stupid people may now also be discriminated against due to the failure of their lobbying efforts."

You know you've been sexually harassed if the boss says, "Hey, baby, how about some action? I can make it worth your while." But sexual harassment is rarely that clear-cut. How can you tell if you've been sexually harassed? Use the following checklist to see whether your legal rights have been violated—whether you're a man or a woman.

Have You Been Sexually Harassed?

You have been sexually harassed if a co-worker or supervisor has:

❑ 1. Made suggestive comments about your appearance
❑ 2. Subjected you to unwanted touching or other physical contact
❑ 3. Subjected you to unwanted sexual jokes or comments
❑ 4. Made overt sexual advances
❑ 5. Showed you sexual graffiti or pornographic pictures
❑ 6. Asked you about your sexual fantasies, preferences, or activities
❑ 7. Repeatedly asked you for a date after you said no
❑ 8. Made sexual innuendoes, jokes, or comments
❑ 9. Made sexual gestures with his or her hands
❑ 10. Made sexually suggestive facial expressions such as licking lips or wiggling tongue.

Don't Monkey Around with Monkey Business

Myth   I can't afford even to take the chance of getting sued, so I'm going to fire anyone who complains. Even if I win the lawsuit, the legal bills will kill me.

Fact   The prevailing party in a Title VII action can recover their attorney's fees from the losing party.

Corporate Mumbo-Jumbo
Uninstalled is the latest euphemism for being fired. Heard on the voice mail of a vice president at a downsizing computer firm: "You have reached the number of an uninstalled vice president. Please dial our main number and ask the operator for assistance." See also *recruitment*.

Watch Your Back!
Never, never, never keep a record of sexual harassment (or any other possible legal action against the company) on your office computer. The files can become part of the case against you, since they are technically company property. In addition, they might be "accidentally" deleted.

How can you handle sexual harassment without getting uninstalled? First of all, recognize that we're not dealing with something trendy here, like a brave, principled rejection of synthetic fibers. Sexual harassment is ugly, violent, and illegal. If you suspect it has happened to you or is happening to you now, follow these steps:

1. Document exactly what has happened. Keep a written record, noting names, dates, and specific details of the incident.

2. Discretely find out if anyone else in the company has had similar experiences with this person.

3. If the behavior continues, contact your human resources department and lodge a formal complaint.

4. Don't let the situation go on too long. In one famous case, the plaintiff argued, "Well, I wasn't offended at the time, but after I got fired for stealing I talked to some people and found out that a reasonable person would have been offended; I decided to sue anyway." Tacky, tacky—and illegal.

5. If necessary, retain your own attorney.

6. Remember that you are protected by law.

Take Cover

And if you're the boss? Increasingly, company owners are trying to protect themselves by developing sexual harassment policies that are consistent with the law. The policies should be formal and written. Then the policies should be applied consistently and fairly. In addition, back up the discrimination policy with a regular training program. Warns one EEOC official, "Any firm that can't show they have a policy against sexual harassment and work to educate employees about the issue are presumed to, in effect, condone it."

The end of the old patriarchal system, in which male bosses behaved as they pleased with female subordinates, has complicated gender relations in American business. To sort out who is misbehaving now, the law must rely on subjective notions of power and court-ship, sex and sensitivity. The best company policy would allow co-workers their freedom and privacy but punish unwanted, harmful behavior. However, that's a lot easier said than done. To date, no one has figured out exactly what that policy should be—least of all the lawyers and judges who keep adding new caveats to the complex sexual harass-ment laws. Our advice? Err on the side of extreme caution.

Political Road Kill: Sexist Language

➤ Babe-o-Rama, get my coffee—and fast!

➤ Hear the one about the dumb blond and the Wonderbra?

It's as obvious as the Great Wall of China that sexual harassment isn't acceptable in today's business world. But sexist language can be much less obvious—and it can pave the way for sexual harassment.

Sexist language assigns qualities to people on the basis of their gender. It reflects preju-diced attitudes and stereotypical thinking about the sex roles and traits of both men and women. Sexist language discriminates against people by limiting what they can do. And if that's not enough, sexist language also annoys and alienates colleagues and clients, can cause legal problems, and perpetuates sexist attitudes. And it's so *rude*.

Let's look at each of these problems in detail.

1. Sexist language annoys and alienates colleagues and clients.

   As you learned in Chapter 13, women have made substantial progress in obtaining jobs in virtually all managerial and professional specialty occupations.

   Since more than half the women in the United States are in the workforce, women are an economic and political power that can't be ignored. Working women get angry (and rightfully so) at co-workers and businesses that stereotype and patronize them with sexist language.

2. Sexist language causes legal problems.

   The law is increasingly intolerant of biased documents and hostile work environ-ments. Since federal law forbids discrimination on the basis of gender, people writing policy statements, grant proposals, or any other official documents must be very careful not to use any language that could be considered discriminatory. Otherwise, they're just looking for a big, fat, juicy lawsuit.

3. Sexist language perpetuates sexist attitudes.

   A steady diet of sexist language encourages women to have low aspirations, to seek *jobs* rather than *careers*, to think the so-called glass ceiling can't be shattered. Sexist language makes it more difficult for people who have been pushed to the margins to enter the mainstream.

Sexist language is so pervasive that it sometimes seems natural. Nonetheless, sexist language sends a message that the only people with power are white middle-class males. More than half of all Americans are of the female persuasion. If you write "he" and "him," you're ignoring half the people in the country. If you talk about doctors as "he's," you're giving the cold shoulder to female medical doctors—more than one-third of all physicians graduating today. Job descriptions with male pronouns automatically disregard more than half the population.

Level the Playing Field: Bias-Free Language

Use *bias-free language* that treats both sexes neutrally. It doesn't make assumptions about the proper gender for a job, nor does it assume that men take precedence over women. Instead, bias-free language uses words and phrases that don't discriminate on the basis of gender, physical condition, age, race, or anything else. It's office politics in action.

Corporate Mumbo-Jumbo
Bias-free language does not discriminate against people on the basis of sex, physical condition, race, age, or any other category. Use bias-free language and visuals (such as posters, bulletins, and handouts).

Here's how to play fair when you write and speak:

1. Avoid using *he* to refer to both men and women.

   Sexist: He knows how to make a great sales presentation.

   OK: Effective salespeople know how to make great presentations.

2. Avoid using *man* to refer to men and women.

   Sexist: Man is a social creature.

   OK: People are social creatures.

3. Avoid expressions that exclude one sex. Here are some of the most offensive examples and acceptable alternatives:

Protect Your Assets
If you need a substitute for a sexist job title, check the U.S. Department of Labor's "Job Title Revisions to Eliminate Sex-and Age-Referent Language from the Dictionary of Occupational Titles."

Out	In
Mankind	Humanity
The common man	The average person
Old wives' tale	Superstition

4. Avoid language that denigrates people.

   Sexist: Stewardess, Male nurse

   OK: Flight attendant, Nurse

The following chart shows the preferred terms for many common occupations:

Out	In
Businessman	The person's specific title
Chairman	Chair, moderator
Foreman	Supervisor
Salesman	Salesperson
Waitress	Server
Woman lawyer	Lawyer
Workman	Worker, employee (or a specific work title)

Always try to use neutral titles that do not imply whether the job is held only by men or women. Many job titles are already neutral, including the following examples:

Accountant	Banker
Doctor	Engineer
Inspector	Manager
Nurse	Pilot
Technician	Assistant

Watch Your Back!
Watch for phrases that suggest women and men behave in stereotypical ways, such as *talkative women, rugged men, giggling girls, rowdy boys*. Expunge such phrases from your writing and speech.

5. Use the correct courtesy title.

   Use *Mr.* for men and *Ms.* for women, with these two exceptions:

   ➤ In a business setting, professional titles take precedence over *Mr.* and *Ms.* For example, on the job use *Dr.* Rozakis rather than *Ms.* Rozakis.

   ➤ Always use the title the person prefers. Some women prefer Miss or Mrs. to Ms.

If you are not sure what courtesy title to use, check in the company's directory and on previous correspondence to see how the person prefers to be addressed. Also pay attention to the way people introduce themselves.

Protect Your Assets
If you don't know the person's gender, you can call the company and ask the receptionist, use the reader's full name in the salutation (Dear J. Rickels), or use the person's position or job title (Dear Supervisor Dingbat).

Other countries are also developing nonsexist courtesy titles for women. Here are some you're likely to find useful:

Country	Unmarried Woman	Married Woman	Neutral
United States	Miss	Mrs.	Ms.
Denmark	Froken	Fru	Fr.
France	Mademoiselle (Mlle.)	Madame (Mme.)	Mad.
Spain	Senorita (Srta.)	Senora (Sra.)	Sa.
Japan	San	San	San

6. Use plural pronouns and nouns whenever possible.

   Sexist: *He* must check all *his* employees' time cards.

   OK: *Supervisors* must check all employees' time cards.

Newspeak

You're not out of the woods yet, bunky. Language can trap you by being *racist* and *ageist* as well sexist. You wouldn't discriminate against people based on their race, age, or disability—and neither will your words. Walk this way:

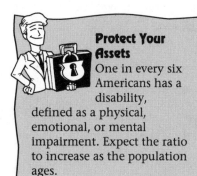

Protect Your Assets
One in every six Americans has a disability, defined as a physical, emotional, or mental impairment. Expect the ratio to increase as the population ages.

1. Refer to a group by the term it prefers.

   Language changes, so stay on the cutting edge. For example, 100 years ago, black people were called "colored." Fifty years later, the term *Negro* was used. Today the preferred terms are *African-American* and *black*. Here are some other changes to put in your Rolodex:

   ➤ Use *Asian,* not "Oriental."

   ➤ Use *Inuit,* not "Eskimo."

   ➤ Use *Latino,* rather than Mexican American, Puerto Rican, Dominican, and other people with Central and Latin American backgrounds.

   ➤ Use *senior citizen* or *senior,* not "old people."

2. Focus on people, not their conditions.

   Biased: mentally retarded

   Nonbiased: people with mental retardation

   Biased: the blind

Nonbiased: people with vision impairments

Biased: cancer patients

Nonbiased: people being treated for cancer

Biased: abnormal, afflicted, struck down

Nonbiased: atypical

3. Only give someone's race if it is relevant. And if you do mention one person's race, be sure to mention the race of everyone else.

Interviewspeak

By the by, it's illegal to ask about race, religion, or marital status on a job interview. Of course, that doesn't stop employers from doing so. Although you're within your rights to say, "I don't think that question is legal," you're more likely to get the job if you use a more low-key dodge (assuming you still want to work for the person). Rephrase the question and treat it as a legitimate request for information. For example:

Question	"Aren't you just looking for a husband?"
Answer	"You may be asking whether I'll stay with the company long enough to justify the expense of training me. Well, I'm not promising to work for you for the rest of my life, just as you're not promising to employ me for the rest of my life. How long I stay will depend on whether my assignments continue to be challenging and whether I can advance in the company."

Fly on the Wall

Lookism is another fact of office life. It is quite common for employers to keep a negative stereotype about race or gender to themselves, but stereotypes about looks seem much more acceptable. Discrimination against overweight women is the most rampant form of lookism.

Just ask former CBS morning personality Kathleen Sullivan. In 1994 she resurfaced as a speaker for Weight Watchers. Before her reemergence, she had been unceremoniously dumped by CBS because of three widely publicized factors: she had gotten a divorce, she had gained weight, and she had let her hair go gray.

Her new position grabbed the media's attention. On an interview with Tom Snyder's CNBC show, Sullivan revealed that her exile had been very painful.

The Least You Need to Know

➤ Flash: Men and women *are* different. But gender has nothing to do with a person's ability to get a job done.

➤ Treat people equally and fairly on the job, regardless of their gender.

➤ Sexual harassment is against the law. Don't do it and don't take it.

➤ Sexist language annoys and alienates colleagues and clients and may cause legal problems.

➤ Use bias-free language.

➤ Avoid sexism, ageism, lookism, and any other discriminatory behavior, even if it doesn't end in *ism*.

Taking the Show on the Road

In This Chapter

➤ Office politics and travel

➤ The global marketplace and business travel

➤ Travel hints to keep you on the top of the heap

➤ Entertainment reports

➤ Why love on the run

Travel Truisms

1. No flight ever leaves on time unless you are running late and need the delay to make the flight.

2. If you are running late for a flight, it will depart from the farthest gate within the terminal.

3. If you arrive very early for a flight, it inevitably will be delayed.

4. Flights never leave from gate 1 at any terminal in the world.

5. If you must work on your flight, you will experience turbulence as soon as you touch pen to paper. Or start to drink your coffee.

6. If you are assigned a middle seat, you can determine who has the seats on the aisle and the window while you are still in the boarding area. Just look for the two passengers you definitely wouldn't want to sit between.

7. Only passengers seated in window seats ever have to get up to go to the lavatory.

8. The crying baby on board your flight is always seated next to you.

9. The best-looking woman/man on your flight is never seated next to you.

10. The less carry-on luggage space available on an aircraft, the more carry-on luggage passengers will bring aboard.

Corporate Mumbo-Jumbo
Frequent business traveler (FBT) is the term for the new breed of worker for whom globalization is a way of life.

Protect Your Assets
Nearly all large companies make travel arrangements through their corporate travel division or a specific travel agency. This system streamlines operations and helps the company get the best deals. If you make your own travel plans, however, we recommend that you cozy up to one travel agency that can become familiar with your travel needs, such as special meal requirements, and seat locations.

Office politics don't end when you take the show on the road. When you travel for business, you're applying your political skills in a new location—with a new set of people and problems. Piece of cake? In your dreams! Traveling for the company has more potholes than a city street. This chapter shows you how to make the most of your out-of-office experiences. You learn how to use office politics to get ahead even when you've lost track of where you are.

New York to California, Three Times Daily

Business trip = 1 part business + 6 parts boredom

Precious hours spent waiting in airports for late planes. Whole nights shot circling the sky in fog, thunder, and lightning. Endless streams of highways, dotted with seemingly identical rest stops. Nights watching television in dismal hotel rooms. Lonely room service meals; greasy burgers grabbed on the run. Days spent schmoozing with clients. Ah, the joys of business travel.

It's all worth it, however, if you get what you want—and you wouldn't if you didn't take flight.

An increasing number of today's workers inhabit a community of air that's responsible only to the imperatives of commerce. The "borderless economy" we hear so much about now means that some business people live everywhere—and nowhere—at once. And with the speed of global communications, they can be anywhere tomorrow. They live and work in a global marketplace that asks them to move as fast as it does. It's not unusual for these workers to log 100,000-plus miles a year. In essence, they are the traveling salespeople of the millennium, toting their personal digital assistants and laptops to intercontinental meetings and clients around the world. Perhaps they're supersonic versions of ancient Bedouin merchants!

Global Worker

How has the work-a-day-world changed? Check out these facts:

➤ In 1932 the busiest airport in the world was Berlin's Tempelhof. About 34,000 passengers per year passed through its doors.

➤ Today more than 35,000 passengers pass through Chicago's O'Hare airport in just three hours—for a total of 70 million people a year.

➤ Dallas-Fort Worth International Airport is larger than Manhattan.

Some of today's new business travelers may not have a real office or even a car, since they do all their work electronically. One social critic has called these traveling workers "resident expatriates" because they live as if they were abroad even when at home. How can you tell if you're a member of this new breed of global workers? Try our little quiz. Write yes or no for each question.

Global Worker Quiz

_____ 1. I check the Cirrus signs to figure out where I am.

_____ 2. I find myself hunting for lunch at 4:00 a.m.

_____ 3. The only TV I watch is CNN.

_____ 4. I rely on World Phones to keep in touch with a partner 17 time zones away.

_____ 5. My phone bill is greater than the national debt of a small banana republic.

_____ 6. When I need to see a dentist, I get on an 11-hour flight.

_____ 7. When I'm asked to identify myself, I give a 16-digit number.

_____ 8. I have 1.5 million frequent flier miles—on every major airline.

_____ 9. If I'm sitting in a chair, I automatically look for the video monitor in the armrest.

_____ 10. I know there's a putting green in the Palm Springs airport, a casino in Amsterdam's Schiphol, and a bowling alley in the Frankfurt airport.

Score Yourself

10–8	yes	What's your nickname—"red eye"?
7–5	yes	If this is Tuesday, it must be Tampa—or was that Tonga?
4–0	yes	You have at least one foot on the ground.

Watch Your Back!
Frequent flyers can get more than just platinum points. Frequent flying can lead to severe back injuries and hearing loss. Injuries caused by objects tumbling from overhead bins result in a significant number of accidents; low oxygen levels in cabin air can cause dizziness.

Protect Your Assets
When you fly, always try to get an aisle seat. It gives you more leg room and freedom to move around the plane. An aisle bulkhead is the closest you can get to comfort without flying business class or first class.

Watch Your Back!
Make sure that the purpose of your travel assignment is to accomplish legitimate business and not to undermine your career or take you out of the loop. Many an unsuspecting worker is sent on a trip and returns to discover an office coup...and a sharp reduction in responsibilities.

Now, perhaps your travel schedule is far less hectic than the one we've described here; nonetheless, it's highly unlikely that you're going to spend your entire career earthbound. Odds are, you're in for some serious business travel.

Shackled to the Shuttle

How closely do you fit the profile of the typical business traveler of today? Compare your reality to these facts:

➤ 55% of all business travelers are married men between 36 to 45 years old

➤ 33% are women

➤ 25% are younger than 35

➤ 25% are not married

➤ 72% work for someone else

➤ 5% take 5 or fewer business trips a year.

➤ 15% take 6 to 10 business trips a year.

➤ 27% take 11 to 20 business trips a year.

➤ 53% take 21 or more business trips a year.

➤ 67% of all single women look forward to business trips.

➤ 48% of all single men look forward to business trips.

➤ 52% of married women dread business trips.

➤ 30% of married men dread business trips.

➤ 63% of all business travelers polled want more comfortable airline seats.

➤ 55% don't drink while they're airborne.

[*Source:* New York Times, *March 8, 1998*]

A Lean, Mean, Travel Machine

Company travel helps you accomplish important business, secure new business, and make key contacts. To make the most of your work on the road (or in the air), travel lean and mean. Translation? When you travel, lean on no one and mean business. Here are some more suggestions that we've learned the hard way:

1. Take seat work.

   Bring some reading material or paperwork with you. Not only will you stave off boredom, you'll squeeze in a little extra work time.

2. Remember sleep, nature's candy.

   Get sufficient sleep the week before the trip. If you're well rested, you'll do better work. You'll also be less likely to get cranky when something goes wrong—and it always does, because that's life.

3. Lay off the booze.

   A few gin-and-tonics may relax you, but they definitely do not make you charming. We have met a lot of drinkers, and even the nicest ones become jerks when soused. It's amazing what 30 to 40 glasses of champagne will do to a person.

   Also, booze or no booze, this is not the time to tell the boss what you thought of the last memo or blast a colleague for a goof-up in the widgets shipment.

4. Carry all essential items with you.

   Essentials include clothing and all business items, such as laptop computers, calculators, disks, slides, books, and hotel information. This way, you can still function if your luggage is lost. Never check important items.

5. Card me.

   Make two index cards with all your travel information on them—your flight numbers, hotels addresses and telephone numbers, rental cars confirmations, and so on. Take one card with you and leave the other with your assistant or an associate. This information helps you reconfirm your travel plans and helps people in the office reach you.

   A little courtesy is the hallmark of good office politics. It shows your consideration and sense of responsibility.

6. Know your itinerary.

   Be sure to bring a copy of your itinerary and leave a copy with your assistant or associate.

7. Travel light.

   If you forget it, you can always buy it or make do. Shampoo makes a great laundry detergent, for example.

Protect Your Assets
Entertain clients in a club, restaurant, or public place—never in your hotel room. You can have a gathering in a hotel *suite*, but be sure it's not intimate.

8. Cover your tracks.

   Be sure to let all your clients know that you'll be on a business trip. The easiest way to do this is by changing your voice mail message. In addition to showing your sense of responsibility, this helps prevent embarrassing slip-ups and thwarts dishonest colleagues from stepping in to save the day.

9. Buy small.

   Try to avoid buying large souvenirs. Not only does this extravagance remind your colleagues that you may have more disposable income than they do, but it also looks astonishingly unprofessional to be lugging home a 10-foot carved horse's head that you just could not live without.

10. Don't brag.

   Resist the temptation to brag to your office-bound colleagues about the wonderful time you had on your last business trip, about how close you and the boss got, and how this will lead to Great Things for your career. We guarantee that the auditor locked in the vault during tax season won't revel in your tales of sinking putts on the Scottish moors between (very brief) meetings. Likewise, the overworked, underpaid systems analyst won't cheer at your account of a $500 dinner.

   When the trip was wonderful, the best political move you can make is zipping your lip. If the trip was a disaster, there's even less reason to spread the bad word. If you have to talk about the trip, be polite and noncommittal.

11. Take care of business.

   Above all, remember that a business trip is just that—a trip to accomplish business. Want to see Goofy and the rest of the gang? Go on your own time. The company is footing the bill to make sure you accomplish certain goals. This is not the time to play tourist—unless it's clearly part of business.

Watch Your Back!
It's never a good idea to eat foods that are unfamiliar, regional, unknown, or unidentifiable. Stay away from mystery meats or anything that resembles what was served in your junior high school cafeteria. Few things put the kibosh on a business trip faster than an upset stomach.

Protect Your Assets
Most companies provide corporate credit cards for employees who travel on company business. The card is to be used for all business-related expenses, such as airfare, car rentals, other ground transpiration, hotels, and meals. Check your company's travel policy for specific information.

Hey, It's on the Company!

According to American Express Travel-Related Services, business travelers spend more than $156 billion a year on "T & E"—travel and entertainment—sometimes with the help of a little creative accounting.

At Sotheby's, the famous auction house, the annual travel and entertainment budget for a single manager during the high-flying 1980s sometimes ran as high as $200,000 a year. But in these days of rightsized management and tighter purse strings, T & E budgets are a lot tighter—and apt to come under much closer scrutiny.

Arguing that management "owes it to me," some employees do a little sleight of hand when it comes to totaling up their travel expenses. Hairdressing appointments, home renovation, traffic tickets, and other personal expenses get buried under such legitimate headings as "meals" or "ground transportation." A little fudging here, a little fudging there—and voila! The company has paid for that new jacket, briefcase, or wallpaper.

Resist the urge to be creative when it comes to filling out your expense report. *Creative accounting* is simply another term for fraud. Your expense report is fact, not fiction. You should be able to explain everything on it. You have our blessing to write a novel, but just don't disguise it as your expense report. Here's what a sample expense report looks like:

	Name: _____	Department: _____					
	Title: _____	Project: _____					
	Date(s) of travel: _____						
	Sun	Mon	Tues	Wed	Thurs	Fri	Sat
Transportation							
air/train	___	___	___	___	___	___	___
car service	___	___	___	___	___	___	___
car rental	___	___	___	___	___	___	___
taxis	___	___	___	___	___	___	___
personal car	___	___	___	___	___	___	___
parking	___	___	___	___	___	___	___
other	___	___	___	___	___	___	___
Lodging							
room charge	___	___	___	___	___	___	___
room tax	___	___	___	___	___	___	___
telephone	___	___	___	___	___	___	___
other	___	___	___	___	___	___	___
Meals							
breakfast	___	___	___	___	___	___	___
lunch	___	___	___	___	___	___	___
dinner	___	___	___	___	___	___	___
other	___	___	___	___	___	___	___
Entertaining	___	___	___	___	___	___	___
Employee signature	_____						
Approvals	_____						
	_____						

Your Cheatin' Heart

Polished and self-assured, Nick spends half his time on the road as a representative for a multinational company. Married for more than 20 years, he's been all over the world: Europe, the Middle East, America, Canada, and Latin America. Traveling for business is often boring and dreary, so Nick has allowed himself some solace. "When I'm on the road, it's like I'm in a parallel universe where adultery doesn't break the rules," he says.

For some, an affair while on a company trip relieves the loneliness of being away from home. For others, it's a way to prove they're still hot. It's a quick thrill, a victimless crime in distant emotional territory.

Watch Your Back!
Be sure to include *original* receipts for all expenses. Otherwise, you run the risk of not being reimbursed for the money you laid out. Ouch! Also, it's a good idea to keep copies of all your receipts and expense reports.

Ever notice that **TR**avel and **TR**ouble both start the same way? Business travel is a minefield of sexual temptation. You're away from home, feeling loose. You're free from the libido-deadening mire of your routine. Add the seductive properties of a hotel lounge, an in-room minibar, and pay-per-view porn, and many workers find themselves unexpectedly engaging in customer relations of the vertical variety. The problem is, after the hokeypokey, your mind is often flooded with regret, especially if the dirty dancing costs you your job.

When you're traveling for the company, remember that you're still in an office setting, even if you're outside the office. This is not the time to make time with your colleagues; share some especially juicy confidences; or let your hair down in any way, shape, or form. Maintain your professional dignity, no matter who's prancing naked in the pool. Even if everyone's drunk, someone will remember the details in the morning. You can bet your bonus on it.

Let's look at a specific example of travel nookie gone astray.

You Play, You Pay

We got this tale from an acquaintance.

I just slept with one of my clients. I know it was a mistake, but we were away on business, and one thing led to another. If my boss finds out, I'll almost certainly be fired. What do I do now?

Here's what we say. What's boinked is boinked. Now it's time for damage control. If the liaison was mutually satisfying and had clearly defined boundaries—meaning it was one-stop shopping and the client doesn't expect future service calls—we wouldn't panic. Chances are, the client isn't going to benefit from the dalliance going public, either. To lessen the odds of becoming the item du jour on the office grapevine, mum's the word. This means no bragging, no knowing winks at the next focus group, and no more interfacing at corporate conferences.

Family Matters

Protect Your Assets
Leave the kids at home, no matter how well be-haved and adorable you think they are. No one ever thinks your kids are as charming, brilliant, and delightful as you do.

Every now and then, you'll get the chance to bring a spouse, significant other, or main squeeze along on a business trip.

If you are invited to bring a spouse on a business trip, be sure to bring your own. Even in this day of mix-and-match marriages, most corporations breathe easier when you arrive with the spouse to whom you are actually wed. We've been on business trips when the Mrs. was the mistress.

➤ If you are heterosexual and single, don't bring your significant other. This is more than some executives and their spouses can handle.

➤ If you are gay, don't bring your significant other. See above.

The Least You Need to Know

➤ Plan on doing at least some business-related travel in your career. It's as unavoidable as Musak, Mickey, and McDonalds.

➤ When you travel, lean on no one and mean business.

➤ Travel well rested, well prepared, and well mannered.

➤ Your expense report is fact, not fiction.

➤ TRavel and TRouble both start the same way. If you play, you'll most likely pay.

➤ If you can bring along a spouse, bring your own.

Part 6
Upward Bound

To get promoted, you're often going to be asked to write your own "Performance Review," an experience not unlike being asked to dig your own grave. Here are 10 self-assessments that employees actually wrote on their Performance Reviews:

➤ *"Planned and held up numerous meetings."*

➤ *"I am a hard worker, but I don't do well with change, such as mergers, acquisitions, downsizing, relocating, and new phone systems."*

➤ *"I have correct and civil relationships with IBM PCs."*

➤ *"I am very dependable, fast leaner."*

➤ *"Typing speed of 40–50 rpm."*

➤ *"You have nothing to loose by promoting me."*

➤ *"Outside activities: A bell ringer for the Salivating Army."*

➤ *"Willing to relocate to a residence in an upscale neighborhood on waterfront, with easy access to mass transit."*

➤ *"I prefer to work alone in maximum privacy."*

➤ *"I am entirely through in my work; no detail gets by me."*

As you can tell, this section also covers how to get a new job…

Soldier of Fortune: Getting Promoted

In This Chapter

➤ Performance reviews

➤ 360-degree reviews

➤ The importance of writing

➤ The art of negotiating

➤ Learning how to listen

➤ The matter of revenge

➤ Setting goals—and achieving them

A mangy looking guy went into a bar and ordered a drink. The bartender said, "No way. I don't think you can pay for it."

The guy said, "You're right. I don't have any money, but if I show you something you haven't seen before, will you give me a drink?" The bartender said, "Deal!" and the guy pulled out a hamster. The hamster ran to the piano and started playing Gershwin songs. The bartender said, "You're right. I've never seen anything like that before. That hamster is really good on the piano." They guy downed the drink and asked the bartender for another.

"Money or another miracle or no drink," said the bartender. The guy pulled out a frog. He put the frog on the bar, and the frog started to sing. He had a marvelous voice and great pitch. A fine singer.

Another man in the bar offered $300 for the frog. The guy said, "It's a deal." He took the $300 and gave the stranger the frog. The stranger ran out of the bar.

The bartender said, "Are you nuts? You sold a singing frog for $300? It must have been worth millions. You must be crazy."

"Not so," said the guy. "The hamster is also a ventriloquist."

You have to be willing to speak up for yourself. In this chapter, you learn all about using performance reviews to set the stage for advancement. Then you learn some effective ways to negotiate for what you want—and deserve.

Judge and Jury

As you hone your skill at office politics, you must learn to expect the unexpected and use it to your advantage. That's why you need cover your bases by doing the best job you can. But remember one of the cardinal rules of office life: appearance = reality. It's not just enough to do a good job—everyone must know that you're the greatest thing since sliced bread, sitcoms, and Stairmasters. But even if the buzz about your work is positive, you still need it in writing. That's where *performance reviews* come in.

Corporate Mumbo-Jumbo

A *performance review* is an assessment of a worker's accomplishments, including such factors as leadership, project management, and expense control. Performance reviews are usually an annual procedure, although they may take place several times a year for probationary employees.

In theory, a performance review is designed to be a positive interaction between a boss and an employee working together to achieve maximum performance. If not handled properly, however, it can be a replay of the Spanish Inquisition. Getting a really bad performance review is like a starring role in the fourth-grade play—the one where you suddenly forgot all your words and froze in horror.

During a performance review, your task is to present your accomplishments in specific detail and your failures in a positive light. No whining, finger-pointing, or throwing sand in someone else's shorts.

Protect Your Assets

Can't remember what you ate for dinner last night, where you put the car keys, and your anniversary—much less how much money you saved the company last quarter by designing an exciting new paradigm? We suggest you keep a running log of all your sterling accomplishments. Also note your problems and how you solved them. Jot down names, dates, and details.

Shoot Yourself in the Foot, Part I

During a performance review, no matter how much good stuff your boss noted, you will always zero in on the one bad thing you did—or didn't do. Like a lemming marching to the sea, you'll throw yourself off a cliff trying to explain your way out of the past year's fiasco. And even if it was an itty-bitty-teeny-weenie fiasco, you'll manage to blow it up to epic proportions. We don't know why this is. Perhaps humans undergoing a performance review have a built-in self-destruct button, like a moth drawn to a porch light. Whatever the reason, it's not a good thing.

Here's our advice: Focus on the big picture. If necessary, ask the supervisor writing your evaluation for time to read it alone. Then set up an appointment to discuss it. Keep in mind that in some companies, managers are expected to have some area in the evaluation that is "in need of improvement." Even if you walk on (unfrozen) water, they are obligated to put in some negative comment. Hey, otherwise, you'd be perfect...and then you'd already have their job.

Shoot Yourself in the Foot, Part II

Absolute truth, like Caribbean vacations, may be a luxury you can't always afford—especially when it comes to performance reviews. The following story illustrates this point. The tale comes from a lowly foot soldier in the minefield of performance reviews.

> At my company, the first round of yearly performance appraisal involves filling out our own evaluation forms. There are a number of categories such as creativity, initiative, growth, and so on. There are spaces on the form for the employee to fill in "strengths" and "growth opportunities." Then a supervisor takes our input and creates our evaluation.
>
> Since I was new to all of this, I made the mistake of being completely truthful. I tried to identify as many growth opportunities as possible. Fortunately, a co-worker looked over my shoulder and stopped me before I finished my attempt at self-immolation. My co-worker explained that management automatically spits back any growth opportunities to employees as examples of poor performance.

Watch Your Back!
Anything that gets put into writing about your work becomes part of your permanent record. Since it usually takes a nuclear blast to remove anything from your permanent record, be very careful of what goes into your performance evaluation. If need be, call in a union representative or attorney during a performance review gone sour to safeguard your rights and reputation—not to mention your job and benefits.

As this story illustrates, if you're not politically savvy, writing your own performance review can be like digging your own grave.

Turnabout Isn't Fair Play

Some companies have sunk to a new level of hell with a "360-degree review." Under this system, each employee gets to review subordinates, colleagues, and the bosses. This process can be just like root canal without anesthesia, only a lot less fun. That's why you need to listen to us. The last thing you want to do is hand in negative evaluations of your subordinates, co-workers, and supervisors.

Corporate Mumbo-Jumbo
A *360-degree review* involves having your performance assessed by your co-workers, subordinates, and supervisors.

Watch Your Back!
Beware of sneak attacks. Unscrupulous companies can ambush employees during performance reviews by setting up adversarial situations. For example, you might be confronted by five supervisors, the human resources chief, and the company attorney at what you assumed to be a meeting just between you and your boss. Always try to find out who will be present at your evaluation so you can come prepared with your own big guns if necessary. If there's a problem, you should have picked up the signs earlier.

Becky was on her deathbed, with her husband Jake at her side. He held her cold hand and tears silently streamed down his face. Her pale lips moved. "Jake," she said.

"Hush," he quickly interrupted. "Don't talk."

But she insisted. "Jake," she said in her tired voice. "I have to talk. I must confess."

"There is nothing to confess," said the weeping Jake. "It's all right. Everything's all right."

"No, no. I must die in peace. I must confess, Jake, that I have been unfaithful to you." Jake stroked her hand.

"Now Becky, don't be concerned. I know all about it," he sobbed. "Why else would I poison you?"

Remember the advice your momma gave you when you were just a tike? It went something like this: If you can't say anything nice, don't say anything at all. A 360-degree review is not the time to get back at your co-workers because they have an office with a window, have nicer shoes, or make more money than you do (and you don't think they deserve *any* of it). It's also not the time to stick it to mailroom staff for reading your last issue of *Soldier of Fortune* magazine and getting mustard on the back cover. And it most definitely is not the time to machine-gun your supervisor, either.

If you're sucked into this swamp, follow these guidelines:

➤ Focus on innocuous topics.

➤ Choose your words carefully. Stay away from loaded words like *unqualified*, *incompetent*, and *knuckle-headed*, even if they are true—especially if they are true.

➤ Never forget that what goes around comes around. You stick it to someone, and odds are they're going to stick it to you. So play nice. No revenge.

Sneak Peak

If you're a newcomer to the wonderful world of performance reviews, you may not have gotten a chance to look at one of these wonderful documents. If you're an old hand, your company may just now be jumping on the bandwagon. Perhaps you're moving on to the Monster Monolithic Company and don't know what to expect by way of assessment. For all these reasons and our genuine love of torture, we hereby present a model performance review, culled from samples used by large and small companies. Expect all this and more as managers increasingly scramble to cover their butts, forestall lawsuits, and maybe even get around to helping workers do their jobs more effectively.

Performance Review

Employee Name _____

Employee's Present Rank and Title _____

Date _____

Manager/Supervisor's Name _____

Instructions: Rank the employee in each category according to the following scale. Include relevant supporting detail.

> 1 = Unsatisfactory
> 2 = Needs improvement
> 3 = Competent
> 4 = Exceeds responsibilities
> 5 = Outstanding

Performance Standards **Ranking and Details**

1. **Job Skills** _____
   Applies skills appropriately
   Understands tasks
   Understands role within company
   Continues training
   Takes initiative

2. **Oral Communication Skills** _____
   Verbal expression clear
   Listens well
   Solicits responses

3. **Written Communication Skills** _____
   Written expression clear
   Writes concisely and clearly

4. **Interpersonal Skills** _____
   Interfaces well with others
   Effective team member
   Promotes open communication
   Manages diversity

5. **Leadership Skills** _____
   Inspires teamwork
   Positive role model
   Confident
   Encourages idealism
   Resolves conflicts well

6. **Ability to Make Decisions** _____
   Analyzes and evaluates choices
   Makes and implements decisions
   Accepts responsibility

7. **Ability to Solve Problems** _____
   Identifies problems
   Analyzes solutions
   Chooses best course of action
   Seizes opportunities

8. **Organizational Skills** _____
   Staff selection skills
   Policy management ability
   Evaluation skills
   Delegates responsibility
   Budget planning
   Expense control
   Maintains deadlines
   Achieves goals

9. **Planning Skills** _____
   Implements change
   Establishes priorities
   Coordinates resources
   Sets schedules
   Maintains schedules
   Manages time well

10. **Creativity** _____
    Innovative thinking
    Original concepts
    Fresh approaches

Overall Performance Rating _____

Summary

1. Strengths

   _____

   _____

   _____

2. Areas for Improvement

   _____

   _____

   _____

3. Personal Growth and Development

   _____

   _____

   _____

4. Next Year's Goals

   _____

   _____

   _____

Employee Response (Attach additional pages if necessary)

   _____

   _____

   _____

Employee's Signature   Date

_____   _____

Supervisor's Signature   Date

_____   _____

See Dick Cringe, See Jane Scream

Most supervisors are not masters of prose. Some can't even string together two words in any logical order. Maybe they slept through 11th-grade English; maybe they're just nincompoops. Whatever the reason for their inability to express themselves in standard written English, it's bad news for you, sweet potato. Why? Because most bosses can't write a coherent sentence; they fall back on space fillers like "the point I am trying to make," "what I mean to say," and "in view of the fact that." Then you get a healthy dose of jargon: empowerment, vision, proactive activity. This kind of review leaves you in a nice pickle because you're not getting any specific guidance. How can you improve your performance if you're not given clear and specific suggestions? Here's what we mean:

What They Wrote	What They Meant
➤ Average	➤ Not too bright
➤ Slightly below average	➤ Stupid
➤ Exceptionally well qualified	➤ No major blunders to date
➤ Active socially	➤ We need to unglue the phone from his/her ear
➤ Zealous attitude	➤ Opinionated
➤ Character above reproach	➤ Still one step ahead of the law
➤ Unlimited potential	➤ Will stick with us until retirement
➤ Quick thinking	➤ Offers plausible excuses
➤ Takes pride in work	➤ Conceited
➤ Stern disciplinarian	➤ Real jerk
➤ Tactful when dealing with superiors	➤ Knows when to keep mouth shut
➤ Approaches difficult problems with logic	➤ Finds someone else to do the job
➤ Keen analyst	➤ Thoroughly confused
➤ Expresses self well	➤ Can string two sentences together
➤ Spends extra hours on the job	➤ Miserable home life
➤ Conscientious and careful	➤ Terrified
➤ Meticulous attention to detail	➤ Nitpicker
➤ Demonstrates leadership	➤ Has a loud voice
➤ Maintains professional attitude	➤ Snobby
➤ Keen sense of humor	➤ Knows a lot of dirty jokes
➤ Strong adherence to principles	➤ Pigheaded
➤ Of great value to the company	➤ Turns in work on time
➤ Unusually loyal	➤ Not wanted by anyone else
➤ Alert to company news	➤ Office gossip
➤ Hard worker	➤ Does it the hard way
➤ Enjoys job	➤ Needs more to do
➤ Competent	➤ Still able to get work done if supervisor helps
➤ Happy	➤ Paid too much

What They Wrote	What They Meant
➤ Deserves promotion	➤ Create a new title to make him/her feel appreciated
➤ Will go far	➤ Relative of management
➤ Should go far	➤ Pa-lease!

Write Angles

You can't get promoted if you're not getting the guidance you need from your bosses. After all, how can you do what they want if you don't have the slightest idea *what* they want? How can you protect yourself against empty performance reviews that lead you down dead-end streets? Learn to write clearly, concisely, and correctly. Write now.

Here are some of the skills you should master:

➤ Spelling

➤ Punctuation

➤ Parts of speech

➤ Pronoun reference

➤ Verb tense

➤ Dangling modifiers

➤ Misplaced modifiers

➤ Parallel structure

➤ Sentence structure

➤ Capitalization

➤ Diction (word choice)

➤ Writing style

Protect Your Assets
Are your grammarphobic? Check out *The Complete Idiot's Guide to Grammar and Style*. It's a complete grammar course that actually makes grammar fun and easy to learn.

Even if you don't have any control over the actual contents of the performance review, if you can write well, you have mastery of your response. When you refute unfair charges and unclear directions clearly in writing, you demonstrate your excellence and desire to contribute to the company. According to some sources, the ability to write well is one of the most important factors in a person's advancement in any company.

Never Assume

Never assume that

➤ The people you work with will cooperate

➤ You understand anyone's motive or agenda

➤ You can't be out on your butt *justlikethat*

You must learn to use office politics to negotiate for the promotions, raises, and other prizes that you want—and deserve.

As you discuss your performance review and your goals with your supervisor, you should

➤ Anticipate key moves.

➤ Recognize hidden power plays.

➤ Assess risk.

➤ Prevent misunderstandings.

➤ Counter intimidation.

➤ Uncover hidden motives.

➤ Handle verbal and emotional abuse.

➤ React appropriately to accusations.

Watch Your Back!
Don't wait to negotiate until you're halfway out the door. As a vital part of your political campaign, you should negotiate whenever necessary to achieve the results you desire in your personal and career goals.

Try these five ideas as well:

1. Encourage and build on offers for advancement, learning new skills, and positions of responsibility.

2. Give concessions that do not destroy your position.

3. Do not be afraid to say no if you know you can do better with another offer. For example, if your boss offers you a promotion in a year and you believe you deserve one now, state your case and support it.

4. Work at gaining trust.

5. Stay flexible and focused.

Remember that in negotiations, timing is everything. Control vital information until it can be used to your advantage. Position yourself to gain the information you need without tipping your hand.

What happens if your boss is playing hardball? How can you recognize these tactics? Hardball negotiators:

➤ Keep their position and insist on what they want

➤ Zero in on your ideas and position

➤ May use personal attacks and dirty tricks

➤ Use stress tactics to throw you off balance

➤ Often have hidden agendas

If your boss is playing hardball, simply stick to your agenda and continue to look for other ways to get what you want. In negotiations, this tactic can be difficult because the hardball negotiator is likely to throw you off course by looking for every opportunity to make conditions more difficult for you. Successful negotiators maintain control over their emotions and look for opportunities to advance their position.

Protect Your Assets
Speaking is a two-way process. It involves not only making contact with the audience but also receiving feedback from them.

How's That Again?

You can't negotiate unless you're really listening to what your boss is saying. It's not enough to be a good speaker; you also have to be a good listener.

There are three main kinds of listening:

1. Empathic Listening

   The purpose with this type of listening is to provide the speaker with emotional support to help him or her come to a decision, solve a problem, or resolve a situation. This type of listening focuses more on emotions than on reason or ethics. As an empathic listener, you can restate the issues, ask questions, and critically analyze the issues.

2. Informational Listening

   With this kind of task, the listener gathers as many facts as possible. The focus is on accuracy of perception. You do this type of listening when your boss asks you questions and offers comments. Informational listening demands that you focus on specific details, distinguish among different pieces of information, and organize the information into a meaningful whole.

Watch Your Back!
Pseudolistening occurs when you only go through the motions of listening. You look like you're listening, but your mind is miles away. *Self-centered listening* is focusing on your own response rather than on the speaker's words (a common mistake to make in a performance review). *Selective listening* happens when you listen only to those parts of a message that directly concern you. Correct these listening problems to enable you to get what you want—and deserve.

3. Evaluative Listening

Here's where you weigh what has been said to see if you agree with it or not. Start the process with informational listening to make sure that you have all the facts. When you are fairly sure that you understand the issues, you can then evaluate them and make decisions based on the facts, evidence, and speaker's credibility. You should use this is the type of listening when you negotiate with your boss.

Get Mad, Get Even, or Get Better: What Would You Do?

Few setbacks in a business career are more painful than getting rejected, whether it's for a project, promotion, or a position. In such situations, it's tempting to following John F. Kennedy's rule: "Don't get mad. Get even." It's especially seductive to sabotage your dog of a boss.

And what's really important? To find out, we polled managers, directors, and CEO's in several different businesses, people we admire for their ability to use office politics skillfully. Here are 12 qualities they look for in effective employees:

Fairness	Honesty	Personal discipline
Thoughtfulness	Maturity	Decisiveness
Objectivity	Intelligence	Determination
Integrity	Sincerity	Trustworthiness

What do you think will help you get where you want to be? To find out, rank these 12 qualities from most to least important.

Most Important	Important	Least Important
_____	_____	_____
_____	_____	_____
_____	_____	_____
_____	_____	_____

Now set about demonstrating these qualities to your co-workers and the powers that be. Remember, citizen, you have the powers of right and good on your side. And good always triumphs over evil.

266

The Least You Need to Know

➤ During a performance review, present your accomplishments in specific detail and your failures in a positive light.

➤ Focus on the big picture.

➤ Learn to write clearly, concisely, and correctly.

➤ When you negotiate, control key information until you can use it to your advantage.

➤ Learn to use good listening skills, including empathic listening, informational listening, and evaluative listening.

➤ Revenge is usually self-destructive. Instead, concentrate on developing and demonstrating your skills.

Chapter 24

When Someone Has to Go— Making Sure It's Not You

In This Chapter

➤ The state of American business

➤ Warning signs of an impending layoff

➤ Ways to survive downsizing, rightsizing, and plain old firings

➤ Mentors and what they can do for you

A friend of ours who works for a large communications firm shared this story:

> After some "downsizing" in our department, a group of us went to the VP and asked about our job security. He replied, "You are 100 percent secure."
>
> Two days later, we got pink slips for a month-end layoff.
>
> The following week the president came to speak to us. He said, "I know you have gotten conflicting information in the past, but yours will be the last layoff for now. That should make you feel better."
>
> It didn't....

This chapter explains how to avoid going down with the ship. First, you learn how to tell if your job is in danger. You find out how to recognize the warning signs of an impending layoff. Then you learn some effective methods for maximizing your chances for staying employed. Finally, you explore the advantages and disadvantages of having a mentor.

I've Been What?

Let's start with a little vocabulary quiz. What do each of the following words have in common?

1. Downsized
2. Restructured
3. Reengineered
4. Made redundant
5. Terminated
6. Dehired
7. Correct-sized
8. Rightsized
9. Selected out
10. Vocationally relocated
11. Payroll adjusted
12. Skills-mixed adjusted
13. Constructively dismissed
14. Given a career-change opportunity
15. Uninstalled

Corporate Mumbo-Jumbo
The term *corporate anorexia* was coined to describe the debilitating business disease resulting from excessive belt-tightening. Some companies have trimmed so much "fat" that their ribs are showing.

Watch Your Back!
It's easy to get complacent about job security. After all, you've been working in the same company for a decade and nothing ever changes. Just because nothing has ever been shaken up before doesn't mean that it will stay the same forever.

The answer? Every one of these terms means the same thing: *fired, canned, booted out, dumped, kicked out, sent packing.* It means you're out on your ear, walking the line, collecting unemployment (if you're lucky). The enormous rise in corporate uncertainty today has resulted in new terms to soften the harsh reality that people are losing jobs and having trouble finding new ones.

Here's a tale we heard from a relative:

> As an intern at a public relations firm, I was eagerly awaiting my performance review to see if I was going to be hired full-time. Three weeks before my review, the office was "restructured," and my cubicle was given to someone else. My new cubicle was in the hallway between the office door and the fire escape.
>
> I complained to my supervisor about my new working conditions.
>
> At my review, I was not hired. "Apparently you can't roll with the punches," the supervisor said.

Our parents believed in the "American dream," the notion that living standards will forever rise, that we'll do better than our parents, and that our children will do better than we've done.

Some say the dream is ailing; some say it's kicked the bucket. "The so-called security of a paycheck is an illusion," reports one worker. "Either you're skilled at answering what the market needs or you're not. If you're not, you're doomed, whether you're in an office at AT&T or an office in your basement."

Your first tactic in protecting your own interests is knowing how to hold on to your own job while others are losing theirs.

Rumble in the Jungle

Here's a story we heard from a person while in line at the post office. (Hey, it's a simple life but we like it.)

> I applied for a job as a child care worker in a day care center. I was hired as a part-time worker and worked for a month until the center needed someone full-time. I took the job and worked there for 4 years!
>
> I came in at six on the days we needed someone to open up early, I stood in as a cook for 60 kids when our cook was ill for a week, and, most important, I was there every day to see the toddlers grow up and move on to school.
>
> When my director decided to move on to another center, she stayed only long enough to welcome the new boss.
>
> At the end of her first day, the new boss came to see me as I was cleaning up a classroom. She said, "I understand you came to the rescue some time ago when the center was short-staffed and really needed you." Then she handed me an envelope and said, "Well, thanks for all your help, but we're not short-staffed anymore."

It's a cold, cruel world, bubba. It's unfortunate but true—the people who work the hardest are often the least aware of what's going on around them. How can you tell if your job is on the line? Here are some ways to see if you're in danger of getting the ax:

1. There's a decreased workload overall.
2. You start getting lousy assignments.
3. Travel and training budgets get slashed.
4. There are no new capital purchases, such as computers.
5. There's much less overtime available.
6. Part-time workers are fired.
7. There are bad rumblings on the office grapevine.
8. The newspaper is full of reports about the bleak future of the industry you work in.

Protect Your Assets
Always remember that consultants get paid for making recommendations, and abolishing your job may be one of their suggestions.

9. You have been criticized directly about your work.

10. Your relationship with you boss changes.

    Bad: Your formerly friendly boss is irritable in dealing with you.

    Worse: Your boss hints that all is not well in La-La Land.

    Worst: Your boss won't see you at all.

11. The boss shows increased interest in the way you work or how work is performed within your group. Typically, when a boss who usually looked for results starts looking at details, it may mean that changes are being discussed at higher levels. This signal rarely means good news for the average worker.

12. Formal studies of workload are being conducted, perhaps by outside consultants.

13. Managers in key parts of the company are let go——and are not replaced.

14. Work previously done by a particular unit is assigned elsewhere.

15. Suddenly, everyone's job is getting shuffled around.

Watch Your Back!
But even if all indicators are bright, never get complacent about your job security, even if you have a contract or tenure. Anyone can get laid off or fired...and nearly everyone has been.

Always watch for the office hatchet. Every company has one. You know who we mean—although outwardly friendly and even mild, the hatchet is the man or woman who wields the ax...and often enjoys it. The hatchet is usually in a clear-cut position of power, but not always. Bosses often happily delegate the job of firing to the office hatchet. The boss stays out of the fray, and you're left wondering how the blow came out of left field.

Nose to the Grindstone

Here's an interesting little tale:

> One day I was called into my manager's office and asked to take the lead on a benchmark project. For the next seven months, I traveled and worked 16 hours a day, seven days a week. My team accomplished the impossible.

> Two weeks later, my manager announced major layoffs. He saved two people in the department, and I was one of them. All my effort had paid off.

One of the best ways to survive a layoff is to avoid the temptation to slack off the job when word starts to fly around that the end is near. Since it's human nature to be concerned and curious, when the rumor mill starts to grind away, some people start spending more time at the water cooler than at their desks. Hey, why bust your butt when you're going to get a pink slip next week?

Simple. Working hard can help you save your job. Until people are actually notified that they're downsized, rightsized, or outsized, no one knows for certain who's in and who's out. It's at this very time that the boss may have orders to prepare a list of the lucky and unlucky ones. Assuming that your boss will have to make choices, you can bet your laptop that it will be made on the basis of who is more valuable to keep (after we save the slot for the boss's nephew, of course). If you're still slogging away, you stand a better chance of being among the saved.

Live and Learn

Here's a nice slap in the face:

> The vice-president of human resources was interviewed for the corporate newsletter. When asked whether there might be layoffs in the future, she responded, "...we must attract and retain only the very best professionals to distinguish ourselves in the marketplace. This means some layoffs will be necessary."

As you can see, staying employed is an ongoing struggle of corporate life today. What if you position yourself to work until you drop from exhaustion, with all your energy, will, and hair long gone? Will that save your job? Well, no. Just working hard is not enough. You have to go one step further.

One good way to stay employed is to learn as many other jobs where you work as you can. Here's what Laurie has to say:

> My Ph.D. is in American and British literature and writing. I was trained to teach all literature classes, genre classes (the novel, the short story, theater, poetry, women in literature, etc.) and all writing classes. Since I now teach at a college of technology, I keep on learning the material I need to become an expert in the specialty classes we offer: Technical Writing, Technical Speech, and Business Writing. I've also learned all about different on-line research techniques, search engines, web sites, and e-mail. This makes me a far more flexible and valuable employee.

The bottom line? The more jobs you know how to do, the more valuable you become to your employer. And what if your skills are ahead of the company's learning curve? Not to worry...just create a need for you and your skills. Show that you're on the cutting edge.

When a company starts throwing workers overboard, your extra skills will make you one of the lucky ones singing "Nearer My God to Thee" in a lifeboat as the ship sinks.

Protect Your Assets
Never turn down any training the company offers, especially if it's free. People with the best chance of survival on the job have the most up-to-date skills, so no matter how much experience you have, take advantage of every chance to learn new skills.

The Sky Is Falling

When it comes to work, always assume the worst so that you'll be prepared for any eventuality. We're not advocating a heavy dose of doom and gloom, but don't delude yourself either. If things look bad, they usually are.

You know you have to pay close attention to the political situation in your company. But you also have to

➤ Stay in the loop. We don't recommend that you become a charter member of the gossip club, but we do suggest you keep your ear to the ground.

➤ Stay visible. Make sure that your accomplishments are recognized. Remember what you've already learned about tooting your own horn.

➤ Position yourself to be heard and seen.

➤ Adapt and get along with people.

➤ Be a little ray of sunshine. If it comes down to it, the bitch-and-moaners are often booted out before the pleasant people. Be positive and proactive, especially toward change.

➤ Keep networking, inside the company and within your industry.

➤ Choice 1: If an onerous task needs doing, offer your services. This attitude shows that you're willing to work extra hard for the home team.

➤ Choice 2: See Choice 1, but wait until someone else has been selected to do the hard work. That way, your willingness will be fully appreciated without any sacrifice on your part. Also, there's no danger that you'll be blamed if the project goes kersplat.

➤ If you're fairly certain that a reorganization will take place, abolishing your group but expanding another, you might want to apply for a job in the other department. Even if your request is turned down, the fact that you applied for a transfer early on can work in your favor. Later, if transfers are being made, the boss may prefer to move you rather than someone else who may be unhappy with a transfer.

➤ Keep your resume up-to-date.

➤ Set aside some money in an emergency fund. It will make you a lot less nervous. You'll do your job better and not drop-kick the pooch.

Watch Your Back!
The particular job you hold may make you vulnerable to a layoff. Many staff positions that don't directly contribute to the bottom line are far more vulnerable to layoffs than sales or production positions are. If your job is in the white-knuckle sector, you might want to consider transferring to a more secure position if the opportunity presents itself. This posturing may mean brushing up on some skills that you can't use in your current position.

Mentor Magic

There's little question that a mentor can be of invaluable assistance to your career goals or for surviving a corporate downsizing. It's nice to have someone looking out for you. However, it's not easy finding a mentor, and it's even harder finding the right one. And in some situations, a mentor can do more harm than good when it comes to surviving the land mines of office politics.

The trick to getting a mentor is to position yourself so that the person you want in senior management informally adopts you as a protégé. How you carry out this plan varies, but we suggest that you seize opportunities to ask the person for business-related advice. Since everyone likes to be considered an expert, ego stroking is likely to fall on receptive ears. Nonetheless, be prudent in your timing. Find a person who takes a genuine interest in your questions and offers you sound, logical advice.

> **Corporate Mambo-Jumbo**
> Sometimes, a business mentor is also called a *rabbi*. Don't ask us why.

Hero of the People

Of course, you want to hitch your wagon to a rising star. Never get allied with someone who is on the way out. You could end up being the one getting the door smacked on your butt. When you target mentors, look for someone who can

➤ Teach you the basics of doing a good job.

➤ Move your career along.

➤ Give you some added job security when it's time to downsize again.

➤ Introduce you to the right people and help you network.

> **Protect Your Assets**
> Since mentors can fulfill different purposes, you may be better off seeking different mentors for different purposes. For example, a senior manager will often smooth your way to the top, while someone closer to your level may be able to teach you the nitty-gritty skills you need to operate the computer.

Swirling Down the Drain

On the down side, mentors can hurt your career as much as help it. It's not just getting the wrong mentor; even the "right" mentor can cause you to go down in flames.

A friend of ours had hooked up with a fabulous mentor, an ambitious soul on the fast track. He took our friend along for a ride, and it was glorious—while it lasted. A few weeks after he got rightsized, she was axed as well. And since they were so closely allied, she had a hard time finding a new job.

The Least You Need to Know

➤ Stay alert to see if your job is in danger.

➤ Avoid the temptation to slack off the job when the end is near.

➤ Learn as many jobs and skills as possible. Stay flexible.

➤ Stay positive and proactive.

➤ Carefully weigh the pros and cons of having a mentor.

When It's Time to Move On

You know you've been working too hard when...

1. You jump-start your car without cables.
2. People test their batteries in your ears.
3. You help your dog chase its tail.
4. You short out motion detectors.
5. People use your hands to blend their margaritas.
6. You're so wired, you pick up AM radio.

7. You walk 20 miles on your treadmill before you realize it's not plugged in.

8. The nurse needs a scientific calculator to take your pulse.

9. You haven't blinked since the last lunar eclipse.

10. You ski uphill.

Everyone has a little job stress, but when your nervous twitch registers on the Richter scale, it may be time to move on. Sometimes, the job fit just isn't right and it's affecting every other part of your life—and not for the better, either. Other times, you're stuck in rank and really frustrated. Maybe you're beginning to feel like your job is about as much fun as working for the Albanian Ministry of Tourism.

Corporate Mumbo-Jumbo
Burnout is a pervasive dissatisfaction with a job, usually caused by feelings of betrayal and helplessness. *Burnout* is more like rust-out—a form of slow oxidation that corrodes your soul.

There are many reasons to move to a new job. In this chapter, you learn how to know when it's time to take a new job—and how using office politics can help you get the one that's right for your talents, interests, and goals.

Running on Empty

Do you feel like a modern-day Don Quixote, tilting at corporate windmills? Have you had enough of the daily grind? Are you trying your hardest, but never getting that raise or promotion? Perhaps you're a victim of *burnout*. Take our simple quiz to find out. For each question, check the answer you think is correct.

Burnout Quiz

True	False	
❏	❏	1. Exhaustion and burnout are the same.
		2. In a high-stress job, burnout is
❏	❏	Inevitable.
❏	❏	Almost inevitable.
❏	❏	Highly likely.
❏	❏	Cannot be determined without more information.
❏	❏	3. The people who are most likely to burnout are those who don't talk about their frustrations.
❏	❏	4. Burnout is contagious.
❏	❏	5. Workers who see themselves as "givers" are less likely to burnout than people who see themselves as "takers."

Answers to the Quiz

1. False. Exhaustion is physical; burnout is a psychological reaction to stress.

2. Cannot be determined without more information. Burnout is not a job disorder; it's a worker disorder. Some people can work for decades in highly stressful jobs without burning out. Why? Because they have developed effective ways to deal with stress. Others, in contrast, burn out faster than Milli Vanilli.

3. False. In most cases, the more you talk about how much you hate your job, the worse you'll feel. This isn't to say you should never talk about your job frustrations. It *is* to say that the more you harp on your dissatisfaction without doing anything about it, the more frustrating the situation becomes.

4. True. Only bad fashion spreads faster than burnout.

5. False. People who see themselves as self-sacrificing can feel just as burned out as people who see themselves as "takers."

Fly on the Wall

Female techies, are you baffled about not being able to crack the "silicon ceiling"? If so, you're not alone. Despite such exciting workplace innovations as unisex bathrooms, the tech industry suffers a distinct lag in leveling the playing field of gender in its workplaces. In 1998, Belkis Leong-Hong, president-elect of Women in Technology (http://www.womenintechnology.com), testified before the House Subcommittee on Technology that women hold only 3 percent of the top jobs in the world of high tech. Further, federal agencies still define careers in science and technology as "nontraditional" careers for women. As a result, the House has commissioned a major study of the "silicon ceiling."

Job-induced stress exists, of course, but far more damaging than stress is your reaction to it. Stress is like exercise: If you begin with a little and practice dealing with that, then tomorrow you'll be able to deal with more.

Now, we're not advocating that you bathe in stress, like a love-struck teenager dunking in cologne. Rather, we're suggesting that few jobs are stress free. (And if you find one that is, please call us. We'll be glad to share it with you or even take it off your hands completely.)

Rx for Burnout

How can you avoid job burnout? Luckily for you, there's a doctor in the house. Here's our prescription:

➤ Realize that whatever the conditions of your job, your mental health is your responsibility. Do whatever relaxes you. Bob plays baseball and volleyball after work; Laurie takes long walks between chapters.

➤ Take care of yourself. Pay attention to your diet. No more diet colas and Twinkies for breakfast (that's lunch, silly.) And exercise (see above).

➤ Take control of your job. Think of work as a problem to be solved, not as a great moral issue in which good (you) is pitted against evil (everyone else).

➤ Try to delegate. Not only does sharing the work take some of the burden off your back, but it also helps build valuable allies. If you need more help, ask for it. (Just make sure you can clearly justify your request to the bean counters.)

➤ Know the real rules in your job. Don't delude yourself into thinking the game is played your way; it rarely is.

➤ Avoid the tendency to place blame, point fingers, and create even more stress for yourself and everyone else. There's enough stress right now, thank you very much.

➤ Stay flexible and open to change.

St. Worker

And while we're on the subject, your 4,000 days of unused sick leave and vacation time aren't evidence of your commitment to the job. Rather, they indicate that you see yourself as a martyr to the cause.

Now, we are *not* advocating that you wait until the end of the fiscal year and then suddenly take all the days you've been squirreling away. We *are* saying that no one ever got a prize for working herself to death. And even if she did, she would be too dead to show up at the dinner.

Take your vacation; you've earned it. The company will manage. And even if it doesn't, you deserve a rest.

Greener Pastures

We really liked this tale from the ledge.

> I work for a company that was trying desperately to attract new Internet users. In an effort to encourage new clients, my manager decided to pay existing customers for successful referrals. If any of our current users convinced a family member or friend to use our service, we would send the referrer a check as a reward.
>
> I took to this program like a stamp to a letter.
>
> Two weeks later I was reprimanded. My manager said I was making the promotion too successful and the company was mailing too many checks.

How can you tell if it's time to move on to a new job? See if any of these feelings have crossed your mind or you've experienced any of the following situations.

1. You really want a promotion, but your chances of a promotion are roughly the same as Pee Wee Herman's of making fullback for the Jets.

2. You were in line for a promotion, but you were passed over for someone else. When you miss out on a promotion, you have to think long and hard about your future with the company. Some people try to rationalize that they will get the next promotion, while others feel quite the opposite. If from any objective standpoint you were the most logical candidate to get promoted and you got passed over like day-old bread, the handwriting is on the wall. If you want to move up the ladder, you might have to move out.

3. You are bored out of your skull. You've asked your boss for more responsibility and requested a transfer to a more challenging position but neither has happened.

4. You have been relegated to the same status as a flea on Rover's tail, thanks to an organizational change.

5. You have had your working hours changed, and your efforts to work out a reasonable compromise have fallen on deaf ears.

6. You have had your responsibilities increased, but your salary has stayed the same. Even worse, maybe you've taken a pay cut, but you're still doing more work than ever.

7. You just can't get along with your boss, despite your best efforts. Some personality conflicts are best resolved by one or both parties going separate ways. If you can't persuade your boss to find another job, maybe it's time for *you* to head out.

8. You took a new job recently, and it wasn't what you expected. Assuming that you've given yourself enough time to get used to a new position, it might even be that the position was misrepresented.

9. You can't stand your coworkers, even after the most generous appraisal.

10. You see that the company is crumbling and management is losing its nerve. A company in extended death throes is no place to be, if you can help it. Bail out, even if your bosses are dabbing their eyes with tear-stained tissues at the thought of your departure.

Watch Your Back!
Don't ignore your feelings when it comes to your career. Sometimes you just have a feeling that it's time to get a different job but nothing has been said or written about your future. Nonetheless, pay attention to your feelings; they're a subtle but reliable indicator of rumblings you may not be able to put into words.

To the Virgins, Make Much of Time

When our friend Lewis started working in 1980, he expected his career to have a few standard perks: an office, frequent promotions, yearly raises, and a pension. "My dad worked in the same company for 20 years," Lewis said. "That's pretty much what I expected to do." That was before Lewis was laid off from corporate jobs three times.

Protect Your Assets
Today's 20-somethings are likely to change jobs, if not careers, many times throughout their lives.

There's a whole new way of looking at jobs, careers, and employment today, babycakes. Now, you are your own company.

"Today, everyone is a contingent worker," says William Bridges, author of *JobShifts: How to Prosper in a Workplace Without Jobs*. Consequently, you have to market yourself—which is best done when you already have a job.

In the Driver's Seat

If you want a new job, always try to look for it while you're still employed. Why? First, because you're already wired in; second, your current employment shows you're in demand. Looking for a new job while you're already on the job can be a tricky business, but being in the workplace gives you a leg up on much of the competition.

The primary advantage? Even in a dead-end job you hate, you probably have the ability to tap into a much broader network of contacts for advise than if you were unemployed. Even more important, they can connect you with potential new employers and colleagues.

Because many employers perceive a job-hunting employee as a drag on office morale and productivity, they'll often confront you about what they (correctly) suspect you're thinking and doing. Therefore, consider being as up-front as possible about your plans. If

Corporate Mumbo-Jumbo
The term *flight risk* describes employees who are suspected of planning to leave a company or department soon.

nothing else (and there is plenty else), telling an employer that you are looking for a new job can often be a bargaining tool for better job conditions. For example, if you tell an employer you are leaving because you want flex time, maybe the company will work something out for you. In addition, there won't be any real surprises—or burned bridges—if you leave the job.

In practice, most people are constantly on the lookout for new jobs and good employers understand this. Whether or not you tell your employer the truth, of course, depends on whether there is anything left to salvage in the relationship.

Mum's the Word

There are potholes to avoid when cruising for a new job from your current desk, however. Above all, you must be cautious about advertising your availability. Don't tell your current bosses that you're looking—unless you want them to start looking for your replacement. And while it may seem obvious, avoid using the company phone, fax, and stationary for job search. Technically, that's stealing.

Above all, when you're dealing with a prospective employer, be sensible about communications, especially at the office. We recommend that you:

➤ Schedule job interviews on your own time.

➤ Avoid phone messages from possible employers (even if you have what you assume to be a completely private voice-mail system). Better to give out your home number and check your messages periodically.

➤ Have all new job-related mail sent to your home rather than to your office.

➤ Make sure the prospective employer recognizes that your application or inquiry is "privileged information" and should remain confidential.

> **Watch Your Back!**
> If your boss happens to pick up on your job search activity and you haven't explained what you're doing, be forewarned: You could be fired.

Networking 101

More than 75 percent of getting a new job is networking—the political skill we've been not-so-gently hammering at you for chapters and chapters. For somebody already out there in the workforce, the way to go is network, network, and network some more. Networking is simply finding the right strings…and pulling them. It's the business of one hand washing another.

> **Corporate Mumbo-Jumbo**
> *Networking* is using personal contacts to help your business and personal life. Networking has been around almost as long as some of the things in the back of our refrigerator.

Here's our quick networking cram course. You can network by:

➤ Taking continuing education courses

➤ Attending conferences in your field

➤ Going to seminars

➤ Continuing work-related travel

➤ Having drinks with colleagues after work

➤ Using World Wide Web sites, such as CareerBuilder

➤ Tapping into online services

➤ Making contacts via e-mail

➤ Joining a community or civic group that draws business people in your field. Traditionally, these have included Rotary, Kiwanis, and Lions, but new ones are starting up just about every day.

➤ Linking up with your trade association. Every group has its own trade association. Laurie, for example, belongs to the Modern Language Association, the American Association of University Women, and United University Professors.

➤ Contacting your alumni associations. Odds are good that some of your high school and college buddies may be able to give you leads on good jobs in your field.

➤ Trying some anti-networking. Yes, you read that right. Remember how you found the love of your life when you swore off love? The same can be true of networking. Sometimes you make your best contacts when you aren't even trying. Plunge into community work, social groups, coach a sport, join PTA, be a scout leader. You'll make valuable contacts and do some good at the same time.

Protect Your Assets
The anonymity and reach of cyberspace makes it even easier to cast a wider net here when looking for a new job.

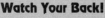

Watch Your Back!
Before you join any professional group, consider what it can do for you. Finding the right group can take some effort. For example, too many members in the group and you might get lost in the shuffle; too few and you might not be able to make any contacts.

But there are right and wrong ways to tap that network, which begins in your own office.

Don't...just walk up to someone in your office and ask if he or she knows about any available jobs.

Do...talk with key people about your skills and general career goals. That way, they'll keep you in mind when they do hear about something that might be right for you. Or down the road, they might introduce you to someone who is in a position to hire you.

Midlife Crisis

Today, the concept of a midlife crisis has become a bit of a cliché. Yet to millions of American workers in their 40s and 50s, a career crisis is all too real. The crisis can be triggered by many things, including a layoff, a divorce, loss of a loved one, or pent-up frustrations.

At certain ages, we may get wake-up calls. It's important to heed those calls, but also to do it in a way that makes sense. For some people, that means making an immediate, dramatic change; for others, it means slower, incremental change.

If you have no clue where to turn next, listen to yourself and others for ideas. For example, analyze compliments people make about you. Think about who you envy and brainstorm about what you want your world to look like in the morning when you wake up.

To get out of a rut, you need to explore, talk, and dream bigger. However, this is not the time to leap without looking. It's not all about jobs or skills. It's really about your life.

Let us warn you against wanting too much from your job in the first place, a danger that can trigger a midlife career crisis. Not everyone is going to get the corner office. You can be ambitious, but if your life is your job, you're going to hit a crisis sooner or later.

Forty and Fired

Sometimes you don't have the luxury of a midlife crisis: one is created for you. It's the middle-age nightmare: you're 40-something and suddenly fired. It probably wasn't a plant closing or something equally dramatic, so you didn't even see it coming. The boss just called you in one Friday, said your division was being sliced in half, and you're out. Now what?

First, take a deep breath. Don't do anything at all for a couple of days. Give the news time to sink it.

After you've begun to accept your fate, the next step is to realize that there is no immediate fix for this situation. Many newly displaced workers want to race right back out into the job market, certain they'll land a new job in a matter of weeks or even days. You may, but usually finding a new job in midcareer requires a campaign.

Corporate Mumbo-Jumbo
GOOD Job is a trendy new acronym for a get-out-of-debt job. It's a well-paying job people take in order to pay off their debts—and a job that they will quit as soon as they are solvent again.

Protect Your Assets
Losing a job typically causes the same kinds of emotions as losing a beloved relative or friend: shock, denial, fear, anger, depression, and, finally, acceptance. One way of coping with these emotions is to mobilize your support system—family, close friends, and trusted colleagues.

Steps to Success

Approach the job search deliberately and carefully, particularly at this vital midcareer point. Take a series of small, practical steps that will put you on the right path toward that next job. Don't procrastinate by painting every room in the house. Instead, try these ideas:

1. Apply for unemployment benefits—even if you don't think you're eligible. Let the unemployment office determine your eligibility.

2. Discuss your situation fully and honestly with your family.

3. Maintain good work habits by rising at a reasonable hour every morning, just as you did before.

4. Consider reaching out for counseling or the kind of impartial, professional advice offered by a search firm. More on this later.

5. Line up your references.

6. Write a preliminary resume or update your previous one to tie your accomplishments to the requirements of the new jobs that you're seeking.

7. Review your financial obligations and finances.

8. Locate a computer you can use if you don't already have one at home.

9. Update your skills—or learn new ones.

10. Don't despair—it's not good for your overall well-being—and it won't help you land a job either. You need to keep confident.

Watch Your Back!
If you've lost your job, do anything and everything you can to avoid wallowing in despair and bitterness. Your attitude can make or break your chances of getting a new job.

One door shuts, but another eventually will open. It will take work and patience, but it *will* happen.

Headhunters

No, we're not talking about the villains in an old jungle movie. *Headhunters* is the slang term for executive search firms. It's a billion dollar industry in America alone.

Corporate Mumbo-Jumbo
Headhunters are executive search firms.

Executive search firms are not the same as personnel services, although they have the same ultimate goal. Personnel agencies generally function by seeking jobs for people who have registered for them. Executive recruiters, in contrast, usually begin with a job description and seek the person who best fits it.

Do you need a headhunter? To find out, see if your qualifications fit this list. Place a check in each category that describes you.

Headhunter Worksheet

- ❏ 1. I am currently at the executive level.
- ❏ 2. I am presently employed and serious about changing jobs.
- ❏ 3. I have been downsized, rightsized, or outsized from my present job in management.
- ❏ 4. I don't want anyone at my present job to know that I am looking for a new executive-level job.

If you are the person seeking a job, it doesn't cost anything to use a headhunter. There is a fee, of course. Usually, it's 10 percent to 35 percent of the year's salary, paid by the company seeking to hire the new employee.

There are hundreds of executive search firms, and each industry has its specialties. Be sure to find the executive search firm that suits your training, interests, and career path. Start by calling your industry trade associations for names. If you are willing to share the confidence, ask other people in your field for names of headhunters they may have used or feel comfortable recommending.

Protect Your Assets

Not making any progress with headhunters? It may not be your fault you're stuck in neutral. There's an unwritten rule that for about two years following a search for a corporate client, the recruiter will consider all of that client's employees untouchable. This practice prevents employee raiding.

The Least You Need to Know

- ➤ Cope with job burnout by learning to relax, taking care of yourself, taking control of your job, delegating work, accepting the real rules in your job, and staying flexible.

- ➤ If you're stuck in rank, bored with work, or hate your co-workers, it may be time to move to a new job. Ditto if you were demoted or the job was misrepresented.

- ➤ Today everyone is a contingent worker; job security is an illusion. Learn how to market yourself.

- ➤ Always try to look for a new job while you're still employed.

- ➤ Network, network, network.

- ➤ Expecting too much from your job can trigger a midlife crisis.

- ➤ Approach the job search deliberately and carefully.

- ➤ *Headhunters* are executive search firms.

Index